THE

AVIATOR'S

BATHROOM

READER

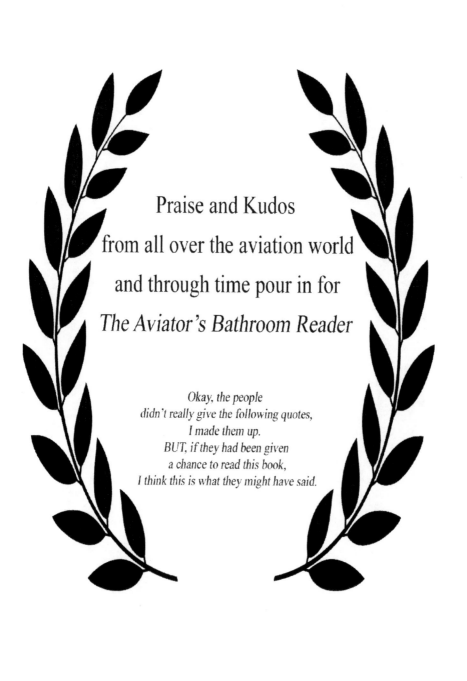

Praise and Kudos

from all over the aviation world

and through time pour in for

The Aviator's Bathroom Reader

*Okay, the people
didn't really give the following quotes,
I made them up.
BUT, if they had been given
a chance to read this book,
I think this is what they might have said.*

"Dieses Buch ist wunderbar. Wen ich zurückkehrte von schiessen einige tapfer und mutige englische Piloten runter und auch ein paar französchische feiglinge. Nach dem Abendessen nehme ich mir die Zeit und geniesse einige Kapitel von den Buch. Lachen hilft mir, mich zu entspannen und lerne dabei auch ein paar Sachen. Ich empfehle das für jeden Piloten, nur natürlich nicht fur die französchisen Flieger."

["This book is wonderful! After returning from shooting down some brave British pilots - and a few cowardly French ones - I sit down after dinner and enjoy a few sections. Laughing helps me relax...and I learn things, too! I recommend this for every aviator...except, of course, the French ones."]

Pour le Merite
"Blue Max"
Prussia
1712 – 1918

- Manfred Freiheer von Richthofen [The "Red Baron" -highest scoring ace in WWI with 80]

"I wish I had this book along on my Atlantic flight. There were a lot of long, boring hours where some entertainment would have been welcome!"

- Charles A. Lindbergh [First to fly solo across the Atlantic Ocean]

---

*"This is the best ****ing book about flying I've ever read! It's got ****hot pilots, stupid ****ing pilots, and a lot of ****ing good lessons we can all learn from. If you don't come away with some ****ing good smarts after reading this, then you're just an *******."*

- Florence "Pancho" Barnes [Movie pilot, adventurer, owner/operator of the "Happy Bottom Riding Club" near Muroc Lake, CA. – now Edwards AFB]

"If my brother and I had this book back then, we would most likely have made our first powered flight in 1902 instead of 1903."

- Orville Wright [Pilot of the first powered takeoff of an airplane]

"I really don't care for all the parts about flying airways, the rules and regulations and stuff. I mean, isn't the sky open and free? That's the way it should always be. The funny parts were okay though, I guess."

- "The Great" Waldo Pepper ['Barnstormer' pilot]

"We need more material like this so when I send my boys over Hitler's Reich they have the knowledge and skill to make it back safe and alive. Send me more assets like this!"

- Frank "12 O'clock High" Savage, BGen [918th Bomb Group, 8th AF]

"You know, I played a number of characters in the movies, all of whom were pilots. And then as a pilot myself I got to fly some of the most up-to-date planes the US Army Air Corps – later the US Air Force – had at the time. Reading this book won't get you a part in the movies, but it may keep you from being mentioned negatively in the newsreels."

- Jimmy Stewart, BGEN, USAF (ret.) [Actor and pilot]

"This book is the best way I've seen to make the mundane knowledge found in the FARs and AIM come to life so it can be recalled by pilots when they need to have it at their fingertips. It will assist in making todays' fliers safer and more capable. And by the way, that story of me saying "Good luck" to Mr. Grindowski when I was standing on the moon is a fabrication: A funny one, yes, but a fabrication."

- Neil Armstrong [First human to set foot on the moon and a true hero]

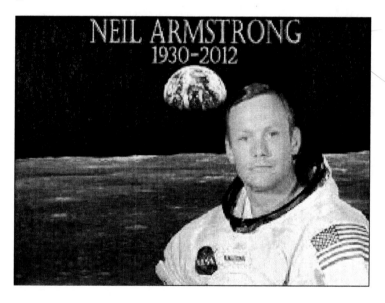

"I offered Drew one million dollars for the rights to his book. I was going to turn it into a blockbuster picture starring my newest bombshell actress. He wouldn't sell. It seems some people just can't be bought: Too bad for him."

- Howard Hughes [mega-billionaire, movie producer and pilot]

"I make the best airplanes of the war and the Allies call them a bad name. Well, in the next one all those "Fokkers" – as you call them – will be flying Messerschmidts. And I'll be sitting at home enjoying books like this one."

- Anthony Fokker (German WWI aeroplane designer/builder]

"Reading; it gives the mind a chance to pause and, with the mind's eye, extend one's awareness far ahead where mere sight cannot take you. I continue on into the black of night; blacker even than over the Sahara on a moonless night; guided only by that small glimmer of light far ahead, which is the dawn. The dawn of my awareness, the dawn in recognizing inspiring passages of knowledge, the dawn of a new day high in the calm before the coming storm that is my life on the ground."

- Antoine de Saint-Exupéry [Author of Conquest of the Air, Night Flight, The Little Prince]

"This book has its ups and downs, like my work."

- Igor Sikorsky [Inventor of the first practical helicopter]

"I wish I had read this book before coming down out of the mountains."

- John Denver [Songwriter and performer, pilot]

"You can't get to fly the big ones until you can fly the little ones. This book will help you do that."

- William Boeing [Airplane designer and builder]

"Okay, you SOB's – read this here book from cover to cover – yeah, the footnotes too – and maybe, just maybe, you'll make it off this stinkin' island and back home to yer loved ones in one piece!"

- Gregory "Pappy" Boyington [VMF-214, WWII Pacific theater ace]

"Chaps, the information you will find herein is bloody good! Remembering what the author presents (although he does get a wee bit 'skanky' at times) may well keep you from becoming 'Fokker Fodder'.

So chin up, Lads, and God Bless the King!"

- Major Billy Bishop, VC, Royal Flying Corps/Royal Air Force [Major Bishop, RAF, was the highest scoring Allied ace of WWI with 72 victories. His son, who flew in WWII, liked to say that between his father and him, they shot down 74 German planes. – Ed.]

―――――――

"Learn from the mistakes of others because you'll never live long enough to make them all yourself."

- James H. "Jimmy" Doolittle, Lieutenant General, USAF (ret.) [Famed pilot, record breaker, leader of the 'Doolittle Raid' on Tokyo in 1942 and another true hero]

―――――――

"As Army Aviator #2 since 1913, I've seen 'em come and I've seen 'em go. The ones who stayed put their all into it; living, breathing, eating and sleeping aviation. This book will help in that endeavor, enrichening the lives of all who dream of a life in the sky."

- Henry H. "Hap" Arnold, General of the Air Force (5 stars)

US Signal Corps 1913
Military Aviator
(Awarded to the first 14 military aviators, of which Lt. Henry Arnold was #2, from his estate.)

THE AVIATOR'S BATHROOM READER

Drew Chitiea
Designated Pilot Examiner
Master Flight Instructor

Colorado Skymaster, LLC
Black Hawk, Colorado

Photographs of the wings and badges pictured herein by Peggy Long.

The wings & badges pictured herein reside in the author's collection.

The Aviator's Bathroom Reader
First Edition
 This novel is a work of fact and fiction. While most of the book is factual, some of the names, characters, quotes may be the product of the imagination or may have been used fictitiously.

ISBN: 0692315888
ISBN-13: 978-0692315880 (Colorado Skymaster, LLC)

I wish to honor my wife Peggy Long, who I met at a time in my life when I was no more looking for a relationship than the man-in-the-moon; you still amaze me all these years later. My best friend and flying partner – I envision Happy Landings to the end of our days.

I also wish to dedicate this book to all who came before in aviation. From the time of Icarus mankind has looked to the sky and wondered: Wondered what it would be like to be up there flying, free as a bird. Only since 1903 have we been able to self-launch a heavier-than-air craft into the wild blue and thus be able to look down on the earth below. Only since then has humankind been able to witness the glory of God's creation from His view - a wonder and miracle indeed! We – myself and all who read this book - are the summation of all of mankind's' dreams for flight. It is you and I - here and now - who are fulfilling the yearnings for flight felt by humans from time immemorial.

We wouldn't have made it this far if not for all those – many "Gone West" with wings folded for the last time - who preceded us. Those men and women who at such great cost learned the secrets and lessons of aviation, then passed them along to the 'nuggets' coming later. From Wilbur and Orville in 1903, through all those who barnstormed, explored, flew and fought, to all who taught and instructed, to all those who insure a future for aviation to this day, I dedicate this book.

Keep 'em Flying!

TO MY READERS

For Those of You with A.I.S. (Acronym Impairment Syndrome)

Throughout this book you will come across many acronyms pertaining to various aviation matters (V.A.M.'s). "B.F.D." you might think, I know 'em all and perhaps even invented a few when I was at (Fill in the blank) back in (Fill in another blank). That might be well and good (W.a.G.) for you old greybeards, but think of the young ones coming along, those foolish new guys (F.N.G.'s) whose heads are yet empty of the wisdom represented by trusty old acronyms (T.O.A.'s).

So when you, my faithful reader (M.F.R.) come across one of those T.O.A.'s, please refer to the Acronyms List (A.L.) of the Appendix Section (A.S.) of this book just to make sure that the meaning you understand of the acronym in question (A.i.Q.) is indeed the actual meaning of the acronym in question (A.M.o.t.A.i.Q.).

This will further your enjoyment of this book (E.o.t.B.) and perhaps even clear up misconceptions of misunderstood acronyms (M.o.M.A.) which have persisted since the days of your being the F.N.G.

DC, HMFWHIC, BH, CO, USA

Oh, there is a dictionary in the appendix section as well, for those words unique to aviation, presented for the same reason.

TABLE OF CONTENTS

FORGIVENESS & PERMISSIONS

I have been collecting the stories, tales, pictures and illustrations found within the confines of this tome (another word for 'chock') for years. Indeed not only does this activity go back into the last century, it goes back into the last millennium as well! I admit I was lax in keeping an exact record of where I found these gems and to whom they can be credited. I was keeping them for my own purposes and pleasures and had no inkling something like this would one day be the result.

There may be copyrighted material in here – if it was so labeled I have tried diligently to obtain the permission of the copyright holder. In many cases (such as for some of the Bob Stevens' cartoons) the creator has 'gone west', the publishing company is out of business and no heirs could be found.

I now prostrate myself at the feet of anyone and/or any corporate entity that holds an unacknowledged copyright for anything found herein. I entreat, implore and grovel to you to allow the continued use of this material as the main purpose for myself as 'author' is not to get rich (In aviation? Surely you jest!) but to pass along the learning, knowledge and wisdom in an entertaining and engaging manner with nothing more than Aviation Safety as the ultimate goal.

I hope and trust that noble cause will meet with your individual and collective approvals.

Drew Chitiea
Terra Incognita, Colorado, USA, Earth, Sol System, Milky Way Galaxy

WHAT THIS BOOK IS ABOUT

A couple had just learned how to send text messages on their cell phones.

The wife was a romantic type; the husband was…well…a pilot.

One afternoon the wife went out to meet a friend for coffee. She decided to send her husband a romantic text message; so she wrote the following:

"If you are sleeping, send me your dreams.

If you are laughing, send me your smile.

If you are eating, send me a bite.

If you are drinking, send me a sip.

If you are crying, send me your tears.

I love you."

The husband texted back to her:

"I'm on the toilet. Please advise."

Kinda brings a tear to the eye, doesn't it? – Ed.

In a way, the story above contains the kernels of why this book was created, to pass along the love of being in the sky and wisdom of the aeronautical ages while also bringing a tear, gleam, sparkle or wistful look to your eye. At the time I write this, I have been flying 44 years: This book was written by pilots for pilots and everyone else who has ever looked skyward wishing they were up there soaring, wheeling about and doing those "hundred things" about which John Gillespie Magee wrote in his famous poem. Of things that groundlings can neither imagine, conceive or visualise.

It matters not whether you are long retired from the cockpit or just beginning your journey through the sky; the fliers of old will recall and remember when strong hands grasped the controls of a fire-breathing steed as they flung themselves skyward. Those coming up the ranks who have yet to experience those particular and peculiar thrills will continue to dream as they prepare and position themselves in readiness for that moment.

As an FAA Designated Pilot Examiner [DPE] I see just about everything out there in the marketplace which is used to glean, gather, collect, collate and present the information necessary to attain an aviation certificate, rating or privilege. Everything the FAA issues or approves is the foundation – all the handbooks, advisory circulars, pilots' operating handbooks (POH), approved flight manuals (AFM), airport facilities directories (AFD) and yes, the Federal Air Regulations (FARs) and Aeronautical Information Manual (AIM). These are the original materials used to develop questions and answers in the knowledge (neé 'written') tests and establishing parameters of acceptable performance in the Practical Test Standards (PTS).

The FAA has allowed that if substantially the same information is presented, then after-market materials may be used for the attainment of a certificate, rating or privilege. Thus one finds the slick Jeppesen books filled with illustrations, graphs, diagrams and such which make a tome three times as thick as the drier but more succinct FAA material(s). Adding to that are ASA materials, the ubiquitous John and Martha King videos, Gleim study guides, any of the training materials found in the Sporty's Pilot Shop catalog and the books by Rod Machado which are virtually exclusive insofar as he brings humor into the mix to make the salient points more relevant and retainable in the mind of the applicant.

In looking around the informational marketplace, I see a plethora of materials – in print and/or digital form – which cover the study for and attainment of a certificate, rating or privilege. Also to be found are excellent resources for specific areas of knowledge and skill retention. These include – but certainly is not limited to – monthlies such as IFR Refresher, Aviation Safety, Flight Training and others which cater specifically to a focused segment of the aviation community. Many magazines – Flying, Plane & Pilot, the "alphabet groups' (AOPA, EAA, IAC, etc.) offerings have within a safety message ("I Learned About Flying From That" is a great example) but which are often overpowered and/or overshadowed by the newest, slickest item to come on the market.

I might enjoy reading about the newest Gulfstream variation or seeing the latest in virtual flight paths and Heads' Up Displays (HUDs), but really – for most of us in General Aviation the closest any of us will get to any of this is seeing one on the ramp or reading about it in the monthly delivered by the post office (I admit, I still cannot get used to 'reading' a magazine on an electronic device. I guess I am firmly ensconced in the 20th century as an "Old Greybeard.").

This is not to say that I eschew the latest device, avionic or cockpit aid in favor of the old steam gauges and a righteously flown NDB approach – since the FAA has allowed iPads into airline cockpits, I also allow any applicant to use in a flightcheck whatever asset they would normally fly with. They therefore must be able to demonstrate use and mastery of the new technology whilst not forgetting aviation's prime directive:

First, always and foremost, fly the plane!

As a DPE I must have enough of a working knowledge of all the different GPS systems, avionics variations and autopilot renditions to maintain a safe testing environment and to determine the applicant knows what he's doing. But all the latest whizzy-gizzy doo-dads cannot take the place of good old-fashioned stick-and-rudder skills when flight ultimately comes down to managing the lift-weight-thrust-drag ratios and basic command and control of the aerospace vehicle when alighting on the firmament with a bodacious and/or squirrely crosswind.

In discussions with other DPEs, CFIs and pilots I have asked the question: "What do you do to retain all the knowledge and skill-level once the flightcheck is passed?" It is a widely known and statistically proven FACT that after the flightcheck is over and the pressure is off, knowledge levels and skills of most every applicant then degrades over time. And of course this is true, if they never did like practising stalls, then when on their own they won't do them again. Didn't like them then, don't like them now, won't like them in the future. And that's not only too bad, but they are doing themselves a disservice; the only way to come to terms with what scares you or makes you uncomfortable is to hit it head on – not shying away and forever having that topic being a 'monster under the bed'.

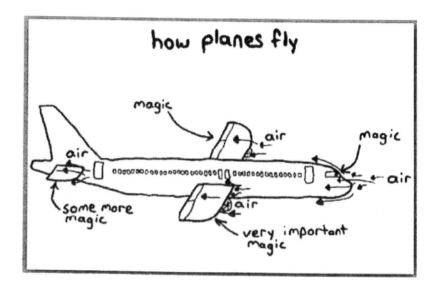

In answering the question posed above, the prevalent answer I hear is "I look back through my study materials I used to get the rating." I'm sorry, but I have to throw the 'BS Flag' onto the field here; I mean really – does any pilot *really* and *truly* open up the Handbook of Aeronautical Knowledge and read for fun? Or even to keep the knowledge fresh? I don't think so. I go through all these resources with regularity because I'm always looking for ways to keep my flightchecks from becoming predictable; I like coming at different subject matters from a different direction.

But really, how many of you have cracked the AIM looking for recommended ways to enter the pattern at a non-towered airport? Think you know all that stuff – ALL that stuff – and what is required to accomplish it? Any of us who have done a long straight-in to the final approach leg at a non-towered airport (and yes, I'm guilty of that too!) have gone against the recommended

procedure. Illegal? No. Unsafe? Perhaps. Imprudent? Yeah…
See what I mean?

So in a long-winded form of "Pretzel Logic" (Think of a pretzel
– nothing is in a straight line but when you get to the end you
have a finished product), I'd like to present the premise of what
this book is all about. It is meant for pilots – primarily General
Aviation pilots (although the military and airline pilots may use
what is found herein when they deign to fly G.A. aircraft) – to
keep their knowledge of aviation rules, regulations and accepted
procedures relatively fresh in their minds. When a situation
arises whilst committing aviation perhaps by having read this
book some synapse closes in the brain and they say to
themselves "Self, what I'm experiencing right now is kinda like
what I read in that book the other day." Then a corrolation is
made between the present experience and the learning which
took place while reading this book and a safe, prudent and legal
(in that order!) course of action can be developed so to insure a
satisfactory outcome to the experience. And as every CFI knows,
the corrolative stage is the highest level of learning.

So there you are – this book is meant to bring and keep you at
the corrolative level of learning about flying and aviation; the
highest and safest level there is. No need to thank me, I'm just
doing this as my civic duty as a citizen of the sky (and the TSA
won't allow me to carry silver bullets any more). *You* are the one

who bought this book. *You* are the one who took it upon yourself to attain, retain and maintain your knowledge at the highest possible level. We aviators are blessed with the freedom of flight; with all the joy, pleasure and satisfaction it brings. However, we cannot forget or let lay fallow the responsibility to be adroit in our knowledge and proficient in our skills. It is a given – it must be a constant.

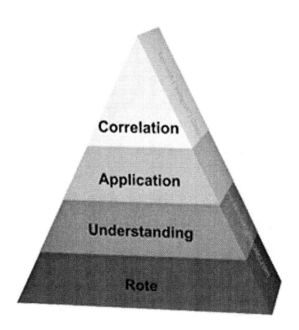

There it is, quite simply, why I collected the materials herein and wrote this book. And I did not do this exclusively – friends sent to me much of what you'll read here. Hundreds of pilots have put pen to paper and fingers to keyboards to present a record for posterity. All I did was collect and collate it over all these years.

Fly high

Fly low

Fly fast

Fly slow

Fly near

Fly far

Disciplined

And free

Always and forever

The best you can be

Live Long and Prosper, Young Skywalker

Okay, okay...I know I'm mixing my metaphors, but you get the idea, right?

So – stay sharp, my friends.

Think about what you're doing when you're flying.

Be always ahead of the airplane.

Be always knowledgable in what you seek.

Be always skillful in what you do.

You are not just a 'Flyboy',

You are a professionally-minded aviator.

Plan always to do your best.

Attention to detail is everything!

Drew Chitiea
Black Hawk, Colorado
2014

And now, without further ado...   Enjoy!

ACTIVITY FOR RETIRED PILOTS

I've had to make one real-life, by-gawd, actual, it's-time-to-leave-now bailout – and was I glad about all the training I had gotten regarding the process! It's an amazing sight hanging there in the harness; the quiet, peaceful floating feeling one has as you watch your (former) valiant steed spin down to impact the earth. It really is quite impressive...until you realize the earth is now coming up at you fast and you're hanging under an old round 24-foot military chute that's gonna set you down like a ton of bricks.

I had been retired for a number of years and was perfectly happy puttering around the house and yard, playing golf and just taking life in general at an easy pace. Yesterday my daughter again asked why I didn't do something useful with my time. Talking about my "doing something useful" seemed to be her favorite topic of conversation. She was "only thinking of me" and suggested I go down to the senior center and hang out with the guys.

I did this and when I got home last night I decided to teach her a lesson about staying out of my business. I told her that I had joined a parachute club. She said, "Are you nuts? You're almost 70 years old and you're going to start jumping out of airplanes?"

I proudly showed her that I even got a membership card. She said to me, "Good grief, where are your glasses! This is a membership to a Prostitute Club, not a Parachute Club."

"I'm in trouble again," I said, "and I don't know what to do... I signed up for five jumps a week."

She fainted.

Retired life is not getting any easier…but it can still be fun and entertaining!

IF AT FIRST YOU DON'T SUCCEED....

Then skydiving is not for you!

FAR Part 105 contains the rules and regulations for the use of parachutes in the sporting sense; the 'when and where's', the repacking rules and so forth. Most of my readers – I believe – have some standards regarding jumping out of a perfectly good airplane; but there just may be some out there who do so anyway.

To them I say: "You're nuts."

Those of us who fly aerobatics know we must wear a parachute when performing the sky-dancing we love to do.

FAR 91.307 Parachutes & Parachuting

(c) Unless each occupant of the aircraft is wearing an approved parachute, no pilot of a civil aircraft carrying any person (other than a crewmember) may execute any intentional maneuver that exceeds:

(1) A bank of 60 degrees relative to the horizon;

(2) A nose-up or nose-down attitude of 30 degrees relative to the horizon.

Here also in (1) & (2) above is the definition of aerobatic flight. I would also add to this exceeding any design load limitations set by the manufacturer. See below:

Crashed Cirrus Data Recorder Tells Aerobatic Tale

The NTSB has determined that two cousins age 23 and 34 were killed in the crash of a rented Cirrus SR-22T on Nov. 13, 2011, near Boynton Beach, Fla., while attempting aerobatics. There were no other occupants aboard the aircraft, which impacted in a marsh. A pilot who witnessed the crash told the NTSB that the aircraft pitched from level flight to a 30-degree nose-up attitude before rolling inverted, reversing the roll and ultimately impacting the ground in an (estimated) 80-degree nose-down condition. Information contained in the aircraft's data recorder largely coincided with that account. It also showed that roll wasn't the aircraft's first.

Data contained by the crash-hardened flight data recording device covered the period from Nov. 11, when the accident aircraft's 34-year-old right-seat pilot signed a rental agreement for the aircraft. It showed that on that day the aircraft was flown for more than 10 minutes below 1,000 feet and for nearly 90 seconds it was flown between 195 and 38 feet. Low-altitude banks of up to 70 degrees were also recorded -- along with a successfully completed 360-degree roll to the left.

The investigation found that the right-seat pilot (who signed the rental agreement for the aircraft) held a commercial certificate with ratings for single- and multi-engine land, rotorcraft helicopter, and instrument airplane and helicopter, all acquired after 2008. His recovered logbooks listed at least 4,384 flight hours with at least 183 in the accident airplane make and model. The investigation also found the pilot had been awarded at least some of his certificates twice. "On Feb. 17, 2006, the pilot had submitted a letter of surrender to the FAA, which constituted an 'unequivocal abandonment' of his commercial pilot certificate," according to the NTSB. The reason for that action was "voluntary surrender in anticipation of FAA certificate action." The NTSB has determined the accident's probable cause to be "the right seat pilot's decision to attempt a low-altitude aerobatic maneuver in a non-aerobatic airplane."

I recall another crash some years ago where a pilot flying a Beech Baron opined to his passengers one day on a trip he thought he could roll the plane. He was talked out of it that day by the other occupant. A few weeks later the pilot did indeed try – and the operative word here is 'try' – to roll the airplane…with three passengers on board. The load limits on the airplane must have been exceeded as the wings separated from the fuselage and the resulting crash killed all four on board.

Limitations are just that – limits! Most everyone can quote the aircraft documentation required to be on board an aircraft prior to flight: The 'O' of 'ARROW' is usually said to be "Operating Handbook".

IT"S NOT!

The 'O' stands for "Operating Limitations" which are <u>contained</u> in the POH/AFM!

Do NOT 'try' aerobatics in a non-aerobatic airplane! If you want to see the world upside-down, search out a qualified school AND instructor. Seriously – your life, and the lives of those who ride with you, depend on it!

IF God had meant for Man to fly, He would have made his bones hollow...and not his head.

AIRCRAFT CRASHES INTO OCCUPIED STRUCTURES

"Oh, the Humanity..."

FAR 91.119 Minimum Safe Altitudes: General

"Except when necessary for takeoff or landing, no person may operate an aircraft below the following altitudes:

(c) Over other than congested* areas. An altitude of 500 feet above the surface, except over open water or sparsely populated areas. In those cases, the aircraft may not be operated closer than 500 feet to any person, vessel, vehicle, or structure."

I find it hard to imagine an outhouse – even a port-a-potty – would not be considered a 'structure'. The balloon pilot in this case was saved from legal action because he was in the act of taking off when this event occurred. The prudent pilot of any aircraft should gain altitude as quickly as possible to avoid becoming a hazard to those on the ground. Drifting along at 5 feet AGL and, in this case, 'discommoding' the occupant(s) of the port-a-potties could very well be construed as "careless and reckless operation of an aircraft" (FAR 91.13). I guess you could call this a 'close encounter of the turd kind.'

* I could not find any definition of the word "congested" in either FAR Pt. 1 or the Pilot-Controller Glossary. It then behooves the wise aviator to err on the conservative side and stay well above and away from the surface of the planet. That's where all the low-level hazards reside…including the FAA. And they are the ones who get to define those pesky words of oblique and obscure meaning when you must stand before a judge at your hearing or trial.

Flying is not dangerous – crashing is dangerous.

AIRLINE CAPTAIN DIES ENROUTE

I recall the first time I flew as part of a crew. The crusty old S.O.B. of a Captain (okay, granted he flew B-17 missions over Germany in WWII, another hundred-plus in F-86's over Korea and a bunch in B-52's early in the Vietnam unpleasantness, so I guess he had earned the right) pointed to the right edge of the radio stack and growled at me, saying: "Kid, ya see this line down the instrument panel? Everything to the left of that is mine!"

"Yessir." I responded.

"Do ya see that self-same line to which I have just referred? Everything to the right of that is mine!" I sat there the entire flight with my hands in my lap...I think all I did on that trip was adjust the cockpit fresh air vent - once.

There was a story, years ago, when a Braniff (?) 747 Captain died enroute from Honolulu to Los Angeles. The First Officer made a routine landing at LAX, did the paper work, and drove home.

In one corner of Operations a group of Captains were huddled, all marveling at how a First Officer was able to land the huge aircraft without the Captain's supervision.

In an opposite corner a large group of First Officers were gathered, all marveling at how the First Officer was able to notice the Captain was dead.

FAR 91.105 Flight Crewmembers at Stations

(a) During takeoff and landing, and while enroute, each required flight crewmember shall –

(2) Keep the safety belt fastened while at the crewmember station.

(b) Each required flight crewmember...shall, during takeoff and landing, keep his or her shoulder harness fastened while at his or her duty station.

The only exceptions to this FAR are; if the aircraft is not equipped with shoulder harnesses or if the crewperson would not be able to perform their duties with the shoulder harness fastened.

So what is meant by this rule even in, say, a Cessna 172? The required crewmember (the PIC) must have attached, fastened or secured their seat belt and shoulder harness about themselves and must keep it fastened during takeoff, cruise and landing; in essence, any time the plane is in motion and the required crewperson is at their duty station.

Now, here's another wrinkle: When practicing instrument approaches with a safety pilot aboard, is the safety pilot a "required crewmember?" The answer – I know you all got this correct – is "Yes." Therefore, the safety-minded and legally-cognizant PIC will insure that any 'required crewmember' comply with this FAR during the course of the flight.

It's probably a good thing the Captain in this story had his belts and harnesses fastened lest he collapsed onto the control column and create a flight hazard for that poor First Officer.

Field Pilot Badge
Austrian Empire 1912 – 1916
Emperor Franz-Josef 1

Aviation is not so much a profession as it is a disease.

AIRLINE HIGH FLIGHT

The first of several "High Flight" [amended] offerings in this book.

AIRLINE 'HIGH FLIGHT':

Oh! I have slipped the surly bonds of gate times

And held rigid by impossible air traffic controllers;

Upward I've climbed and joined the congested skies

Of fixes, missed approaches and done a hundred things

My passengers did not care for delays, turbulence and held

In the holding pattern low on fuel. Waiting there,

I've chased the schedules and flung

Myself against management and union rules.

Up, up the long ascent in seniority list

I've topped and gone on to the next aircraft

Hoping that I do not get furloughed.

And, while with worried mind I've trod

The difficult sanctity of regulation,

Waiting for the FAA inspector, who thinks he's God.

- Brian Carver

In honor of Captain Phillip Valente

(Lifted without remorse from the QB <u>Beam</u>, June 2012)

Pilot, Military Airship, Officer
France
Collar insignia
1912 – 1922

Always keep an 'out' in your back pocket.

AIRLINE JOB DESCRIPTION

Co-pilots and First Officers – those poor hapless souls who occupy the right seat in airplanes requiring a 'crew' – are expected to back up the actions of the Captain, contribute via CRM to safe flight and basically be a good [and quiet] wingman. A good Captain will welcome this crewmember to the flight deck; a poor one may be described below.

An old USAF buddy of mine became a co-pilot for TWA when he mustered out. When anyone asked him what he did at the airline, he replied:

"I was the sexual advisor to the Captain."

"You were the WHAT?" was the usual response.

"Yeah," he continued, "He used to tell me 'If I want any fucking advice from you I'll ask for it."

When you see a crew standing together, how can you tell who the Flight Engineer is? Say "Traffic, 12 o'clock" and he'll look to his left.

Defined, CRM is the "...method for addressing, assessing and improving human behavior within the aviation context. Aeronautical Decision Making (ADM), situational awareness, resources and workload management are primary CRM disciplines used to counter errors and threats."

Crew Resource Management (CRM), while originally developed within and by the airline industry, can certainly be used to good effect in General Aviation. If you are flying with another pilot, conduct a 'preflight briefing' as to who is the PIC, who has what duties, who will do what in the event of an emergency, etc. You can develop and customize the briefing to your needs, the capabilities of the airplane and the mission requirements.

If you are flying with a 'civilian' (non-flying person), brief them thoroughly as to what you have planned for the flight, the weather (turbulence) you may potentially encounter, and then give them one or two jobs to do – looking for and calling out traffic is the most basic. Depending on their experience level, you can assign all sorts of cockpit chores to involve that person in the management of the flight. You create a 'crew' environment for the flight, you involve that person in the conduct of the flight and you just might create a spark of interest which downstream turns into another pilot joining the ranks. It's all good.

The worst day of flying beats the best day at work.

AN AVIATION FABLE

Politically incorrect as Hell: But you knew that when you bought this book, right? There surely is a woman pilot's rebuttal to this, but I haven't seen it. If one of you lady pilots can come up with one, I'll include it in the second edition...if there is one.

Once upon a time, a pilot asked a beautiful Princess, "Will you marry me?"

The Princess said "NO!!"

....and the pilot lived happily ever after and rode motorcycles, made many deployments, got good promotions and duty stations, made love to skinny big-breasted women, hunted and fished and raced cars, went to men's clubs, dated women half his age, drank Whiskey, Beer, Tequila & Rum, did shooters and Flaming Hookers and never heard bitching, never paid child support or alimony, hosed cheerleaders, movie star wanna-be's and barmaids and kept his house and guns; never got cheated on while he was at work or on a deployment; all his friends thought he was friggin' cool as hell; he had tons of money in the bank.

And he always left the toilet seat up.

My #1 FAVORITE regulation:

FAR 91.3 Responsibility and Authority of the Pilot in Command

(a) The pilot in command of an aircraft is directly responsible for, and is the final authority as to, the operation of that aircraft.

(b) In an in-flight emergency requiring immediate action, the pilot in command may deviate from any rule of this part to the extent required to meet that emergency.

The reg goes on to say that upon the request of the Administrator a report on the deviation shall be submitted in writing to the Administrator. More importantly, do NOT compromise safety of the flight if you, as PIC, deem that action to be unsafe. If Tower asks "Expedite to the next turnoff" do not put you or plane at risk by rushing the after-landing process in order to comply. If it can be accomplished safely, then yes, comply. If unable, that's the way it goes; if the airplane on short final behind you must make a go-around, so be it. If ATC tells you to do something and you feel safety would be compromised, the phrase "Unable" works well. You will then be asked "State your intentions?" but you always have a 'Plan B' for everything you do in an aircraft, don't you?

You cannot be lost if you don't care where you are.

ANYBODY CAN DO ANYTHING IN AN AIRPLANE...ONCE!

NTSB Part 830 Notifications and reporting of Aircraft Accidents or Incidents

830.2 Definitions

Aircraft Accident means an occurrence associated with the operation of an aircraft which takes place between the time any person boards the aircraft with the intention of flight and all such persons have disembarked, and in which any person suffers death or serious injury, or in which the aircraft receives substantial damage.

Substantial Damage means damage or failure which adversely affects the structural strength, performance or flight characteristics of the aircraft, and which would normally require major repair or replacement of the affected component. Engine failure or damage limited to an engine if only one engine fails or is damaged, bent fairings or cowling, dented skin, small punctured holes in the skin or fabric, ground damage to rotor or propeller blades, and damage to landing gear, wheels, tires, flaps, engine accessories, brakes or wingtips are not considered "substantial damage" for the purpose of this part.

I would wager the B-24 in the picture could be included under the definition of "aircraft accident". Believe it or don't a gear-up landing is NOT considered an 'accident'.

NTSB Part 830.5 Immediate Notification

The operator of any civil aircraft...shall immediately, and by the most expeditious means available, notify the nearest NTSB office when:

(a) An aircraft accident or any of the following listed serious incidents occur:

(1) Flight control system malfunction or failure

(2) Inability of any required flight crewmember to perform normal flight duties as a result of injury or illness

(3) Failure of any internal turbine engine component that results in the escape of debris other than out the exhaust path

(4) Inflight fire

(5) Aircraft collision in flight

(6) Damage to property, other than the aircraft, estimated to exceed $25,000 for repair … or fair market value in the event of total loss, whichever is less

So, if you are involved in such an event AND you survive, you are required to notify the nearest NTSB office immediately and by the most expeditious manner possible. May you never be there.

Let's do a 360 and get the Hell outa here!

AT THE AMEs

If you can find an AME who is also a pilot, good on ya! They will help keep you flying until the last day you possibly can.

I recently went to the AME for my flight physical. After exhaustive lab tests, he said I was doing 'fairly well' for my age. (I just turned 60.)

A little concerned about that comment, I couldn't resist asking him, "Do you think I'll live to be 80?"

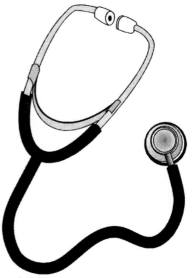

He asked: "Do you smoke tobacco, or drink beer, wine or hard liquor?" "Oh no," I replied, "and I don't do drugs, either!"

Then he asked: "Do you eat rib-eye steaks or barbecued ribs?"

I said: "Not much... my former doctor said that all red meat is very unhealthy!"

"Do you spend a lot of time in the sun, like playing golf, sailing, hiking, fishing or bicycling?" "No, I don't," I said.

He asked: "Do you gamble, drive fast cars, or have a lot of sex?" "No," I said. He was quiet for a few seconds, and then asked:

"Then, why do you even give a shit?"

Just about every certificated pilot – save balloonists, glider and Light Sport pilots – are required to possess a medical certificate when exercising the privileges we've earned. When visiting the AME we pretty much leave things up to him/her when determining our fitness to fly. Have you ever wondered just what it is they're looking for, and the range of acceptable standards allowed? Well, a slow read through FAR 67 will enlighten you no end.

You will be amazed that "Bifoveal fixation and vengeance-phoria relationships"- FAR 67.103(f) - can be a cause for concern in the minds of most AME's. I know I don't want to be anywhere near the person who has that problem!

A medical application may be denied if a person has "a personality disorder that is severe enough to have repeatedly manifested itself by overt acts." - FAR 67.107(a)(1) Hell, every pilot has those; it occurs every time we fly. What's the big deal?

If one must arise several times during the night for that 'nocturnal relief mission', does that mean I have to declare "A transient loss of control of the nervous system without satisfactory medical explanation of the cause."? FAR 67.109(a)(3) Would having two beers at dinner be a 'satisfactory medical explanation?' Jeez, I sure hope so. Otherwise, I'm sunk.

Related Reading: FAR 67, AIM section 8

Class & Pilot wing
Women's Auxiliary Service Pilot (WASP)
US Army Air Corps
1942 – 1945
(These were awarded to Mary Strok)

The medical profession is the natural enemy of the aviation profession.

AUSSIE PILOT REQUESTS HELP

A few years back I consulted on a few projects at Jeppesen, one of which was a program for a Chinese airline 'ab initio' flight training course. This was to be administered to their 'best and brightest' down under outside Brisbane, Australia. (BTW: Half of the first class had never even driven an automobile prior to commencing their flight training...but that's another story) Our contact down there sent me this. Now, their rules are but slightly different than ours – but see if you can count the rules violations in this. I gave up trying. Don't mind the 'misspellings', it's just the Aussie version of what passes for 'English' down under.

Cheers Mate!

G'day!

I am writing to you because I need your help to get me bloody pilot's license back. You keep telling me you got all the right contacts. Well now's your chance to make something happen for me because, mate, I'm bloody desperate. But first, I'd better tell you what happened during my last flight review with the CAA Examiner.

On the phone, Ron (that's the CAA d***head), seemed a reasonable sort of a bloke. He politely reminded me of the need to do a flight review every two years. He even offered to drive out, have a look over my property and let me operate from my own strip. Naturally I agreed to that. Anyway, Ron turned up last Wednesday. First up, he said he was a bit surprised to see the plane on a small strip outside my homestead, because the "ALA" (Authorized Landing Area), is about a mile away. I explained that because this strip was so close to the homestead, it was more convenient than the "ALA," and despite the power lines crossing about midway down the strip, it's really not a problem to land and take-off, because at the halfway point down the strip you're usually still on the ground. For some reason Ron seemed nervous. So, although I had done the preflight inspection only four days earlier, I decided to do it all over again. Because the prick was watching me carefully, I walked around the plane three times instead of my usual two.

My effort was rewarded because the colour finally returned to Ron's cheeks. In fact, they went a bright red. In view of Ron's obviously better mood, I told him I was going to combine the test flight with some farm work, as I had to deliver two "poddy calves" from the home paddock to the main herd.

After a bit of a chase I finally caught the calves and threw them into the back of the ol' Cessna 172. We climbed aboard but Ron, started getting onto me about weight and balance calculations and all that crap. Of course I knew that sort of thing was a waste of time because calves like to move around a bit particularly when they see themselves 500-feet off the ground! So, it's bloody pointless trying to secure them as you know. However, I did tell Ron that he shouldn't worry as I always keep the trim wheel set on neutral to ensure we remain pretty stable at all stages throughout the flight.

Anyway, I started the engine and cleverly minimized the warm-up time by tramping hard on the brakes and gunning her to 2,500 RPM. I then discovered that Ron has very acute hearing, even though he was wearing a bloody headset. Through all that noise he detected a metallic rattle and demanded I account for it. Actually it began about a month ago and was caused by a screwdriver that fell down a hole in the floor and lodged in the fuel selector mechanism. The selector can't be moved now, but it doesn't matter because it's jammed on "All tanks," so I suppose that's Okay.

However, as Ron was obviously a nit-picker, I blamed the noise on vibration from a stainless steel thermos flask which I keep in a beaut little possie between the windshield and the magnetic compass. My explanation seemed to relax Ron, because he slumped back in the seat and kept looking up at the cockpit roof. I released the brakes to taxi out, but unfortunately the plane gave a leap and spun to the right.

"Hell" I thought, "not the starboard wheel chock again." The bump jolted Ron back to full alertness. He looked around just in time to see a rock thrown by the prop-wash disappear completely through the windscreen of his brand new Commodore. "Now I'm really in trouble," I thought...

While Ron was busy ranting about his car; I ignored his requirement that we taxi to the "ALA," and instead took off under the power lines. Ron didn't say a word, at least not until the engine started coughing right at the lift off point, and then he bloody screamed his head off. "OhGawdOhGawdOhGawd!"!"

"Now take it easy Ron," I told him firmly. "That often happens on take-off and there is a good reason for it." I explained patiently that I usually run the plane on standard MOGAS, but one day I accidentally put in a gallon or two of kerosene. To compensate for the low octane of the kerosene, I siphoned in a few gallons of super MOGAS and shook the wings up and down a few times to mix it up. Since then, the engine has been coughing a bit but in general it works just fine, if you know how to coax it properly.

Anyway, at this stage Ron seemed to lose all interest in my test flight. He pulled out some rosary beads, closed his eyes and became lost in prayer (I didn't think anyone was a Catholic these days). I selected some nice music on the HF radio to help him relax. Meanwhile, I climbed to my normal cruising altitude of 10,500-feet. I don't normally put in a flight plan or get the weather because, as you know getting FAX access out here is a friggin' joke and the weather is always "8/8 blue" anyway. But since I had that near miss with a Saab 340, I might have to change me thinking on that.

Anyhow, on leveling out, I noticed some wild camels heading into my improved pasture. I hate bloody camels, and always carry a loaded .303, clipped inside the door of the Cessna just in case I see any of the bastards.

We were too high to hit them, but as a matter of principle, I decided to have a go through the open window. Mate, when I pulled the bloody rifle out, the effect on Ron, was friggin' electric. As I fired the first shot his neck lengthened by about six inches and his eyes bulged like a rabbit with myxo. He really looked as if he had been jabbed with an electric cattle prod on full power. In fact, Ron's reaction was so distracting that I lost concentration for a second and the next shot went straight through the port tyre. Ron was a bit upset about the shooting (probably one of those pinko animal lovers I guess) so I decided not to tell him about our little problem with the tyre.

Shortly afterwards I located the main herd and decided to do my fighter pilot trick. Ron had gone back to praying when, in one smooth sequence, I pulled on full flaps, cut the power and started a sideslip from 10,500-feet down to 500-feet at 130, knots indicated (the last time I looked anyway) and the little needle rushed up to the red area on me ASI.

What a buzz, mate! About half way through the descent I looked back in the cabin to see the calves gracefully suspended in mid-air and mooing like crazy. I was going to comment to Ron on this unusual sight, but he looked a bit green and had rolled himself into the fetal position and was screamin' his freakin' head off. Mate, talk about being in a bloody zoo. You should've been there, it was so bloody funny!

At about 500-feet I leveled out, but for some reason we kept sinking. When we reached 50-feet, I applied full power but nothin' happened. No noise - no nothin'. Then, luckily, I heard me instructor's voice in me head saying "carb heat, carb heat." So I pulled carb heat on and that helped quite a lot, with the engine finally regaining full power. Whew, that was really close, let me tell you!

Then mate, you'll never guess what happened next! As luck would have it, at that height we flew into a massive dust cloud caused by the cattle and suddenly went I.F. bloody R, mate.

Crikey, you would have been really proud of me as I didn't panic once, not once, but I did make a mental note to consider an instrument rating as soon as me gyro is repaired (something I've been meaning to do for a while (now). Suddenly Ron's elongated neck and bulging eyes reappeared. His mouth opened wide, very wide, but no sound emerged.

"Take it easy," I told him, "we'll be out of this in a minute." Sure enough, about a minute later we emerged, still straight and level and still at 50-feet.

Admittedly I was surprised to notice that we were upside down, and I kept thinking to myself, "I hope Ron didn't notice that I had forgotten to set the QNH when we were taxiing." This minor tribulation forced me to fly to a nearby valley in which I had to do a half roll to get upright again. By now the main herd had divided into two groups leaving a narrow strip between them. "Ah!" I thought, "There's an omen. We'll land right there." Knowing that the tyre problem demanded a slow approach, I flew a couple of steep turns with full flap. Soon the stall warning horn was blaring so loud in my ear that I cut its circuit breaker to shut it up, but by then I knew we were slow enough anyway. I turned steeply onto a 75-foot final and put her down with a real thud. Strangely enough, I had always thought you could only ground loop in a tail dragger but, as usual, I was proved wrong again!

Halfway through our third loop, Ron at last recovered his sense of humor. Talk about laugh. I've never seen the likes of it. He couldn't stop. We finally rolled to a halt and I released the calves, who bolted out of the aircraft like there was no tomorrow. I then began picking clumps of dry grass. Between gut wrenching fits of laughter, Ron asked what I was doing. I explained that we had to stuff the port tyre with grass so we could fly back to the homestead. It was then that Ron really lost the plot and started running away from the aircraft.

Can you believe it? The last time I saw him he was off into the distance, arms flailing in the air and still shrieking with laughter. I later heard that he had been confined to a psychiatric institution - poor bugger!

Anyhow mate, that's enough about Ron. The problem is I got this letter from CASA withdrawing, as they put it, my privileges to fly; until I have undergone a complete pilot training course again and undertaken another flight proficiency test. Now I admit that I made a mistake in taxiing over the wheel chock and not setting the QNH using strip elevation, but I can't see what else I did that was a so bloody bad that they have to withdraw me flamin' license. Can you?

Bob Guthrie
Oonadata Station
Northern Territory

What you know is not so important as what you do
with it.

AVIATION 101

Every industry has pithy sayings and aviation is no different. Gathered here are some having more pith than most. I can remember years ago landing at a smaller non-towered airport in my Citabria. Just as I touched down, I had to sneeze; when I looked up I was going between the runway lights out into the grass. No big deal, right? (See Rule #5) I was a mile from the line shack where I was meeting some flying buddies – they couldn't have seen that, right? WRONG! As I taxied up, they all stood up and applauded! I told them that any lesser-skilled pilot would have taken out a runway light. They didn't buy that, either. Oh, well...there are unbelievers among us still...

1. It is best to keep the pointy end going forward and the greasy down as much and as long as possible.

2. Takeoffs are optional; landings are mandatory.

3. Flying is not dangerous; crashing is dangerous.

4. Generally, if you push the stick/yoke forward, the houses get bigger. If you pull the stick/yoke back, they get smaller. Unless you pull the stick/yoke all the way back

and keep it there, then everything gets bigger as it goes 'round and around. (e.g. "House-Barn-House-Barn")

5. The quality of the landing is inversely proportional to the number and importance of the people watching experiencing it.

6. The survivability of the landing is inversely proportional to the angle of arrival (Low angle = high survivability, and vise-versa).

7. Keep looking around – there's always something you missed.

8. Obey gravity, it's the law! (Gravity always wins)

9. You can only tie the record for low flying.

10. Any pilot who relies solely of terminal forecasts can be sold the Brooklyn Bridge. If they rely solely on winds aloft forecasts, they can be sold Niagara Falls.

11. Always fly the airplane with your head, not just your hands. The airplane should never get to a place in space and time that your mind hasn't gotten to at least ten minutes earlier.

12. Learn from the mistakes of others for you will never live long enough to make them all yourself.

13. In an airplane, you are always a student.

FAR 91.119 Minimum Safe Altitudes

Except when necessary for takeoff or landing, no person may operate an aircraft below the following altitudes:

(a) Anywhere: An altitude allowing, if a power unit fails, an emergency landing without undue hazard to persons or property on the surface.

I have not found a definition of the word 'undue' in relation to the word 'hazard' in my studies, so if you are charged with 'flat-hatting' across terra firma, guess who gets to define those words? Yep, the prosecuting attorney at your hearing or trial. Be ever-so-wary of low-altitude flying – that's the word to the wise.

Do not spin this aircraft! If a spin occurs, it will return to earth without further attention on the part of the aeronaut."

- Curtis-Wright *Flyer* handbook, circa 1910

AVIATION MONKEY

We can joke about things like this because we're insiders. Those not cut of this cloth had better keep their pie-holes shut (a tip o' the cover to Gunnery Sergeant R. Lee Ermey, USMC [ret.] for that descriptive euphemism). But when all Hell goes into the hand basket in a hurry, we sure look to the Skipper for guidance: Hell, our lives depend on it.

A guy walks into a pet store and was looking at the animals on display.

While he was there, an engineer from the local airport walked in and said to the shopkeeper, "I'd like a Line Service monkey, please." The clerk nodded, went to a cage at the side of the store and took out a monkey. He put a collar and leash on the animal and handed it to the engineer, saying, "That'll be $1,000." The engineer paid and left with the monkey.

Surprised, the first customer went to the shopkeeper and said, "That was a very expensive monkey. Most of them are only a few hundred dollars. Why did that one cost so much?" The shopkeeper answered, "Ahhh…that was a line service monkey. He can park, fuel, and service all types of aircraft, conduct all required ground ops testing, rig aircraft flight controls, and all with no mistakes. He's well worth the money."

With his interest piqued, the customer then looked around and spotted a monkey in another cage with a $10,000 price tag. "That one's even more expensive! What can it do?" he asked. "Oh, that one is a "Maintenance Supervisor" monkey. He can instruct at all levels of aircraft maintenance, supervise all corrective and preventive maintenance programs, supervise a crew and even do most of the paperwork: A very useful monkey indeed." The customer continued to look around the shop a little longer and found a third monkey in a cage. The price tag read $50,000. Reading that, the customer said, "$50,000!!!! Holy smoke, what does this one do?"

"Well", the shopkeeper said, "I've never actually seen him do anything but drink beer, screw the girl monkeys, and play with his dick, but his papers say he's an airline captain!"

FAR 61.3 Requirements for Certificates, Ratings & Authorizations

(a) Pilot Certificate. No person may serve as a required pilot flight crewmember of a civil aircraft...unless that person –

(1) Has a pilot certificate...in that person's physical possession or readily accessible in the aircraft when exercising the privileges of that certificate.

(2) Has photo identification in that person's physical possession or readily accessible in the aircraft when exercising the privileges...

(c) Medical certificate. A person may serve as a required flight crewmember...only if that person holds the appropriate medical certificate...that is in the person's physical possession or readily accessible in the aircraft.

I'd like to meet the AME willing to examine, let alone issue a medical certificate to, one of those monkeys.

Flight Mechanic's Badge
Czechslovakia
1947 - 1953

Never trade skill for luck.

AVIATIONS GREATEST LIES

Another 'Top Ten' list...except there are 30 of them this time. I've seen these on posters, t-shirts, coffee mugs [in really, really small print] and elsewhere where pilots and aviators gather. Who among us hasn't heard someone say at least one of these at some time? I know I'm guilty of at least three [Hell, no, I'm not going to tell you which ones!]. Well, enjoy... Oh, and by the way, these are for humorous and illustrative purposes ONLY...not necessarily 'rules'; more like 'guidelines'.

'Aviations Greatest Lies' Countdown

30. Of course I know where we are

29. I've got the traffic in sight

28. I've got the field in sight

27. I thought *you* took care of that

26. I just completed the annual...everything's perfect

25. I fly every day…I don't need recurrent training

24. We'll be home by lunchtime

23. Your plane will be ready by 2 o'clock

22. I can fly the box it came in

21. No need to look it up…I've got it all memorized

20. Most of my time is actual instrument

19. Sure, no problem, I've got 1,000 hours in that make/model

18. This plane outperforms the book by 20 %

17. We shipped that part yesterday

16. All you have to do is follow the book

15. Yes, I'm just 22, but I've got 6,000 hours, a 4-year degree and 2,500 in Lears

14. If we get just a little lower, I'll bet we can see the runway lights

13. Don't worry about weight and balance…she'll fly just fine

12. The weather is going to clear to VFR by the time we get there

11. I broke out right at minimums

10. I only need these glasses for reading

9. All that turbulence spoiled my landing

8. I fixed it right…it must have failed for some other reason

7. I have no interest in flying for the airlines

6. We'll be on time, maybe early

5. Me? I've *never* busted minimums

4. We in aviation are overpaid, underworked and well-respected

3. Pardon me, Miss…have you seen my Learjet keys?

2. I'm from the FAA and I'm here to help you

1. I'm *so* happy to see you here! (in reference to #2 above)

You will never do well if you stop doing better.

AVIATORS NIGHT BEFORE CHRISTMAS

Who-ever came up with this penned a classic. Let there be peace on earth...but keep your ammunition dry, just in case.

AVIATOR'S NIGHT BEFORE CHRISTMAS

T'was the night before Christmas, and out on the ramp,
Not an airplane was stirring, not even a Champ.
The aircraft were fastened to tie downs with care,
In hopes that - come morning - they all would be there.

The fuel trucks were nestled, all snug in their spots,
With gusts from two-forty at 39 knots.
I slumped at the fuel desk, now finally caught up,
And settled down comfortably, resting my butt.

When the radio lit up with noise and with chatter,
I turned up the scanner to see what was the matter.
A voice clearly heard over static and snow,
Called for clearance to land at the airport below.

He barked his transmission so lively and quick,
I'd have sworn that the call sign he used was "St. Nick."
I ran to the panel to turn up the lights,
The better to welcome this magical flight.

He called his position, no room for denial,
"St. Nicholas One, turnin' left onto final."
And what to my wondering eyes should appear,
But a Rutan-built sleigh, with eight Rotax Reindeer!

With vectors to final, down the glideslope he came,
As he passed all fixes, he called them by name:
"Now Ringo! Now Tolga! Now Trini and Bacun!
On Comet! On Cupid!" What pills was he takin'?

While controllers were sittin', and scratchin' their heads,
They phoned to my office, and I heard it with dread,
The message they left was both urgent and dour:
"When Santa pulls in, have him please call the tower."

He landed like silk, with the sled runners sparking,
Then I heard, "Left at Charlie," and "Taxi to parking."
He slowed to a taxi, turned off of three-oh,
And stopped on the ramp with a "Ho, ho-ho-ho..."

He stepped out of the sleigh, but before he could talk,
I ran out to meet him with my best set of chocks.
His red helmet and goggles were covered with frost,
And his beard was all blackened from Reindeer exhaust.

His breath smelled like peppermint, gone slightly stale,
And he puffed on a pipe, but he didn't inhale.
His cheeks were all rosy and jiggled like jelly,
His boots were as black as a crop-dusters' belly.

He was chubby and plump, in his suit of bright red,
And he asked me to "fill it, with hundred low-lead."
He came dashing in from the snow-covered pump,
I knew he was anxious for drainin' the sump.

I spoke not a word, but went straight to my work,
And I filled up the sleigh, but I spilled like a jerk.
He came out of the restroom, and sighed in relief,
Then he picked up a phone for a Flight Service brief.

And I thought as he silently scribed in his log,
These reindeer could land in an eighth-mile fog.
He completed his pre-flight, from the front to the rear,
Then he put on his headset, and I heard him yell, "Clear!"

And laying a finger on his push-to-talk,
He called up the tower for clearance and squawk.
"Take taxiway Charlie, the southbound direction,
Turn right three-two-zero at pilot's discretion"

He sped down the runway, the best of the best,
"Your traffic's a Grumman, inbound from the west."
Then I heard him proclaim, as he climbed through the night,
"Merry Christmas to all! I have traffic in sight."

The most dangerous part about flying is the drive
home from the airport.

AVOIDING MIDAIR COLLISION

Most mid-air collisions occur during VFR conditions near airports [who would have thought that was so?]. The main point being when approaching or departing an aerodrome, one had better be alert. Refer to the diagrams in the AIM regarding traffic pattern operations:

AIM 4-3-3 Traffic Patterns

1. Enter the pattern in level flight abeam the runway mid-point at pattern altitude [1,000'agl unless otherwise noted]

2. Maintain pattern altitude until abeam the approach end of the landing runway while on the downwind leg.

3. Complete the turn to final at least ¼ mile from the runway/

4. [During takeoff] Continue straight ahead until beyond the departure end of the runway.

5. If remaining in the traffic pattern, commence the crosswind turn beyond the departure end of the runway within 300' of pattern altitude.

6. If departing the traffic pattern, continue straight-out or exit with a 45° turn [left or right in the same direction as the traffic pattern] beyond the departure end of the runway, after reaching pattern altitude.

No, this is NOT how airplanes are made!

The occupants of these airplanes are extremely fortunate; they all walked away from an event that usually has fatal consequences. Recently in my local airspace this same thing happened resulting in two fatalities and one hospitalization. The one person who survived told me all that was felt was a 'bump' and then the airplane lost power. The pilot was barely able to maintain control over the airplane as it fell to earth. The other airplane wasn't as lucky; it lost a wing, killing the student and instructor on board.

Most midair collisions occur near airports on VFR days. Reducing the risks of a midair collision requires you:

1. **USING** your radio to make <u>accurate</u> position reports.

2. **LISTENING** to your radio to envision where others are.

3. **LOOKING** for signs of another airplane, e.g. sun glinting off the airplane, a flash of movement out the corner of your eye, an airplane shadow on the ground that   isn't yours, etc.

4. **REALIZING** that not every pilot will use their radio even if they have one on board AND there are antiques out there without radios as well.

5. **ENTERING & DEPARTING** traffic patterns at non-towered airports per the recommendations found in the AIM [4-3-2 & 4-3-3]

6. **PERFORMING** all maneuvers in the pattern 'by the book' and following SOP's so others may count on you to do things as expected; hopefully you can count on them for the same.

7. **STAYING** alert to potential and possible traffic conflicts [e.g. an instrument approach to the departure end of the runway you intend to use, someone announcing   a   long straight-in to either end of the runway you intend using, someone in an emergency doing something non-standard to get back to the airport, etc.

8. **KEEPING** your head on a swivel.

WWI pilot's maxim:

Keep looking around; beware the 'Hun in the sun.'

"Captain Eddie" Rickenbacker, US Air Service 1918
(October 8, 1890 – July 23, 1973)
US top-scoring WWI ace with 26 victories
Awarded the Congressional Medal of Honor

AIM 4-3-5 Unexpected Maneuvers in the Airport Traffic Pattern

There have been several incidents in the vicinity of...airports that were caused primarily by aircraft executing unexpected maneuvers. [Controllers and other pilots] can anticipate minor maneuvering [but] cannot anticipate major maneuvers...

This section of the AIM is a good read for guidelines in operating an aircraft near airports. The universal use of SOP's makes everyone's job a lot easier and safer. I have experienced on more than one occasion the terror that instantly comes when faced with another pilot doing something non-standard – like long unannounced straight-ins to the other end of the runway in use – and having to perform unusual attitudes and recoveries at low altitude in the traffic pattern. When confronted, these people are self-righteous, defensive or oblivious/clueless to the hazards they've created.

Once, when performing touch-and-goes in my Super Decathlon, the tower controller asked me to "Make a 360 for spacing." I asked "Would you like that horizontally or vertically?" You <u>*know*</u> *what his answer was.* ☺

Luck may stand in occasionally for skill, but not consistently.

B-1 BOMBER FOR SALE

And now, on the lighter side…

About 14 years ago a B-1 bomber was in here (Billings, MT) doing practice approaches and touch and goes. On one of the landings the pilot sets his brakes on fire. He taxis in, and the airport parks him on a taxiway and then puts cones around him until parts and mechanics can be brought in from Ellsworth AFB the next day.

The next day is a Saturday, which doesn't have much going on, so we get to laughing in the tower that maybe somebody should hang a For Sale sign on the plane. We convince one of our guys who's well known for doing things like this that it would be a good idea.

So he takes off for the hardware store to buy a For Sale sign. On the way back he stops at a car dealer and gets one of those "As is/No Warranty" signs that hang in all used cars. On that sign was written something like low miles, new engines, needs brakes and tires. Those signs were taped together, and off goes our hero.

He climbs over the fence, leaving some skin on the barbed wire, and makes his way the 1000 feet or so to the aircraft. As he's doing that, we see a couple of airport vehicles starting to gather with the recently arrived mechanics as well as the plane's crew.

Not looking good for our intrepid airplane salesman. He gets to the nose wheel and tapes the sign to the nose strut.

Then he starts to make his way back from the plane as the vehicles start to head out from the shop on the way to the bomber. Somehow he makes it without being seen.

The vehicles arrive at the plane, and of course notice the sign right away. The Air Force guys are in stitches, funniest thing they've seen in a long time. Airport guys are not sure what to think. Airport management is livid as they've been tasked with security.

Pretty soon a camera appears and all the Air Force guys are taking pictures of each other by the sign.

Our hero is back in the tower now, and notices the bomber's commander is talking on a cell phone. Our guy gets on the radio to the airport truck and asks for that guy's phone number. As soon as he finishes that call, our guy calls the aircraft commander. When he answers, our guy says "I'm calling about the plane you have for sale." The aircraft commander about falls over from the laughter. It just so happened that the chief photographer for our local newspaper is a pilot and he may have been called prior to the sign being placed. He was told to get up here with a big lens.

An article showed on the front page of the Sunday paper. When that came out, the Colonel running Ellsworth called the airport director and read him the riot act, wondering what kind of dog and pony show he was running up there.

We were later informed by the crew that the sign was framed and is now permanently mounted inside the aircraft. Hard to have <u>that</u> kind of fun anymore.

Any comment regarding how well things are going – or in regards to tailwinds of any velocity – will immediately get things going in the opposite direction.

B-25 MOON

This is one of 'those' photos that will never make the cover of FLYING magazine, no matter how good the focus, the symmetrical composition and the feeling of flight as evidenced by the blur of the propeller blades. Maybe I'll include this as 'Miss June' in the Aviator's Bathroom Reader wall calendar.

FAR 91.105 Flight Crewmembers at Stations:

(a) During takeoff and landing, and while enroute, each required flight crewmember shall –

(1) Be at the crewmember station unless the absence is necessary to perform duties...or in connection with physiological needs; and

(2) Keep the safety belt fastened while at the crewmember station

I'm fairly sure 'mooning' the camera ship is outside the normal performance of one's duties and certainly cannot be construed as being in "connection with physiological needs". However, of even greater importance is:

FAR 91.107   Use of Safety Belts & Shoulder Harnesses

(a) Unless otherwise authorized by the Administrator –

(1) No person may take off a U.S. registered aircraft (exceptions) unless the pilot in command ensures that each person on board is briefed on how to fasten and unfasten that person's safety belt and, if installed, shoulder harness.

(2) No pilot may cause to be moved on the surface, take off or land a U.S. registered civil aircraft (exceptions) unless the pilot in command of that aircraft ensures that each person on board has been notified to fasten his or her safety belt and, if installed, his or her shoulder harness.

This seems so basic, so elementary, so common-sensical; Why do I include this?

In all the PTS's for all the certificates and rating, there is a requirement that the PIC conducts a passenger briefing prior to flight. In reality, as you can read in the regulation above, the briefing <u>must</u> be conducted even before the aircraft begins to move about the surface! I was told about a local examiner (NOT me) who failed a flightcheck (after the ground portion had been accomplished) after the plane had taxied five feet! It was because the (commercial AMEL) applicant failed to ensure the safety belts and harnesses were fastened and the examiner was briefed on how to fasten and unfasten them.

You may consider this a B.S. reason to bust a flightcheck, but these briefings are in the regulations and are MANDATORY! Why do you think the airline flight attendants pay such close attention to this every time they brief the passengers prior to pushback? Because it's REQUIRED! You, as PIC, are obliged to brief each and every passenger on how to fasten and unfasten the safety belts and shoulder harnesses. You <u>must</u> ensure they are fastened prior to that craft moving even one inch on the surface. If you do no other task informing your passengers of the safety requirements, do this one.

A thorough passenger briefing might sound like this:

"Here are your safety belts and shoulder harnesses. To attach them, insert the metal end into the buckle and to tighten, pull the strap. To release the safety belt lift up on the buckle tab.

There are two exits on this C-172 Heavy* (point to them). To latch the door*, push down on the handle, to release and open the door lift up on the handle. In the event of an off-airport landing, exit the aircraft to the rear and we'll meet up 50 yards behind the airplane.

Please keep your feet off the rudder pedals as they are a flight control, and do not pull back on the yoke as it also is a flight control.

We have cabin heat and fresh air ventilation available.

Please ensure your safety belt (and shoulder harness) remains attached and snug the entire flight.

So sit back, relax and enjoy the flight."

* Customize these parts per the aircraft you're flying that day.

Croatia Army Pilot
1941 – 1944
A short-lived independent Croatian air force arose from a dismembered Yugoslavia and allied itself with Nazi Germany. They did not last long, being decimated on the Russian Front.

Airspeed, Altitude, Brains: Any 2 are required for a successful flight.

BALLS TO THE WALLS

The term "I've got the balls to the wall" has its origins in the early days of flight when the throttle(s), propeller and mixture controls had round balls on the end to afford the pilot a better grip. Pushing the throttles full forward towards the instrument panel to provide maximum power and thus speed equated to: Balls to the Walls.

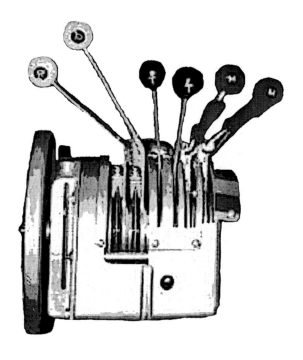

St. Louis Approach to United: "United 123 best forward speed to the marker, you're number one."

United 123 (male voice): "Roger, balls to the wall."

St. Louis Approach to American: "American 4321, you're number two behind a United 737, follow him, cleared visual, best forward speed."

American 4321 (female voice): "Well I can't do balls to the wall, but I can do wide open."

-Radio silence-

Unidentified Pilot (male voice): "Is American hiring?"

FAR 91.117 Aircraft Speed

(a) Unless otherwise authorized by the Administrator, no person may operate an aircraft below 10,000 feet MSL at an indicated airspeed of more than 250 knots (288 mph)

(b) Unless otherwise authorized, no person may operate...at or below 2,500 feet AGL within 4 nm of the primary Class C or Class D airport...more than 200 knots (230 mph)

(c) Unless otherwise authorized, no person may operate...in the airspace underlying Class B airspace or in a VFR corridor...through Class B airspace...more than 200 knots (230 mph)

So to recap:

- Under 10,000' MSL, keep it below 250 knots (288 mph)

- Within 4 nm of the primary Class C or D airport, stay below 200 knots (230 mph)

- Under Class B airspace or while transiting through a VFR corridor, remain below 200 knots (230 mph)

This DC-3 is the wind indicator at the Whitehorse, Yukon Territory, Canada airport. It is so finely balanced a wind of just 4 knots will cause the airplane to turn into and face the wind.

"Keep the aeroplane in such an attitude that the air pressure is directly in the pilot's face." - Horace C. Barber, 1912

BECAUSE I FLY

BECAUSE I FLY

I laugh more than others,

I look up and see more than they do.

I know how the clouds feel,

What it's like to have the Blue in my lap;

To look down on birds,

To feel freedom through the stick.

Who but I can weave through God's outstretched arms

And then feel the blessing of His presence?

Who else has seen the unclimbed peaks from above?

The rainbow's secrets?

The real reason birds sing?

Because I fly

I envy no-one on earth.

- Anonymous

Aviate, Navigate, Communicate – in that order.

BIBLICAL ADMONITIONS FOR AVIATORS

I have a passable relationship with Biblical studies and have been looking for some time – casually, I admit – for the chapter and verse from where these truisms were first spake unto us by the prophets of old. They were then written – no doubt in hieroglyphics at first – on papyrus and handed down to the Greek soothsayer Aeronauticus, the Roman Stentorian Gluteus Maximus all the way to the King James version quoted here, which explains the archaic language of 'Ye Gud Olde Dayz'. Take heed, ye skyfarers, and transgress them not.

1. As the operator who giveth wrong numbers, so respected is he who lavishly extolleth his own exploits in the skye.

2. He mayeth enlarge upon the dangers of his adventures, but up the sleeve of his listeners shall be heard the tinkling of silvery laughter.

3. Let not thy familiarity with thy craft breed contempt, lest thou become exceedingly careless at a time when great care is required for thy well-being.

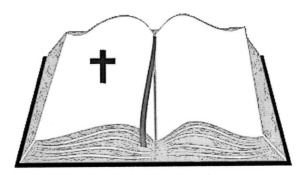

4. Obey with fervor the laws and observe prudence thereto. Spin thou no lower than 1,500 cubits above the firmament and stunt not above thine own domicile, for the hand of the Law is heavy and reacheth far and wide throughout the land.

5. Incur not the wrath of thy commander by shirking thy duty to the rules, for he who observeth not the SOP's shall be cast unto Supply, Administration or verily even becoming the PLO.

6. Let not thy prowess in the heavens persuade thee that others cannot do even as thou doest; for he that showeth off whence the public can see – and thereby tells tales about thee - is an abomination unto his fellow pilots.

7. More praiseworthy is he who can touch tail-skid and both main wheels upon the firmament at the same time than he who loopeth and rolleth 'til some faire young damsel stares in amazement at his daring.

8. He who breaketh an undercarriage in a forced landing may, in time, be forgiven; but he who runeth out of fuel shall be despised forever.

9. Beware of the aircraft driver who taketh off without looking behind him for there is no health in such a person and, verily, their days are numbered.

10. Clever skyfarers take the reproofs of their instructor with rapt attentiveness, confessing their dumbness and regarding themselves with humor. They then try again, profiting by the wise counsel and taking naught offense at aught that has been shewn unto them.

11. As is a postage stamp that lacketh glue, so are words of caution to a Foole: They adhere not and verily go in one ear and outeth the other, for there is nothing 'twixt and 'tween to stop them.

12. Hearken unto the teachings of yon Grey-beards and forsake not the practice of prudence for in truth the reckless shall inhabit the earth for only a short spell.

13. Look to thy left and to thy right as thou journey through the heavens lest thy friends buy drinks for thy widow and console her in other ways.

14. Hear instruction; be wise, take it to heart and refuseth it not so thou canst soareth with the eagles. Yee length of days and a life of peace shall be added unto thee.

Truly superior pilots are those who use their truly superior judgment to avoid those situations requiring their truly superior skills.

Thanks, Spence! - ed.

BLOWING IT BY NOT FLYING

I KNEW there was more to life than food, shelter and clothing! I plan to follow this guy's lead and fly more...that way I can save more for other 'fun' stuff – like the bathroom renovation my sweetie wants to do.

For a number of years I was afraid to calculate my exact flying expense. A few years ago I finally decided to get right down to the facts and came up with the following information. This may not relate directly to your expenses but I believe it is worthwhile considering my approach.

First I calculated my fixed expense; what I pay if I never fly a minute each year. First the hanger expense; I figure this is less than I would pay for an apartment for a girlfriend on the side and I am far less likely to get shot by my wife so I figure in the long run I am saving money considering a divorce and medical expenses. Next I looked at insurance. When I considered that I pay car insurance, medical expense, Social security expense, deductibles, life insurance and countless extended warranty policies/insurance it became clear to me that what I pay for airplane related insurance is such a small percentage that it is hardly worth considering. I help with my own annuals and all maintenance so that is worth something; perhaps a few thousand dollars saved each year. As I see it all of my fixed expense ends up being an actual savings of perhaps $5,000 per year (I don't work cheap you know).

When it comes to variable expense I first look at fuel. AV gas is around $5.50 per gallon while auto gas is only $3.00. With this in mind, I feel comfortable in saying that it is only $2.50 more to buy AV gas. Therefore, It seems to me that if I burn 12 gallons per hour then fuel to fly only cost me $30 per hour and if I can split that expense with a passenger that goes down to only $15 dollars per hour out of pocket. Oil is another factor to consider. I figure that I lose a couple of quarts of oil over the side every hour due to leeks and I burn about one quart per hour. With this in mind it is easy enough to figure that if I burn one quart and don't burn the two quarts that leek out then I actually come out ahead one quart per hour so oil shouldn't be considered an expense.

Now comes the good part. If I have a savings of $5,000 per year on fixed expense and it only cost $15.00 per hour to fly, I can fly 200 hours per year for $3000 of my savings and realize an actual savings, in pocket, of $2,000 per year which I can put into savings.

If I didn't have an airplane I would not be able to save the $5,000 each year so I would have no savings. As it is, I get to fly and I am able to put back the $2,000 for tougher times which we will surly need as time goes by. Therefore, I cannot afford to not have an airplane. Having an airplane and not flying it is not good for the engine so the 200 hours flying time is something I must do to protect our $2,000 annual savings.

This is how I explain the cost of flying to my wife.

Works for me.

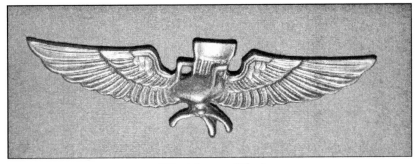

'Chairborne Pilot'
US Navy (unauthorized)
1960 –

Keep flying the airplane until all the moving parts
stop moving.

BLUE ANGELS HOLD FIRST-EVER OPEN TRY-OUTS

PENSACOLA, FL.

Harold Enderby's friends say that when he first saw the Navy's televised announcement that the Flight Demonstration Squadron, better known as the Blue Angels, would be holding open tryouts for the first time in its history, the lifelong aviation buff turned to his fellow sanitation workers at Doug's Dugout Bar-N-Grill and said, "Mark my words - I'm going to be a Blue Angel if it's the last thing I do."

And this Sunday, that dream came true for an incredible 43 seconds, as Enderby got the chance to fly the famed Blue Angels' F/A-18 Hornet directly into the tarmac during the first day of the Navy's most dramatic and colorful audition program ever.

Since 1946, the Blue Angels have recruited only elite military fighter pilots. But this week and this week only, the Navy is giving the public a rare treat: allowing ordinary, everyday citizens a chance to try out for the world's premiere precision flying team. Memorial services for Enderby, along with five other late aspiring aviators will begin Friday and continue throughout the week.

Crowds line up for the chance to fly a supersonic jet:

"Some of these folks may not have worked their way through four years of the Naval Academy, 10 years of flying missions as a naval aviator on three different carriers, two sessions at the fighter school at Miramar, and another 18 months of special aerobatics and flight operations here at Pensacola like I did but they sure had spirit," Blue Angel member Johnny "Crash" Krewsh said. "They gave it their all and that's what counts. My hat is off to them, and to their surviving family members."

With would-be pilots lining up by the thousands and crowds predicted to grow even larger over the next six days, the excitement and death toll are both expected to rise.

"It was quite a sight to see so many citizens arriving at the airbase entrance just hours after the initial announcement," said Lt. Cmdr. Maxfield "G'night, John-boy" Walton, the officer in charge of registering and interviewing the excited applicants, as well as contacting their next of kin. "Who knows? Your old math teacher, a cab driver, the guy in the next cubicle who can't seem to do anything right anybody could be the next Chuck Yeager. Now this is their chance to strap themselves into at $41 million 1,200 mile-per-hour airplane and show us what they can do."

By mid-afternoon, the Blue Angels had whittled down the list to an elite, still-breathing few.

Though some of the amateur Angels who got into the cockpit suddenly realized they didn't know what they were doing and jumped right back out, Navy officials said all who put aside their fears or lack of experience or physical disability to climb aboard a fighter jet were stars today.

The once-in-a-lifetime tryouts will continue throughout the week. But long after the flames resulting from this unique recruiting experiment have died which FEMA personnel said should happen within 10 days the fire of these plucky applicants' enthusiasm will shine on.

The enthusiasm of Erin Rappaport, a Springfield, IL eighth-grader who played flight simulators on her PlayStation and impressed Naval flight teams when she sat in the F/A-18 Hornet's cockpit for the first time and already knew, or could guess, at the functions of many of the jet's 188 different controls.

"That sounds just like Erin," said Rappaport's math teacher, Janice Billingsly. "We'll miss her very much."

Erin wasn't the only special person who flew here today; she wasn't the only female, or the only person to crash next to Pino's Pizza on Grove Avenue, or even the youngest. But, witnesses said, she displayed incredible grit and a can-do attitude to her classmates who were inside eating pizza when she tried to fly by and wave.

Officials also singled out the determination of San Dimas, CA's Alfred K. McAllister affectionately described by Blue Angels flight instructor Harmon "Golfer" Links as a "hell of a tough old guy who took off and just kept going.

"We almost couldn't find enough phone books for him to sit on, and he decided against the helmet because it knocked off his glasses," Links said. "But what a trooper. He never once looked back. Radar finally lost track of him about 200 miles out over the Gulf of Mexico, still climbing." "I think he thought he got to keep the plane!" Links added. "If we ever locate and recover the wreckage, we hope to give him the proper burial he deserves."

Others noted the beaming face of Peter Collsworthy, a foreman at an Akron, OH cement plant for the past 25 years, who got the biggest roars from the crowd by far. "He may have flunked the 'near-miss' part of the high-speed aerobatic pass, causing the bailout of a man with 17 years' flight experience when he sheared the wing off of Cmdr. "Wild Bill" Hickok's plane, vomited into his helmet, panicked, inverted the aircraft with the throttles maxed, and hit Mach 1 just before crashing into the Gulf with almost a full load of fuel," Blue Angels commanding officer Brock "Violins" Saxon said.

"But he nailed the steep climb and the steep dive, and he certainly had showmanship. If there's one thing I keep telling my cadets, it's that you can't teach enthusiasm. I think we all learned a little something about the power of raw enthusiasm here today."

"That crowd was rocking out to 'Danger Zone' when he plummeted into the Gulf at the speed of sound," said Lois Collsworthy, Peter's widow. "That would have meant a lot to him. He always loved that song."

Military Pilot
Italy
1922 – 1943
('A' was attached to the wings of 24 pilots who made a highly-publicized Atlantic crossing in 1933)

Death is a small price to pay for looking 'Shit Hot'

BREAKING NEWS REPORT

Okay, okay...put any airline/service/etc. in the place of those mentioned here.

A wealthy retired American Airlines pilot narrowly escaped serious injury recently when he attempted horse-back riding with no prior experience. He had mounted the horse unassisted and the horse immediately began moving. As it galloped along at a steady and rhythmic pace, the pilot began slipping sideways from the saddle.

Although attempting to grab the horse's mane, he could not get a firm grip. He then threw his arms around the horse's neck but continued to slide down the side of the horse. The horse loped along, seemingly oblivious to its slipping rider. Finally, losing his grip, he attempted to leap away from the horse and throw himself to safety. His foot became entangled in the stirrup, and he was at the mercy of the horse's pounding hooves as his head and upper body repeatedly struck the ground.

Moments away from unconsciousness and probable death, to his great fortune a retired UAL captain, working as a greeter at Wal-Mart to supplement his meager retirement, observed the situation and quickly unplugged the horse.

THE CAT & DUCK METHOD OF IFR FLYING

I first heard of this years ago when it was printed in some flying magazine now long-forgotten. I ran across it in an old file cabinet down in the basement collecting dust.

1. Place a live cat on the cockpit deck. Because a cat always remains upright and lands on its feet, it can be used in lieu of an Attitude Indicator ("Artificial Horizon") and needle and ball (turn coordinator) instrument.

2. Watch which way the cat leans to determine pitch and whether or not one is flying wing low. This will allow you to fly straight-and-level with complete accuracy and confidence.

3. A duck is utilized for final approach and landing segment of the flight because of the fact that any sensible bird would not be flying in conditions in which you find yourself. Merely hurl the duck out the window and follow it to the ground.

4. There are some limitations to using this method for instrument flight but by rigidly following these items, a certain level of success can be attained which will not only amaze you, startle your crew, astonish your passengers and leave the occasional tower controller with an open mouth.

a. Get a wide-awake cat. Most cats do not wish to stand for longer periods, so it may be prudent to carry along a dog of some kind to keep the cat at full attention to its duties.

b. Make sure your cat is clean. Dirty cats will spend the time washing themselves: trying to follow a cat undertaking such activities will result in slow rolls, inverted flight and the occasional flat spin. You can see this is most unprofessional and may cause consternation among the passengers.

c. Use an old cat. Young cats have 9 lives; an older, used-up cat with but one or two lives left has much more to lose and therefore will be more dependable and trustworthy.

d. Avoid using stray cats. Try to obtain one of 'good moral character' (*like all ATP's, right? –*ed.) because you will be spending a lot of time together.

e. Beware of cowardly ducks. If the duck perceives you are using a cat to stay upright, it will refuse to leave the airplane without the cat. Ducks are no more better on instruments than you are.

f. Get a duck with good vision. Near-sighted ducks sometimes fail to see they are 'on the gauges' and will go flogging off into the nearest hill or mountainside. Very near-sighted ducks will not recognize they have been tossed out of the plane and will plummet to earth in a sitting position. This is the most difficult maneuver to follow in an airplane.

g. Get a land-loving duck. A duck who likes water will wander off to the nearest lake, river or stream for its final approach – you won't like the outcome.

h. Choose your duck carefully. It is easy to confuse a duck with a goose; while they are very competent instrument fliers, geese seldom wish to go the same direction you do. If your 'duck' seems to be heading for either Canada or Sweden, you can assume your goose is cooked and therefore…[see - Acronyms: KMAG YOYO]

There are 3 simple rules for making good landings – unfortunately, no-one knows what they are.

CHECKED NOTAMs?

These pictures were sent to me by a buddy serving in 'the sandbox' and illustrates what can happen when NOTAM's are not checked prior to flight. In this case, there was a rather large chunk of concrete removed from a runway and due to be replaced the next day. The removal of that section – coincidentally right in the middle of said runway and even more coincidentally right at the normal touchdown landing zone – and a night flight inbound to that base resulted with a C-130 heavily damaged and a runway OTS longer than planned. And most likely some remedial training and a nasty note in the AC's 201 file.

FAR 91.103 Preflight Action

Each pilot in command <u>shall</u> before beginning a flight, become familiar with <u>all</u> available information concerning that flight. [my underscoring, -ed.]

AIM 5-1-3 Notice To Airmen (NOTAM) System

a. Time-critical aeronautical information which is either of a temporary nature or not sufficiently known in advance to permit publication on aeronautical charts or in other operational publications receives immediate dissemination via the national NOTAM system.

Note: (1) NOTAM information is that aeronautical information that could affect a pilot's decision to make a flight. It includes such information as airport or aerodrome primary runway closures, taxiways, ramps, obstructions, communications, airspace, Navaid status changes, ILS's, radar service availability and other information essential to planned enroute, terminal or landing operations.

There are four (4) types of NOTAM's:

1. NOTAM D

For all navigational facilities (airports) that are a part of the National Airspace System (NAS). All NOTAM D's must have one of the following Keywords as the first part of the text after the location identifier: Runway; Taxiway, Ramp, Apron, Aerodrome, Obstruction, Navigation, Communications, Services, Airspace, Other aeronautical information.

2. FDC NOTAM's

Amend such things as published IAP's and other current aeronautical Charts. They also include TFR's.

3. POINTER NOTAM's

Issued to highlight or point out another NOTAM to assist users in cross-referencing important information. Keywords in these must match that/those in the NOTAM being pointed out: If related to TFR's keyword must be 'Airspace'.

4. Special Use Airspace (SUA) NOTAM's

Issued when SUA (e.g. MOA's, MTR's, etc.) will be operational outside the published scheduled times.

Observer's Badge
Prussia
1913 – 1918

Airspeed is Life – Altitude is Life Insurance.

CLOAKED AIR FORCE ONE

I couldn't care less about your political leanings, this IS funny!

[And the more I hear about politics the more I become an anarchist]

Go Falcons!

USAF General:"Mr. President, we've just invented an invisibility cloak for air Force One."

Obama:"You're kidding me, right?"

USAF General:"No, Sir. The plane will be invisible for its maiden flight. Would you like to ride along, sir?"

Obama:"Darn right I would!"

USAF General:"Have a nice flight, sir."

It is far better to break ground and fly into the wind
than the other way around.

COMPANY MEMO

Once again, there are some of ~~us~~ you out there with 'way too much time on your hands.

Dear Co-worker:

The airline industry is in a crisis. Its business model doesn't work with the current price of fuel and the existing level of capacity in the marketplace. We need to make changes in response.

While there have been several successful fare increases, those increases have not been sufficient to cover the rising cost of fuel. As fares increase, fewer customers will fly. As fewer customers fly, we will need to reduce our capacity to match the reduced demand. As we reduce our capacity, we will need fewer employees to operate the airline. Although these changes will be painful, we must adapt to the reality of today's market to successfully navigate these difficult times.

Therefore, a program to phase out the more senior pilots by the end of the current fiscal year, via retirement, will be placed into effect immediately.

Under this plan, senior pilots will be asked to take early retirement, thus permitting the retention of the new-hires who represent our future.

This program will be known as SLAP (Sever Late-Aged Pilots). Pilots who are SLAPPED will be given the opportunity to look for jobs outside the company. SLAPPED Pilots can request a review of their employment records before actual retirement takes place.

This review phase of the program is called SCREW. SCREW (Survey of Capabilities of Retired Early Workers). All pilots who have been SLAPPED and SCREWED may file an appeal with upper management.

This appeal is called SHAFT (Study by Higher Authority Following Termination). Under the terms of the new policy, a pilot may be SLAPPED once, SCREWED twice, but may be SHAFTED as many times as the company deems appropriate.

If a pilot follows the above procedure, he/she will be entitled to get: HERPES (Half Earnings for Retired Personnel's Early Severance) or:

CLAP (Combined Lump sum Assistance Payment).

As HERPES and CLAP are considered benefit plans, any pilot who has received HERPES or CLAP will no longer be SLAPPED or SCREWED by the company.

And, once again, thanks for all your years of service with us.

When a flight is going incredibly well, something was forgotten.

WHY THE CO-PILOT DOES THE PREFLIGHT

The Preflight Action regulation (FAR 91.103) quoted elsewhere in this book mentions "...becom(ing) familiar with all aspects of the flight..." Mark Twain once observed that "Once you have a cat by the tail, you learn some things that cannot be learned any other way." If you learn enough things the correct way, times you get to upgrade to the left seat and have your new co-pilot go through the same IOE you did

Well, for one reason, it's because they're expendable…just like 2nd Lieutenants.

Expendable (adjective) [ik spéndeb'l]

1. Not worth preserving or saving for reuse

2. Easily sacrificed or dispensed with

Field Pilot Badge
Austria-Hungarian Empire 1917 – 1918
Emperor Karl

DOUGLAS "WRONG-WAY" CORRIGAN'S COMPASS ROSE

I happened on the compass rose seen in the first picture one day while scanning some street maps. The quality of the photo is bad as I took it with my cellphone, then had to wait six months to get someone's assistance in downloading it. The picture is NOT reverse printed as you can legibly read "S MACGREGOR WAY" and the scale marker right-way around. It reminded me of this story and some excuses I've heard over the years about reasons why ~~my~~ some students got 'lost' on a cross-country.

As for Douglas "Wrong Way" Corrigan, he was an accomplished aviator prior to his adventure of July 17 – 18 1938. He had applied several times for permission to fly the Atlantic and was turned down by the authorities every time. He finally said he was going to fly non-stop from New York to California and they allowed him to depart.

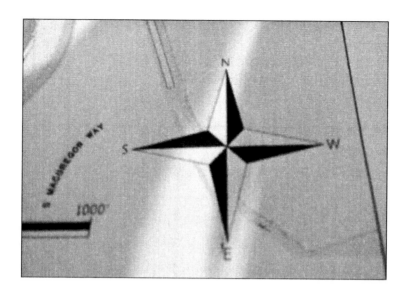

Taking off eastward in a heavy fog (!) he was expected to make a westward turn and head to California. 26 hours later, he dropped out of the clouds to find himself over water. Knowing it was too soon in the flight to be the Pacific, he looked at his compass in the dawn's early light and 'discovered' he had been following the wrong end of the needle. His plane had a compass sitting on the floorboards where the entire azimuth and both ends of the needle could be seen.

He landed at Baldonnel Airport, Dublin, Ireland after a 28-hour, 13 minute flight.

He was repeatedly questioned (interrogated?) by authorities on both sides of the Atlantic about his 'mistake' but he never, to his dying day (9 December 1995), ever changed his story. He was hailed as a hero upon his return to the USA as his escapade brought some relief and humor to the depths of the Great Depression. In New York City, he was given a ticker-tape parade down Broadway with an estimated crowd over 1 million lining the street, more than had turned out to see Charles Lindbergh 11 years earlier.

The points I wish to make after all of this are as follows:

    1. PLAN your flights carefully.

    2. FLY your flights close to the plan.

    3. P-7 at all times! (See Acronyms)

4. Check your DG against your magnetic compass early and often, especially when IFR and even more often if you're in IMC.

5. When you have nothing to do (!?) in the cockpit, check 'em again!

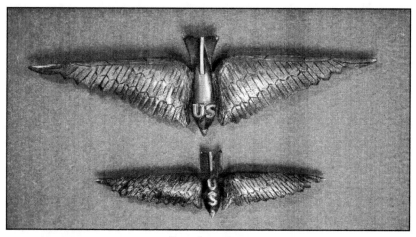

Bombardier
US Army Air Service
1917 – 1918

"IFR" flying:
"I Follow Rivers, Roads & Railways"

DC-10 QUALIFICATION EXAM

For a while in my checkered path to "The Top", I was an instructor at a major airline in the DC-10 fleet. These 'Jurassic Jets' had the old steam gauges and the navigational system – while state of the art then – didn't have half the power of today's hand-held GPS. Notwithstanding that fact, we had to be 'up' on many subject areas. Here, then, is the -10's qualification exam. Go ahead and attempt this; take all the time you need...and then some.

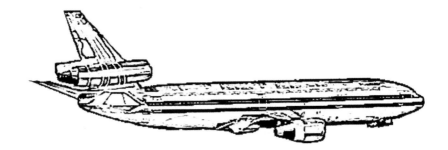

History:

You are transporting the Pope on his tour. Discuss the history of the Papacy from its origins to the present day concentrating especially – but not exclusively – on its social, political, economic, religious and philosophical aspects and impact on Europe, Asia, the Americas and Africa. Be concise and specific. Extra points if you use Latin [NOT Italian].

Medicine:

You have been provided with a razor blade, some gauze and a bottle of scotch: Remove your co-pilot's appendix. Do not suture your work until it has been inspected. You have 15 minutes.

Public Speaking:

2,600 riot-crazed aborigines are storming your aircraft. CALM THEM. You may use any ancient language except Latin or Greek.

Music:

Write a piano concerto putting into music the sound of a greaser landing on a snow-packed runway. You will find a piano under your chair.

Education:

Develop a fool-proof and inexpensive educational system that takes a rebellious drop-out teenager from the streets to the First Officer's seat in 200 flight hours. Use any instructional aids except the educational principles of Piaget and the videos of John and Martha King.

Psychology:

Based on your knowledge of their works, evaluate the mental and emotional suitability of the following to become a Line Check Airman for your company: Ramses II, Richard the Lionheart, Tsarina Catherine the Great and Kaiser Wilhelm II. Support your evaluations with quotes from each person making appropriate references. It is not necessary to translate.

Sociology:

Estimate the sociological ramifications that might accompany the end of the world. Discuss these in terms of management policies and procedures found in your FOM. Construct an experiment to test your theory.

Biology:

Create life. Develop more than two sexes. Present theories as to the suitability of each sex to adequately accomplish the duties of a flight attendant, baggage handler and corporate headquarters middle manager.

Engineering:

The disassembled parts of a Garrett turbo-prop engine have been placed in a box beside your desk. Included is the instruction manual written in conversational Sanskrit. You must build the engine and bolt it on the airframe today. Be prepared to conduct the flight test with the First Officer from the Education portion of this exam.

Political Science:

There is a red phone on your desk. Launch all the B-52's in the Strategic Air Command [SAC]. Send them to any unfriendly nation or target of opportunity using the navigational equipment found in your DC-10 circa 1975.

Epistemology:

Take a position for or against the Validity of Aerodynamics. Explain this to the Chief Pilot and the Line Check airmen of your fleet. You receive extra points if no-one falls asleep during your presentation.

Weather:

Describe in detail your knowledge of the sky from the ground up to and including FL 600. Include natural and para-normal phenomena. Be clear and concise.

General:

Prepare an essay on a) why you exist, b) what you are doing here presently and 3) your future plans. A single paragraph on each topic will suffice.

Aviation Rule #1: First & Foremost – Always Fly the Plane.

DON'T QUIT

It's sad how many people begin flying lessons and do not finish. My wife – before I met her – almost did so because of the criticism heaped upon her by 'well-meaning' associates who found fault and deficiencies in everything she did. She's a deliberate learner, someone who has to understand just about everything at a given point in her training before going on to the next subject, task or maneuver. She finally told everyone to "F.O." – Foxtrot Oscar – and went her own way to earn her wings and an Instrument Rating. We in aviation have to, we MUST, encourage and support those who want to join us in this endeavor. If you know of a Student Pilot, give them a copy of this. And give them all the support you, and your flying friends and associates, can give them. The continued existence and success of our industry and the activity we love depends on it.

When things go awry, as they sometimes will,
When the road you're trudging seems all uphill,
When the funds are low and the debts are high,
And you want to smile but can only sigh,
When cares are pressing you down a bit,
Rest if you must, but DO NOT QUIT!

Life is strange with its twists and turns
As all of us sooner or later learns.
And many a striver turns about
When they might have won had they stuck it out.
Don't give up 'though the pace seems slow,
You likely are to succeed with one more go.

Success is failure turned inside out:
The silver lining in the clouds of doubt.
And you can never tell how close you are,
It may be near when it seems so far.
So stick with it when you're hardest hit,
It's when things seem that worst that
YOU MUST NOT QUIT!

- Author Unknown

Czechoslovakia Observer
1930's
When the country was betrayed by the Munich Agreement in
1938, the Czech personnel scattered across Europe to fight the
Nazis. This badge came cased, made in Prague in the late '30's.

DRONE PILOT AWARDED PURPLE HEART

Yeah, all you Cold – and Hot – Warriors…it's coming to this. A comfy chair in air conditioned comfort thousands of miles from the AoO wearing a green bag and scarf.

NELLIS AFB, NV (The Global Edition)–

When an electrical fire disabled Colonel Jack "Van Go" Vandermulen's Predator drone, the 65-year old veteran pilot exclaimed "Mayday! Mayday! We're going down! We're going down!" while sitting at his cubicle, sources close to his office confirmed.

Witnesses stated Vandermulen began violently pulling and pushing the various ergonomic levers under his seat in an apparent attempt to "eject" himself. Unable to trigger an ejection, the pilot called out: "Jammed! Alternate bailout. I'm outta here!" and rolled abruptly over the right armrest of his chair.

"Oh, crap," he said after impacting the concrete floor at the North Dakota Air National Guard Station in Fargo, ND. His then un-piloted drone, armed with two Hellfire missiles, reportedly crashed into an Afghanistan hillside some 6,743 miles away.

Meanwhile Air Force officials have been at a loss to explain the pilot's bizarre behavior. However, one drone crew member, who wished to remain anonymous, said there were some early warning signs, "We should have suspected a problem when he [Vandermulen] showed up for the mission in a leather bomber jacket, helmet, and goggles."

The Air Force later issued a statement admitting that Vandermulen was part of a new classified program dubbed "Balding Eagles," utilizing seasoned military airmen to fill the government's growing need for drone pilots.

The program has come under intense scrutiny following the incident. Concern has mounted at the highest levels of the DOD that similar events might occur with other aging pilots.

But USAF defenders of the program argue that this isolated case must not be used to bar all older pilots from flying unmanned drones.

In an article appearing in next month's AARP Magazine titled "The Baby Boom Bombers," author Christine Timmel argues that "With key accommodations such as post-it-note reminders and fun brain teasers during mission planning, aging pilots can continue leading successful Predator drone attacks."

Vandermulen is currently being treated for a broken right hip. No word yet from the Air Force as to when Vandermulen will return to duty.

Breaking News Concerning UAV's:

Unfortunately, the US government can no longer afford to employ actual pilots.

Starting next year, an elite group of high scoring X-box veterans will be remotely piloting the US fleet, from their bedrooms in California.

As long as it's ok with their mom.

'Tis best to keep the pointy end going forward and
the greasy side down.

EARACHE REMEDY

It's good practice to have some gum, caramels or chewables along when taking a non-pilot flying. If there's any ear distress during the descent (in the old non-pressurized DC-3 days, the stewardess – yes, she was a stewardess then – came down the aisle with a tray of mints for the passengers), they can exercise their jaw and Eustachian tubes in their ears to relieve any discomfort. In my flightbag I have a pack of Juicy Fruit gum – "Best if sold by November, 1998" – it should still be good, right?

During a commercial airline flight a retired Air Force pilot was seated next to a young mother with a babe in arms. When the baby began crying during the descent for landing, the mother began nursing the infant as discreetly as possible.

The pilot pretended not to notice and, upon disembarking, he gallantly offered his assistance to help with the various baby-related impedimentia. When the young mother expressed her gratitude, the pilot responded: "Gosh, that's a good looking baby...and he sure was hungry!"

Somewhat embarrassed, the mother explained that her pediatrician said nursing would help alleviate the pressure in the baby's ears. The Air Force pilot sadly shook his head, and in true aviator fashion exclaimed:

"And all these years, I've been chewing gum."

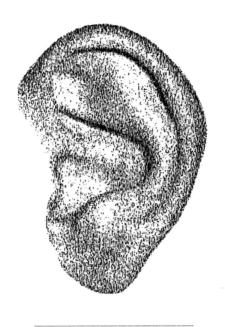

AIM 8-1-2 Effects of Altitude

(b) Ear Block

This section addresses the hazards of flying too soon after an illness affecting the Eustachian tubes – the connection between the throat and inner ear that allows the air pressure within the ear canal(s) to equalize with the outside air pressure. It describes causes of the problem and the various ways and means to alleviate the symptoms.

I once flew too soon after a cold and upon descending from the wild blue the pain increased dramatically and I was deaf for three days.   Scared me to death!   Paragraph 5 of this section recommends if the blockage does not clear up shortly after landing, a physician should be consulted. This is another reason to insure the "IM SAFE" medical checklist [AIM 8-1-1 paragraph i] is followed.

If you fly with someone who does not tell you – or because you didn't ask them about their fitness to fly – then they likely will experience what happened to me. PLUS – they may have only treated the symptoms of their illness; they are still germy as ever. I guarantee if you fly with someone still fighting off a cold or other such illness you'll be sick in three days.

(c) Sinus Block

Whereas an ear blockage can be recognized by pain in the ears, a sinus blockage will be felt behind and above the eyes and/or inside the upper cheekbones.   The same recommendations detailed above also apply.

Given a choice, go for the more conservative option.

EVACUATION PROCEDURE

While there is little in the FAR/AIM to guide the General Aviation pilot on this procedure, it is important enough to consider and discuss.

First off, be sure to brief your passengers on how to fasten and unfasten the seatbelts and shoulder harness [FAR 91.107]. You MUST ensure they know how to do this – never assume they do - then CHECK they are fastened prior to any aircraft movement.

Secondly, instruct them on how to operate the door(s) in the event of a possible event. Do NOT say 'crash landing' as this will get their knickers in a knot even before you start the plane.

Use 'comfortable words' to describe things:

"If we need to make an 'off-airport' landing…"

"If I need you to exit the plane quickly…"

You can use humor:

"If the cabin is filling up with water…" (Assuming you're not flying anywhere near a large body of water)

"If the Aero-Zombies make a try for us, you can exit the aircraft quickly by doing this…"

Just make sure your passengers know how to exit the aircraft and *where* to meet up. Fifty yards *behind* the plane is a great place for a head-count, confab and debrief.

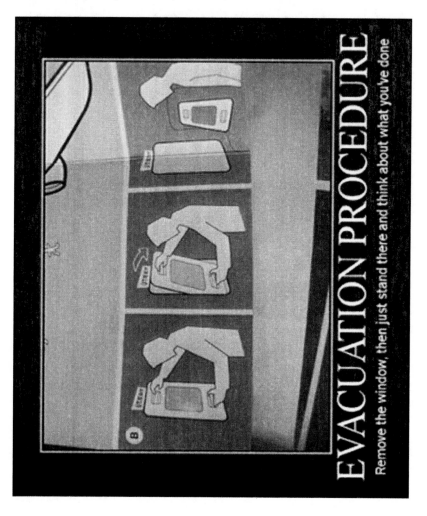

And so, at the beginning of each day, consider that ATC, the weather-guessers, mechanics, supervisors...and birds...are all trying to kill you. Your job is to not let them.

FAA INQUIRY RESPONSE

Another letter – this one to the FAA – along the lines of the "Aussie Pilot Requests Help" found elsewhere in this compendium. As with that one, I gave up trying to enumerate the number of FAR violations; perhaps one of you good readers can enlighten thereupon. Anyway, enjoy!

Inspector Carl N Frank
Flight Standards District Office
Oklahoma City, OK

Dear Mr. Frank:

Here is the letter you asked me to send you about my flight back in December. First of all, I would like to thank that very nice, older fellow you had with you yesterday, you know, the one who took my student pilot's license and told me I wouldn't need it any more. I guess that means that he is giving me my full-fledged pilot's license. After all that happened yesterday, I have earned it. You should watch that fellow though. After I told him about the flight, he seemed quite nervous and his hands were shaking. He said he had never heard anything like it before.

Anyhow, here is what happened. The weather has been so bad here in Ardmore since I soloed last week that I had not been able to go flying. But yesterday I wasn't about to let low ceilings and visibility, and a little freezing drizzle stop me from flying up to Oklahoma City and back. I was pretty proud of having soloed in only 6 hours, so I invited John Winters, my next door neighbor, to go with me.

We planned to fly up to Oklahoma City Will Rogers airport, which, as you know, is less than 100 miles from Ardmore. There is this excellent restaurant on Meridian just north of I-40 that serves absolutely wonderful char broiled steaks and the greatest mixed drinks.

Well, on the way to the airport the road was icy and our car slid in the ditch. I can see why they say that the most dangerous part of a trip is the drive to the airport. My neighbor was a little concerned about the weather, but when I reminded him once again about those steaks and the booze that we would soon be enjoying, he seemed much happier.

When we arrived at the airport there were still a few snow showers around but the freezing drizzle had almost stopped. I checked the weather and was assured that it was solid IFR all the way. I was delighted the weather was so good. When I talked to the man who runs the airport, I found out that the airplane I had been flying was covered with ice. You can imagine my disappointment. Just then a friendly young line boy suggested that I take one of the airplanes that was in the hanger. I told him to pull one out. I saw immediately that it was very much like the Cessna 150 I have been flying. I think he called it a 337. He told me it was also made by Cessna. I noticed right away that it had two tails, but I didn't say anything because, well, I was in a hurry. Oh yes, it had a spare engine too.

I unlocked the door and we climbed in. I began looking for the place to put the key. Now I don't want to get anyone in trouble, but it shouldn't be necessary to get out the airplane manual and follow the checklist just to fly an airplane. That's ridiculous. I never saw so many dials and needles and knobs and handles and switches.

As we both know, they have simplified this a lot in the 150. I forgot to mention that I did file a flight plan with the guy in the tower. He said I would need to because of the weather. When I told him I was flying a pressurized Skymaster (that's what is said on the control wheel) he said it was all right to go up Victor-163 all the way. I don't know why he called it a victor; I guess that's just his pet name for an interstate highway. And besides, it is I-35 Not 163. But those fellows try to do a good job. They told me a lot of other stuff too, but you know how much red tape there is when you deal with the government.

The takeoff was one of my best, and as I carefully left the pattern just the way the book says it should be done, I noticed that the Skymaster doesn't climb as good as the 150. The tower told me to contact Fort Worth Center. I dialed in the frequency that he gave me but it seemed kind of silly to call them since I wasn't going to Fort Worth. Just then there must have been some kind of emergency because a lot of airline pilots began yelling stuff at the same time and made such a racket that I turned my radio off. You'd think that those professionals would be better trained. I-35 was right under me, and since from that I knew that I was on course, I went right on up into the clouds. After all, it was snowing so hard by now that it was a waste of time to look outside, you could only see about a quarter of a mile.

Going into the clouds was a bad thing to do, I realized, since my neighbor undoubtedly wanted to see the scenery, especially the snow cover on the Arbuckle Mountains ahead of us. But everyone has to be disappointed some time, and we pilots have to make the best of it, don't we?

It was pretty much smooth flying, and with the ice and snow that seemed to be forming all over the windshield, there wasn't much to see. I will say that I handled the controls quite easily for a pilot of only six hours. My computer and pencils fell out of my shirt pocket once, but sometimes these things happen I am told. I don't expect you to believe this, but as one time my pocket watch was standing straight up on its chain. That was pretty funny, and I asked my neighbor to look, but he just kept staring straight ahead with sort of a glassy look in his eyes. I figured that he was afraid of heights, like all non-pilots are. By the way, something was wrong with the altimeter. It kept winding and unwinding all the time.

Finally I decided we had flown about long enough to be in Oklahoma City. I had it all worked out on my E6B computer. I am a whiz at that computer, but something must have gone wrong with it, since when I came down to look for the airport there wasn't anything there except a lot of houses. Those weather people had sure been wrong too. It was real marginal conditions, with a ceiling of about 100 feet. You just can't trust anybody in this business except yourself, right? Why, there were even thunderstorms going on, with an occasional bolt of lightning. I decided that my neighbor should see how beautiful it was, and the way the lightening seemed to turn that snow on the roof tops all yellow; and the roof tops were so close that it looked like you could just reach out and touch them. But I guess he was asleep, having gotten over his fear of height, and I didn't want to take him up.

Anyway, just then I had an emergency. The front engine ran out of gas. It really didn't worry me since I had read the book, and knew right where the other ignition switch was. I just fired up the spare engine on the back and we kept on going. This business of having two engines one in front and one in back is really a safety factor. If one quits, the other is right back there ready to go. Maybe all airplanes should have two engines. You might suggest this and get an award (we could split the cash). As pilot-in-command, I take my responsibilities very seriously. It was apparent that I would have to go down lower and keep a sharp eye in such bad weather. I was glad that my neighbor was asleep because it was pretty dark under the cloud, and if it hadn't been for the lightning flashes it would have been hard to read the road signs through the ice on the windshield. The landing lights were not very bright either, You would think they would have melted the ice that covered them but they didn't. Several cars ran off the road when we passed, and you can sure see what they mean about flying being a lot safer than driving.

To make a long story short, I finally spotted Tinker Air Force Base, and since we were already late for cocktails and dinner, I decided to land there. It being an Air Force base, I knew it had plenty of runway, and I could already see a red-colored light in the control tower, so I knew they were still celebrating Christmas and we were welcome. Somebody told me that you can always talk to these military people on the international emergency frequency, so I tried it, but you wouldn't believe the language I heard. Those people ought to be straightened out by somebody, and I would like to complain as a taxpayer. Evidently they were expecting somebody to come in and land, because they kept talking about clearing the airspace for some damned stupid, incompetent SOB up in the clouds.

I wanted to be helpful so I landed on the taxiway to be out of the way in case that other fellow needed the runway. A lot of people came running out waving at us. It was pretty evident that they had never seen a Skymaster land on a taxiway before. That general with the nasty temper was real mad about something. I tried to explain to him in a reasonable manner that I didn't think the tower operator should be swearing at that guy up there, but his face was so red that I think he must have a drinking problem.

Well, that's about all. After your two FAA inspectors left, the weather got really bad so I got one of the Air Force guys to drive me to where I could rent a car to drive back home. I never did get my steak and drinks. My neighbor stayed there at the hospital there in Oklahoma City. He can't write you a letter just yet because he's still not awake. Poor fellow, he must have the flu or something. Let me know it you need anything else, and by the way, send my new pilot's license airmail special delivery.

Very truly yours,

Glenn Endsley

The future in aviation is the next 30 seconds: Long-term planning is the next hour and a half.

FAREWELL

This is the farewell letter from a Commander to his squadron, circa early 21st century. He details much of what has gotten – and is getting - in the way of a warrior's fighting spirit, the commitment to duty and the will to win. Can't say I blame him for his thoughts – these days there is a great disturbance in the Force. And I'm not just meaning the USAF. 'Nuff said. Names and particulars have been omitted because this leader – and those who served with and under him – doesn't need any more grief than the current state of affairs. Refer to "PO" in Appendix: Acronyms.

And again, I include something that's not 'PC' – refer to the Appendix: Acronyms. If 'sensitivities' are offended, tough – it's MY book. I'll include what I want.

Some of you know that I was recently "retired" as the XXX Fighter Wing Commander. The decision was made by Brig Gen [First name, Last name], the [state] Air Commander, who replaced me because he "just wants to change the culture at the XXX" - not for cause or performance or any other reason. This officer never commanded anything bigger than an Air Control Squadron, and somehow he wound up in charge. Heck, the guy probably got beat up in grade school every day. I think it is indicative of what is happening in our Air Force and reinforces what [First name, Last name] and the anonymous author have to say below.   Well, I also have something to say about our changing Air Force and its quickly disappearing Fighter Pilot culture.

How many scope-dope drone operators does it take to change a light bulb? Two: One to change the bulb - and one to kiss my ass. That's right. I said "Kiss my ass." 'Cause I've had it. The air superiority fighter and its PILOT are not dead and the Chinese are so far not impressed with drones.   I am tired of Fighter Pilots suffering at the hands of all the pencil pushing REMF's and ladder-climbing opportunists and shitty non-rated managers (who think they are leaders) just because the Air Force is currently more interested in feelings and sexual orientation than fighting. Not all officers have what it takes to lead warriors, yet too many of them are in charge in our military. At this rate we may lose the next real war. These shit-bird officers need to be run out of leadership positions and get out of my face already. We have too many people in our military that feel the need to play political victim and go to court instead of just dealing with it themselves.

No one can have any kind of fun anymore. Men and women can't flirt, hug, look at anyone sideways, or drink beer out of mermaid mug because of you "victims" and your lawyers. Are you happy? And while I'm at it, Fighter Pilots, who are willing to die so that we can have low prices at the gas pump and shop at the mall, should be able to throw the wildest parties they can manage without one uptight biddy coming in and stopping it. There were scads of women at the '91 Tailhook party who were having the time of their lives, voluntarily being just as debauched as any of the men were. Everyone who flew a plane, or even knew someone who flew a plane, knew how wild those parties were and what went on. What does our society expect - a prayer service? It's worse now than it was then. "Victims" need to just throw some punches of their own whenever guys, gals, lesbos, or homos get out of line. Doesn't our tax money go to teach all of our military how to fight?

I'm not trying to make the idiotic "she had it coming" argument here, which would go something like "of course they grabbed her breasts, look how big they are." Plus, just reaching out and grabbing some boob is wrong no matter what. When I was at Tailhook, even at our most drunken admin parties we never acted like that. No matter how hard I try I can't think of an excuse good enough to do something like that. But it's still nothing to lose a career over or get your panties in a wad. Besides, fighter pilots are supposed to be aggressive assholes. That's how we used to train them. I don't know about you, but I don't want a military of fighter pilots who are gifted at giving sensitivity seminars. I want mad-dog, rabid killers going to battle for me and mine. Man or woman.

When our homeland is threatened by Middle-Eastern Muslim radicals, or when we want to force our form of government on some poor, unsuspecting poppy growing shit hole, or when uppity North Korean despots develop nuke weapons, I want to be able to call on men and women who like to fight and drink. I want an officer who knows how to whack some drunk in the balls when he grabs her tits, not call a press conference and a lawyer. If you're a wimp who doesn't know how to find the exit at a rowdy party, go fly a kite - not a jet fighter. Fighter Pilot should always be capitalized because it is a hard-earned title. So there! Perhaps it really is time for me to retire.

BGEN (ret.)

Much of what you think you know is incorrect.

FIGHTER PILOT'S HEAVEN

"Oh, there are no Fighter Pilots in Hell..."

Everybody's a lieutenant, except God... He is a General!
You only come to work when you are going to fly.
You fly three times a day, if you wish, except on Friday.
You never run out of gas.

You never run out of ammo.

Your missions are one hour long (or longer if you desire) and no briefings are ever required.

Sorties are air-to-air or air-to-ground, your choice.

You shoot the gun on every mission...

There are no check rides.

It is always VFR, and there are never any ATC delays.

You can fly out of the MOA and down to 10 feet AGL...if you want.

There are no "over G's."

Never any 'Fatals'....I mean.....you are already there!

There is never any SOF duty.

You always fly overhead landing patterns with initial approach at 20 feet, then break left.

You can go cross-country anytime you desire...the further the better...

There are no ORI /UEIs.

"Happy Hour" begins at 1400 hours and lasts until 0200+ hours.

The bartenders are all friendly with big bosoms.

Beer is free, but whiskey costs a nickel.

The bar serves only Chevas Regal, Jack Daniels and Beefeaters...plus 500 kinds of beer.

The Girls are all friendly and each Aviator is allowed three...

There are no fat women, and the thin ones look like Sophia Loren.

Country and Western music is free on the jukebox.

You never lose your room key and your buddies never leave you stranded.

The sun always shines, and you can put your hat in your pants pocket.

Flight Suits are allowed in the Officers Club at all times.
The BX always has every item you ask for, most being free.
There are never any crosswind landings, and the runways are always dry.

Control Tower flybys for wheels-up checks can be made at 600 kts.

There are never any noise complaints.
Full afterburner climbs over your house are encouraged.
ERs always contain the statement, "Outstanding Officer."

There are no additional duties.
Friday Happy Hour is mandatory.
There are no flight surgeons.
There are no Staff Jobs.

Functions requiring mess dress attire never occur.
All air traffic controllers are friendly and always provide priority handling...

The airplanes never break.
"ACE" status is conferred upon all

"Happy Hour Landing" – Two for the price of one.

FIRST MILITARY AIRPLANE SOLICITATION LETTER

Note the date of this letter; it is 4 years and 6 days since the Wright Brothers' first flight on 17 December 1903! And as a side-note, 65 and one half years after the Wright flight, Neal Armstrong made his "One small step for a man" off the Lunar Excursion Module (LEM) sitting on the moon at 'Tranquility Base' and the "one giant leap for mankind."

December 23, 1907

Signal Corps Specification, No. 486

Advertisement and Specification for a Heavier-Than-Air Flying Machine

To The Public: Sealed proposals, in duplicate, will be received at this office until 12 o'clock noon on February 1, 1908, for furnishing the Signal Corps with a heavier-than-air flying machine.

The flying machine will be accepted only after a successful trial flight, during which it will comply with all requirements of this specification.

It is desirable that the flying machine should be designed so that it may be quickly and easily assembled and taken apart and packed for transportation in army wagons. It should be capable of being assembled and put in operating condition in about one hour.

The flying machine must be designed to carry two persons having a combined weight of about 350 pounds, also sufficient fuel for a flight of 125 miles.

The flying machine should be designed to have a speed of at least forty miles per hour in still air. ...

Before acceptance a trial endurance flight will be required of at least one hour during which time the flying machine must remain continuously in the air without landing. It shall return to the starting point and land without any damage that would prevent it immediately starting upon another flight. During this trial flight of one hour it must be steered in all directions without difficulty and at all times under perfect control and equilibrium.

The expense of the tests to be borne by the manufacturer. The place of delivery to the Government and trial flights will be at Fort Myer, Virginia.

It should be so designed as to ascend in any country which may be encountered in field service. The starting device must be simple and transportable. It should also land in a field without requiring a specially prepared spot and without damaging its structure.

It should be sufficiently simple in its construction and operation to permit an intelligent man to become proficient in its use within a reasonable length of time.

The price quoted in proposals must be understood to include the instruction of two men in the handling and operation of this flying machine. No extra charge for this service will be allowed.

It has been said two wrongs don't make a right – but two Wrights can make an aeroplane.

FIXED WING CHECKLIST

I came across this checklist when I was at Kenmore Air Harbor in Seattle to retrieve a client's DeHaviland DHC-2 Beaver. It was pinned to the wall of the maintenance hangar and, suffice to say that while...ahhh...creative in terminology, it pretty well covers what needs covering. Here's to all the old L-20 drivers out there!

✓ Two long things that stick out from either side.

✓ Things that go up & down on the things that stick out from either side.

✓ Three wheels [or two floats].

✓ Two little pedal thingys.

✓ Two steering wheels [one, if applicable]!

✓ One operator's manual.

✓ Levers that make the plane go fast.

✓ The gizmo that lets us talk to the folks in that high building with lots of glass.

✓ Coffee [& cups].

✓ The doodads that snap together so we don't fall out of our seats.

✓ All the dials & arrows & stuff that tells how high we are, how fast we're going and stuff.

✓ The hickey-doos on the things that stick out from either side that help us slow for landing.

✓ [If amphib equipped] The switch that makes the wheels on the floats go up & down.

✓ The gadget we can turn on to make the airplane fly all by itself.

✓ The thing that looks like a TV screen with a line going round & round inside it that keeps us from flying into cumulo-granitus clouds.

✓ The written speech we give to passengers when the going gets rough.

✓ Book of Common Prayer AMEN!

FAR 91.103 Preflight Action

Each pilot in command shall, before beginning a flight, become familiar with all available information concerning that flight. This information must include –

(a) For a flight under IFR or a flight not in the vicinity of an airport, weather reports and forecasts, fuel requirements, alternatives available if the planned flight cannot be completed, and any known traffic delays of which the pilot in command has been advised by ATC.

If one re-reads this regulation, you can find some requirement words; 'shall', 'all', 'must', etc. Hmmm…'all' available information? Like Venus lining up with Mars and the moon to create extra-high tides? What exactly do they mean?

There's just so much to consider.

You bet. Another thing – I defy anyone reading this book to come up with the official definition of the word 'vicinity*'. I can't find it anywhere. So God forbid you have an event and the prosecuting attorney alleges you were not 'in the vicinity' of an airport, you can argue all you want but it is they who get to define that word. And it will NOT be in your favor!

———————

A smart, prudent and safety-conscious pilot will either have produced a weight-and-balance for the airplane loading for that flight, the weather briefing information, and a TOLD (Takeoff and Landing Data) card with the runway lengths of airport(s) one intends to use…OR will have some pro-formas already created to use.

* Since this was written, one enterprising CFI [Michael Shannon at Denver's Aspen Flying Club] found 'vicinity' defined for weather – as in 'Showers in the vicinity'. THERE vicinity means within a 5 – 6 statute mile radius from the reporting station. Thanks Mike!

However - I still stand by my recommendation for prudence in interpreting the intent of this regulation.

Army Pilot
US Army Air Service
1917 – 1918
"Dallas"wing

Without fuel, pilots are just pedestrians.

FLYER'S FABLE

A bit far-fetched (but I can see it) and with a moral...of sorts. Always tell the truth – you therefor won't have to remember the lies you told.

One day, while an old pilot was cutting the branch off a tree high above a river, his axe fell into the river.

When he cried out, the Lord appeared and asked, "Why are you crying?"

The aviator replied that his axe had fallen into water, and he needed the axe to supplement his meager pension.

The Lord went down into the water and reappeared with a golden axe.

"Is this your axe?" the Lord asked.

The aviator replied, "No."

The Lord again went down and came up with a silver axe. "Is this your Axe?" the Lord asked.

Again, the aviator replied, "No."

The Lord went down again and came up with an iron axe. "Is this your Axe?" the Lord asked.

The aviator replied, "Yes."

The Lord was pleased with the aviator's honesty and gave him all three axes to keep, and the aviator went home happy.

Sometime later the aviator was walking with his woman along the riverbank, and his woman fell into the river.

When he cried out, the Lord again appeared and asked him, "Why are you crying?"

"Oh Lord, my woman has fallen into the water!"

The Lord went down into the water and came up with ANGELINA JOLIE. "Is this your woman?" the Lord asked.

"Yes," cried the aviator.

The Lord was furious. "You lied! That is an untruth!"

The Pilot replied, "Oh, forgive me Lord. It is a misunderstanding. You see, if I had said 'no' to ANGELINA JOLIE, You would have come up with CAMERON DIAZ. Then if I said 'no' to her, you would have come up with my woman. Had I then said 'yes,' you would have given me all three. Lord, because of my airline's bankruptcy I am an old man not able to take care of all three women in a way that they deserve, that's why I said yes to ANGELINA JOLIE."

And God was pleased.

Moral of this story is: Whenever a Pilot lies, it is for a good and honorable reason, and only for the benefit of others! (Right...?)

To err is human, to forgive Divine – neither of which is corporate policy.

FLYING A ROUND ENGINE

This was passed on to me by Colonel Ed Huber, USAF (ret.) who I met while employing Skyraiders in the 69th SOG. A mighty airplane, 7 hard points per wing, 1,400 mile range and can stay aloft longer than any pilot's bladder can hold out. It served most notably in the Vietnam altercation where – as callsign "Sandy" – the pilots flying them provided air cover for the 'Jolly Green Giant' helicopters of air rescue fame.

"No man left behind."

God bless 'em all…every one.

Starting, Taking Off & Flying a Radial Engine in an AD-6 Skyraider:

Be sure you drain both sumps [you can refill your zippo while doing this]. Look out the left side of the oily cockpit canopy and you will notice a very nervous man holding a huge fire bottle. Nod to this person…

Starting:

1. Crack throttle about ¼ inch

2. Battery ON

3. Magnetos ON

4. Fuel boost ON

5. Hit starter button [the 4-blade 13' 6" prop will start a slow turn]

6. Begin to bounce your finger on the primer button. This act requires finesse and style; it is much like a ballet performance. The engine must be caressed and seduced into starting.

7. Act One: Belching, banging, rattling, backfiring, spluttering, flame and black smoke from the exhaust stacks shoots out about 5 feet [fire bottle person is very pale, looks like he wants to run away, and has the nozzle at the ready position]

8. When the engine begins to 'catch' on the primer, move the mixture to Full Rich. The flames emitting from the exhaust will stop and be replaced with white smoke [fire bottle guy beginning to look relieved]. You will hear a throaty roar that is like music to the ears. Enjoy the macho smell of engine oil, hydraulic fluid and pilot sweat.

9. Immediately check the oil pressure and hydraulic gauges.

10. The entire airplane is now shaking, shuddering and vibrating from the engine torque and prop RPM [the engine is a Wright R-3350 that develops 2,700 HP]

11. Close cowl flaps to warm engine prior to taxi

12. Glance occasionally at the 300 different levers, gauges and gadgets, fiddle with those that require fiddling

13. Call Ground Control to taxi to the duty runway

Taking Off:

1. Check both magnetos ON

2. Exercise the propeller

3. Cowl flaps OPEN

4. Double-check temps and pressures

5. Crank in 1.5 degrees right rudder trim to help your leg with engine torque during takeoff

6. Tell the tower you are ready for the duty runway

7. Line up on the runway and lock the tailwheel [for sure!]

8. Add power SLOWLY as with a monster engine and prop the airplane really wants to turn left [NEVER add power suddenly! There is not enough right rudder in the world to hold it straight]

9. Add more power and add more and more right rudder until your leg begins to tremble

10. Expect much banging, belching and farting as the airplane roars down the runway; some of this will be coming from the airplane

11. Push the stick forward to lift the tail when it "feels right", then pull back when it feels righter to lift the airplane off the ground

12. Gear up. Adjust power and prop to climb setting

13. Close cowl flaps and keep an eye of the CHT gauge

14. Adjust power as needed or turn on the supercharger

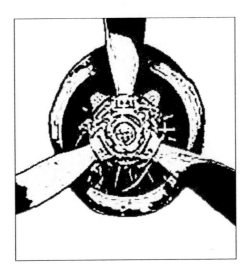

Flying With a Round Engine:

1. Once you reach altitude, which is not very [about 8,000' msl], reduce throttle and prop to cruise settings

2. The next fun thing is to slowly reduce the mixture control until the engine just about quits. Ease the mixture forward just a scoosh and this is best mixture

3. While in cruise the engine will sound like it's going to blow up or quit at any minute; this keeps the pilot occupied by scanning the gauges for the least hint of trouble

4. Moving the various levers and gadgets to coax a more consistent sound concentrates the mind wonderfully

5. At night or over water the engine will make noises you have never heard before. Refer to step 4

6. Looking out of the front of the cockpit, you notice the clouds have a soft, slightly blurry glow. This is due to the oil on the cockpit canopy

7. Seeing lightning in the clouds ahead increases pucker factor by about 10 as you cannot fly high enough to get over them and if you try to get under the clouds you will die in turbulence, so –

> A. Secure everything in the cockpit that isn't secured, get a good grip on the stick, turn on the deicers, tighten and lock your shoulder harness, and hang on

> B. You will then have a ride that exceeds any 'terror' ride at the amusement park. You will also discover that the airplane can actually fly sideways while inverted.

8. Once through the weather, call ATC and in a deep, calm voice advise them you have 'slight turbulence' in your sector

9. Scan the aircraft to see if all the major parts are still intact and attached. This includes any popped rivets

10. Do the controls still work? Are the gauges and levers still in proper limits?

11. Fumble for the relief tube [because you really need it] being extremely careful with the lower zipper of the flight suit

12. Carry on with the mission

It is better to die than to look bad; but it is possible to do both.

FLYING A ROUND ENGINE vs. FLYING A JET:

I've been blessed through my aviation career to have hand my hands controlling a number of fine – and one not-so-fine – tailwheel airplanes, from the smallest single-engine [Skyote] to a DC-3. Each one required – no...demanded – full attention when performing takeoffs, landings and ground maneuvering. But when airborne – where there is nothing over the top of your head but clear blue – I'm as close to Heaven as I can get without actually entering that big pilot's lounge in the sky.

1. To be a 'real' tailwheel pilot you must have flown a taildragger for an absolute minimum of 500 hours.

2. Large round engines smell of gasoline, rich oil, hydraulic fluid, sweat and are not air conditioned.

3. Engine failure to a jet pilot means something is wrong with the air conditioning.

4. When a jet takes off, there is no noise in the cockpit.

5. Landing a jet requires a certain airspeed and altitude – at which you cut the power and drop like a rock onto the runway. Landing a taildragger requires finesse, lots of prayer, body English, pumping of the rudder pedals and a lot of nerve.

6. After landing a jet, it travels straight down the runway.

7. Landing a taildragger is like riding a wild mustang – it might decide to go just about anywhere, including back the way it just came! Gusty winds encourage this behavior.

8. You cannot fill your Zippo lighter with jet fuel.

9. Starting a jet is like turning on a light bulb – one flick of the switch and its running.

10. Starting a round engine is an artistic endeavor requiring prayer, cuss words and sometime meditation.

11. Jet engines don't break, lose oil or catch fire very often – which leads to boredom and complacency.

12. A round engine may blow an oil seal ring, gasket or header, burst into flame, splutter for no apparent reason or plain old quit at any moment. This results in heightened pilot alertness and awareness at all times.

13. Jet engines smell like a kerosene lantern at a scout camp outing.

I knew I was in trouble when the tower asked me to climb to field elevation.

F.O. HAS B.O.

C'mon, folks – you can't make this stuff up! The skeptic in me says "Nah, it's a put-on." The realist in me says "It could happen."

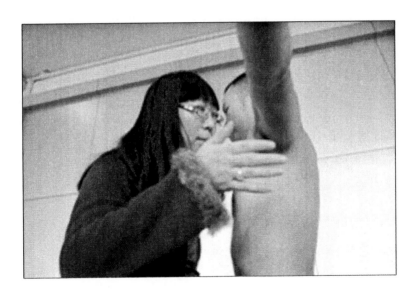

Chinese Airline Judges Pilot Candidates by Armpit Odor

A Chinese airline has sparked controversy after it was reported it included a zero-body-odor requirement in its pilot recruitment tests. Applicants had their armpits sniffed by company staff, to check for any bad smells.

You think requirements stink in your line of work? Think again. Chinese company Hainan Airlines demanded to smell under the arms of students interviewing as trainee aircrew. Obviously, there were other requirements as well, including 20/20 vision, a maximum height of 1.87 meters and a very good knowledge of the English language, but meeting them and failing the bad odor test meant instant elimination for candidates.

"I passed everything, but I was doomed by my armpits, which are always a bit whiffy", said one of the applicants.

Asked about the purpose of this unusual requirement, one of the Hainan Airlines testers said "our staff works very closely with the public, and no passenger wants to smell a pilot's armpits. And if they can keep their cool with this test, they aren't going to sweat in the cockpit." The photos below paint a pretty clear picture of how the BO test was conducted.

Everyone knows airlines choose their flight attendants mainly based on looks, and as unfair and misogynistic as that sounds, it does make some sense, whereas judging candidates by their armpit odor seems just dumb. But look at it this way, if one of the approved candidates ever crashes a plane, at least they'll smell nice doing it…

If you're going to be cooped up in a close cockpit environment for a length of time, good hygiene is a must – even if you aren't looking for a job in China.

Flying is not a Nintendo game: You cannot push a button and start over.

FORMATION ETTIQUETTE

I recall some years ago Pilot B saw his friend – Pilot A – out flying and 'thought' he would bounce him; that is, perform a mock attack. As it came to light in the post-mortem investigation, Pilot A was undertaking an IPC with an instructor and was using a view-limiting device at the time. Just as Pilot B made his pass, Pilot A turned his airplane...and a mid-air occurred. All three people died. Please keep this in mind if you are contemplating something like that – and do NOT do it! If you want to fly formation, complete formation training offered by a well-qualified and experienced school.

FAR 91.111 Operating Near Other Aircraft

(a)No person may operate an aircraft so close to another aircraft as to create a collision hazard.

(b)No person may operate an aircraft in formation flight except by arrangement with the pilot-in-command of each aircraft in the formation.

(c)No person may operate an aircraft, carrying persons for hire, in formation flight.

FULL STOP OR TOUCH-AND-GO?

A policeman friend told me a story making it around the station house. Seems someone in another jurisdiction had pulled someone over for doing a 'California stop' past a stop sign. The driver became belligerent when telling the officer there wasn't any difference between slowing down and stopping. One thing lead to another and the driver was pulled from the car and was being struck soundly about the head and shoulder with the officer's billy club. The officer then asked the now submissive driver "What do you want me to do? Slow down or stop?"

The officer got some administrative time off...the driver got 30 days – after he was discharged from the infirmary.

THIS
MIGHT BE A FULL STOP LANDING

FAR 61.57 Recent Flight Experience: Pilot in Command

(a) General Experience

...No person may act as pilot in command of an aircraft carrying passengers or of an aircraft certificated for more than one crewmember unless that person had made at least three takeoffs and landings within the preceding 90 days, and

(ii) If the aircraft to be flown is an airplane with a tailwheel, the takeoffs and landings must have been made to a <u>full stop</u> in an airplane with a tailwheel.

(b) Night takeoff and landing experience

(1) ...no person may act as the pilot in command of an aircraft carrying passengers during the period beginning 1 hour after sunset and ending 1 hour before sunrise, unless within the preceding 90 days that person has made at least three takeoffs and landings to a <u>full stop</u> during that period beginning 1 hour after sunset and ending 1 hour before sunrise. [Editor's underlining]

I have to date over 5,000 hours of dual given; while instructing takeoffs and landings, I first require full stop taxi-backs. I want the student to experience, understand and master the entire sequence of events of both the takeoff and landing processes. Besides, since over 56% of all GA accidents occur during takeoffs and landings [most all of them loss-of-directional-control] they need to train their focus, attention and skill-acquisition on that. I do not want them to rush the cockpit activities transitioning from landing phase to takeoff phase. This distracts them from the primary task of maintaining directional control. Only when they can perform all cockpit tasks without taking their eyeballs and attention away from directional control do I allow them to move into touch-and-goes.

If you are learning [or teaching in] a retractable-gear single or multi-engine airplane, I recommend performing full-stop taxi-backs. IF you perform touch-and-goes, I STRONGLY advise performing them only with <u>extreme</u> caution, high paranoia* and attention-to-detail. More than once if I hadn't been on 'Red Alert' my student would have raised the landing gear during roll-out instead of the flaps. There is just too much to do in a retractable and/or twin with a high risk of doing something wrong, out of sequence or not at all. It has even occurred as I've administered flight checks to nervous applicants. In complex and/or twin-engine airplanes, taking your time to perform after-landing checks during taxi-backs then properly setting up the airplane for takeoff is crucial. It can save a lot of embarrassment, coming up with a deductible ($$$) and dealing with the accompanying FAA paperwork.

United States Army Air Corps – Crewmember
1941 – 1947

* Murphy's Law of Flight Instruction: If a student can do the wrong thing at the wrong time, they will.

FUTURE PILOT

When I started flying the regulation read "Eight feet between bottle and throttle." Set your beer on the wingtip and by the time you get to the cockpit you're legal.

Oh, and do NOT touch the helmet on the bar of the O-Club! (Recalling the 'Check Six' at Nellis AFB)

One thing you do NOT want to hear in the cockpit, *"Hey, hold my drink and watch this!"*

FAR 91.17: Alcohol or Drugs

No person may act, or attempt to act, as crewmember of a civil aircraft –

(1) Within 8 hours after the consumption of any alcoholic beverage;

(2) While under the influence of alcohol;

(3) While using any drug that affects the person's faculties in any way contrary to safety; or

(4) While having an alcohol concentration of .04 or greater in a blood or breath specimen.

As a DPE, I question applicants on this regulation; they usually can recite the numbers (8 hours, blood level of .04), but most have overlooked the 'gotcha' in this regulation. That is (2) and (3) above, while under the influence. Years ago an organization, I believe it was the USAF, did a study on this. (Notice the regulation stipulates 'civil aircraft'. Hmmm). Anyway, the researchers discovered the subjects performed worse during the hangover period than they did at the height of the drunk.

So for all you 'Two Party' aficionados out there (one on Friday night and one on Saturday) keep in mind it ain't just the 8 hours between bottle and throttle. If you happen to get pulled over – and convicted – of a DUI or DWI, you MUST report it to the FAA [see FAR 61.15 (c)] within 60 days and must also note the fact of conviction on your application for a medical certificate.

And do not refuse to take a breath-a-lizer test for a peace officer. Failure to do those things mentioned above has resulted in certificate denials, suspensions and even revocations. Even a history of non-alcohol related motor vehicle violations will invite the attention (all negative) of the FAA. No drink or party is worth that; either drink with extreme moderation with food in your stomach or, better yet, arrange for a designated driver. Best still, do not drink anything alcoholic within 24 hours of flying.

Related Reading: AIM section 8-1-1 d, FAR 67.7 and FAR's 61.15 (c) & (d) and 61.16

Pilot-Observer
Germany
1939 – 1945 Denazified
(After 1957 WWII veterans were allowed to wear old decorations & awards so long as no NAZI symbology was evident. The owner of this badge removed the swastika which hung under the eagle's claws.)

FAA regulations prohibit drinking within 8 feet of the airplane and smoking within 50 hours of the flight; or is it the other way around?

THE GAY FLIGHT ATTENDANT

This was sent to me by an airline Captain friend of mine who specifically requested – upon pain of death, I might add – that his name, the flight attendant's name and especially the airline NOT be mentioned if I was going to use this. In fairness to all concerned, and notwithstanding the personal predilections of those involved, flight attendants perform an immensely necessary [and often thankless] duty in achieving and maintaining a high degree of superb service to the flying public in general and aviation safety in particular. A sense of humor by all concerned can make otherwise mundane matters go better.

My flight was being served by an obviously gay flight attendant, who seemed to put everyone in a good mood as he served the food and drinks.

As we prepared for landing, he came swishing down the aisle and told the passengers: "Captain Marvey has asked me to announce that he'll be landing the big scary plane shortly, so lovely people, if you could just put your trays up, that would be super."

On his trip back up the aisle, he noticed this well-dressed Middle Eastern looking woman hadn't moved a muscle. "Perhaps you didn't hear me over those big brute engines but I asked you to raise your trazy-poo, so the main man can pitty-pat us on the ground."

She calmly turned her head and said, "In my country, I am a Princess; I take orders from no one."

To which (I swear) the flight attendant replied, without missing a beat: "Well, sweet-cheeks, in my country I'm a Queen, so I outrank you. Tray-up, Bitch!"

She complied.

If you crash because of bad weather, when they bury
you it will be beautiful, clear & calm.

GET IN GOOD WITH YOUR DPE

In reality, the best way to 'get in good' with your examiner is to be prepared. Having a case of test jitters is okay, even normal; we examiners know how to recognize the difference between that and not having your shit together. We come prepared for success – I arrive at a flightcheck looking forward to the applicant dazzling me with their knowledge and aeronautical prowess. A 'bust' just means more paperwork – for us and for the applicant. None of us like that. Practice, drill, roll-play with your instructor, anything it takes to know the material backwards, forwards and inside-out. If you can walk away from a flightcheck – with your new certificate in hand – saying "Well, THAT was an anti-climax." Then you were properly prepared. Everyone likes that – guaranteed!

10 WAYS TO GET IN GOOD WITH YOUR DPE:

10. Let them know your psychiatrist said you are okay to get back in the air.

9. Bring some heavy-metal music so he won't have to listen to that annoying tower chatter.

8. Demonstrate your stick-and-rudder skills by doing a barrel-roll right after take-off.

7. Tell him your 'psychic friend' said it was a good day to fly.

6. Show them the trick where you turn the Master Switch off to save on Hobbs time.

5. Tell them there's a BIG tip in it for them if you pass ["Know what I mean?" Wink...wink]

4. When you buzz the tower, be sure to put it on their side of the plane so they can wave to all their FAA buddies up there.

3. Show them the cool design you made by drawing lines between all the airports on the sectional.

2. Tell them that old joke about the traveling salesman and the FAA Examiners' daughter.

And the #1 way to get in good with your FAA flight Examiner?

1. Bring them a bottle of good scotch. [Hey…works   for me!]

One way, really and truly, to get on the good side of your DPE is to show up PREPARED!

To do this you must first expend a little energy in doing some research; first of all, read every single page of the appropriate Practical Test Standards (PTS) for the certificate or rating for which you're going for.

I mean every, single page!

There is much in the 18 – 24 pages of preface that will enlighten you and give you exact and precise knowledge as to what is or is not acceptable performance, the equipment you must bring to the flightcheck, the type of airplane and its qualities and/or capabilities, etc.

If you want to see the exact guidance we DPEs must operate under, go to www.faa.gov and enquire about "Order 8900.2" or you may just Google that, it comes up both ways.

Go to chapter 7 and find the certificate/rating of interest to you and read exactly how we must conduct that particular flightcheck.

NOW you have a real good idea as to what to expect.

You may also consider each Task to decide whether this can be examined in the ground portion (oral) or during the flight portion. If during the ground portion, practice answering each sub-topic (a, b, c, etc.) VERBALLY. Does your answer sound clear, concise and correct? If so, go on to the next item. If your answer sounds confused, vague, wandering or downright incorrect –

You need to practice more.

THAT'S how you 'get in good' with your DPE!

...and keep in mind there is NO <u>financial</u> reason in the world why you can't pass your next flightcheck!

AVIATION MALADY: "GET-THERE-IT IS"

Cartoon © 1990 by Bob Stevens
TAB Books, Inc., Blue Ridge Summit, PA 17294
First edition

One of the factors judged in several flight tests – as stated in the respective Practical Test standards (PTS), is for the Pilot in Command (PIC) to make a "...competent go, no-go..." decision based either on the actual weather report(s) or the one given by the Examiner specifically for that exam. This is the easy part; for if the weather is bad enough, the applicant states they would not fly in those conditions – a 'no-go' situation – and all is well. Both the pilot and the aircraft are safe and sound sitting on the ground all warm and toasty.

But there is a trap in making a 'go' decision, and that is embedded deeply in the inherent nature of a pilot. See, pilots are optimists: We are going to place ourselves into a vehicle built by the lowest bidder assuming the maintenance is up to standards, launch into an un-natural, inhospitable and occasionally even hostile environment, trusting that everything will operate as expected with no surprises enroute, and we'll arrive at our intended destination on time, with no worries. The prudent pilot should – no, must – exert discipline throughout the flight to constantly make "Continue, Don't Continue" decisions in regards to that flight.

If, as a VFR pilot, the lowering cloud ceiling is forcing lower and lower altitudes - turn around and leave that area. If the haze is making the distance over the nose where the ground is visible get closer and closer to the aircraft – perform a 180° turn and get to the nearest airport.

A study was made some years ago looking at the scenarios just mentioned. Non-instrument rated Private Pilots were placed in a simulator and then conducted a VFR trip. Next, the same trip was performed but with deteriorating weather conditions the closer the subject got to the destination. Long story short, it was found that when VFR pilots found themselves in Instrument Meteorological Conditions (IMC), they had – on average – 126 seconds to live: That is just over two minutes before loss of control and a resultant (fatal) crash. That's the average! Some subjects lost control within 10 seconds; some lasted as long as five minutes. But they all – every one – ultimately lost control, crashed and 'died'.

A motel for a night or two is far cheaper than a deductible. It is infinitely less expensive than a burial plot. If you are a VFR-only pilot, do NOT press on into IMC! Do NOT let 'Get-There-Itis' have the upper hand in your judgment factoring. Good Aeronautical Decision-making – and your life – depends on it.

Military Pilot
France
1913 - 1915

Learn from the mistakes of others; you will never live long enough to make them all yourself.

GOT GEAR?

Landing gear up is a hugely embarassing moment – however, no-one has ever died of embarassment, it's being inundated by the paperwork afterwards that does them in! So below I have detailed what my very first I.P. had me do, each and every time I turned final. It's kept me from just such an embarassing moment more than once.

Some years back I was taxiing out and saw a friend – who flew an award-winning twin Beech (Beech 18) – make a go-around. He added power, got a climb going, raised the gear and made another pattern circuit. I now am on the Alpha taxiway abeam the touchdown markings and here he comes – with the landing gear up! I was trying to get the radio changed to the tower frequency but was too slow; I watched both propellers start chipping away at the runway and the plane belly-flop onto the runway. It truly was a sad and sickening sight. Folks, you cannot check gear down too many times; and if you are flying a straight-leg airplane, get in the habit anyway – you won't always be flying fixed gear planes.

Rarely are gear-up accidents fatal, or even injurious; however, forgetting to extend the "Runway Noise Suppressors" affords several entities (NTSB, FAA and the insurance company for just

3) the opportunity to examine you, your skills, currency, proficiency, logbook entries, airworthiness…and on and on and so-forth and so-on. Get the picture?

My first IP had me say – out loud so he could hear it – EVERY time I turned final: "Final turn, final gear check – down and green. Prop Max RPM." Since I was flying a fixed-gear, fixed-prop airplane I had to ask why. He said, "You won't always be flying one of these. Some day (maybe) you'll be in faster, more complex airplanes and doing this will save you the occasion of stating your name, rank and serial number to the Board of Inquiry". He went on further to say that if I didn't say that phrase and physically simulate the act of gear down; I had to pay him $1 (big money in those days!) I think I had paid him $5 or $6 by the time he was through with me. But to this day I always say that phrase, out loud, at that point in each and every flight.

If I'm completing an instrument approach, at 500' above minimums I say "Five hundred to minimums, final gear check, down and green. Prop max RPM" then I can focus completely on the last, most demanding portion of the IAP – flying under exacting control until I see the runway environment or decide to go missed.

I also was taught to keep my hand on the landing gear lever until I saw <u>and was sure I saw </u>the green light(s) indicating gear down and locked. If there were no green light(s), I had a gear malfunction. And if the gear MALF really IS caused by some mechanical issue, you of <u>course</u> are intimately acquainted with the Emergency Gear Extension checklist in the AFM/POH, right?

Better higher than lower; better faster than slower.

GRADING LANDINGS

There are innumerable "Top Ten" lists; a night-time talk-show host presents one almost every night. Of course, there are very likely more examples but 'top ten' sounds more onomatopoetic [look that up in your Funk and Wagnall's!] than anything else.

The top ten ways to spot a really bad landing:

10. Passengers appear shorter than before takeoff.

9. Skid marks left on runway pavement [and in pilot's underwear].

8. You're cleared to land three times without ever making a go-around.

7. The scraping noise you heard was the trailing edge of the flaps.

6. You're commended for a perfect four-point landing…and the airplane has only three wheels.

5. Laughter is heard during every tower transmission for hours.

4. Rescue workers meet you at the gate [tie-down] and ask how many casualties there are.

3. The propeller has that snazzy new Q-tip look.

2. Max power required to taxi to the gate [tie-down].

1. The line crew refuels your high-wing airplane...without needing a ladder.

Pilots flying under IFR but in VMC do NOT have a priority for the runway just because they are flying under IFR. [See AIM 5-4-26]. I recall having my hands and feet full helping a student land a tailwheel airplane in a strong crosswind and we took more time on the runway than usual, causing a Lear to go-around. As they went around one of the Lear crew radioed "Thanks a lot, taildragger!" That made me P.O.'d and I responded with: "Hey, Jerk, YOU come land this thing in this crosswind!" He kept quiet and tower never said a word.

In the Airplane Flying Handbook [FAA-H-8083-3A], pgs. 8-11 & 12-17 detail the principles and techniques for making go-arounds or rejected landings. Remember, if the approach is destabilized for any reason and/or the PIC does not like the way the approach is turning out – GO-AROUND! The airplane was meant to fly and you are safe in the middle of the sky. Then, sort things out in your mind and either make another attempt, approach a different runway or even fly to a different airport if the conditions are too overwhelming. I guarantee no-one will think the less of you for that; and it sure beats having a bent airplane and/or possible injuries.

As a DPE, I once had a Private Pilot applicant perform three go-arounds in a row. He was all apologetic saying he just didn't like the way the approach was setting up. I told him "I will NEVER second-guess an applicant on matters of safety if they opt for the more conservative choice." And I will ride along on go-arounds all day long. Do NOT be afraid to make a go-around if you think you must. And don't think about if you should or shouldn't too long – just DO IT!

Remember that 56% of all GA accidents occur during takeoffs or landings. The key to a good landing is a good approach: The key to a good approach is good airspeed control: And the key to good airspeed control is good procedures.

Poland Air Gunner
1919 – 1039
In 1919 Poland was carved from the remains of the Imperial Prussian and Russian empires. Sandwiched between two mortal enemies, its fate was determined by WWII and the Iron Curtain until 1989.

The survivability of the landing is inversely
proportional to the angle of arrival.

GROUNDSPEED CHECK

I had the pleasure – and honor – of hearing Brian Shul up close and personal at our QB hangar meeting one evening. This pilot had overcome terrible injuries to fly again; and fly not just any old airplane out there, but an SR-71 Blackbird! He had other fantastic stories to tell about the capabilities of this amazing airplane; of outrunning surface-to-air missiles and beginning to slow down 600 miles away in order to rendezvous with a tanker – and overflying him as they were still too fast! I heartily recommend his website; while his book isn't cheap, it will be the focus of interest in your hangar library.

GROUNDSPEED CHECK:
By Brian Shul

Former sled (SR-71 Blackbird) driver.

There were a lot of things we couldn't do in an SR-71, but we were the fastest guys on the block and loved reminding our fellow aviators of this fact. People often asked us if, because of this fact, it was fun to fly the jet. Fun would not be the first word I would use to describe flying this plane—intense, maybe, even cerebral. But there was one day in our Sled experience when we would have to say that it was pure fun to be the fastest guys out there, at least for a moment.

It occurred when Walt and I were flying our final training sortie. We needed 100 hours in the jet to complete our training and attain Mission Ready status. Somewhere over Colorado we had passed the century mark. We had made the turn in Arizona and the jet was performing flawlessly. My gauges were wired in the front seat and we were starting to feel pretty good about ourselves, not only because we would soon be flying real missions but because we had gained a great deal of confidence in the plane in the past ten months. Ripping across the barren deserts 80,000 feet below us, I could already see the coast of California from the Arizona border. I was, finally, after many humbling months of simulators and study, ahead of the jet.

I was beginning to feel a bit sorry for Walter in the back seat. There he was, with no really good view of the incredible sights before us, tasked with monitoring four different radios. This was good practice for him for when we began flying real missions, when a priority transmission from headquarters could be vital. It had been difficult, too, for me to relinquish control of the radios, as during my entire flying career I had controlled my own transmissions. But it was part of the division of duties in this plane and I had adjusted to it. I still insisted on talking on the radio while we were on the ground, however. Walt was so good at many things, but he couldn't match my expertise at sounding smooth on the radios, a skill that had been honed sharply with years in fighter squadrons where the slightest radio miscue was grounds for beheading. He understood that and allowed me that luxury. Just to get a sense of what Walt had to contend with, I pulled the radio toggle switches and monitored the frequencies along with him. The predominant radio chatter was from Los

Angeles Center, far below us, controlling daily traffic in their sector. While they had us on their scope (albeit briefly), we were in uncontrolled airspace (Above FL600 is Class E airspace – ed.) and normally would not talk to them unless we needed to descend into their airspace. We listened as the shaky voice of a lone Cessna pilot who asked Center for a read-out of his ground speed. Center replied: "November Charlie 175, I'm showing you at ninety knots on the ground." Now the thing to understand about Center controllers is whether they were talking to a rookie pilot in a Cessna, or to Air Force One, they always spoke in the exact same, calm, deep, professional tone that made one feel important. I referred to it as the "Houston Center voice." I have always felt that after years of seeing documentaries on this country's space program and listening to the calm and distinct voice of the Houston controllers, that all other controllers since then wanted to sound like that and that they basically did. And it didn't matter what sector of the country we would be flying in, it always seemed like the same guy was talking. Over the years that tone of voice had become somewhat of a comforting sound to pilots everywhere. Conversely, over the years, pilots always wanted to ensure that, when transmitting, they sounded like Chuck Yeager, or at least like John Wayne. Better to die than sound bad on the radios.

Just moments after the Cessna's inquiry, a Twin Beech piped up on frequency, in a rather superior tone, asking for his ground speed in Beech. "I have you at one hundred and twenty-five knots of ground speed." Boy, I thought, the Beechcraft really must think he is dazzling his Cessna brethren.

Then out of the blue, a navy F-18 pilot out of NAS Lemoore came up on frequency. You knew right away it was a Navy jock because he sounded very cool on the radios: "Center, Dusty 52 ground speed check." Before Center could reply, I'm thinking to myself, hey, Dusty 52 has a ground speed indicator in that million-dollar cockpit, so why is he asking Center for a read-out? Then I got it, ol' Dusty here is making sure that every bug smasher from Mount Whitney to the Mojave knows what true speed is. He's the fastest dude in the valley today, and he just wants everyone to know how much fun he is having in his new Hornet. And the reply, always with that same, calm, voice, with more distinct alliteration than emotion: "Dusty 52, Center, we have you at 620 on the ground."

And I thought to myself, is this a ripe situation, or what? As my hand instinctively reached for the mic button, I had to remind myself that Walt was in control of the radios. Still, I thought, it must be done—in mere seconds we'll be out of the sector and the opportunity will be lost. That Hornet must die, and die now. I thought about all of our Sim training and how important it was that we developed well as a crew and knew that to jump in on the radios now would destroy the integrity of all that we had worked toward becoming. I was torn.

Somewhere, 13 miles above Arizona, there was a pilot screaming inside his space helmet. Then, I heard it—the click of the mic button from the back seat. That was the very moment that I knew Walter and I had become a crew. Very professionally, and with no emotion, Walter spoke: "Los Angeles Center, Aspen 20, can you give us a ground speed check?" There was no hesitation, and the replay came as if was an everyday request. "Aspen 20, I show you at one thousand eight hundred and forty-two knots, across the ground." I think it was the forty-two knots that I liked the best, so accurate and proud was Center to deliver that information without hesitation, and you just knew he was smiling. But the precise point at which I knew that Walt and I were going to be really good friends for a long time was when he keyed the mic once again to say, in his most fighter-pilot-like voice: "Ah, Center, much thanks, we're showing closer to nineteen hundred on the money."

For a moment Walter was a god. And we finally heard a little crack in the armor of the Houston Center voice, when L.A. came back with, "Roger that Aspen. Your equipment is probably more accurate than ours. You boys have a good one." It all had lasted for just moments, but in that short, memorable sprint across the southwest, the Navy had been flamed, all mortal airplanes on freq were forced to bow before the King of Speed, and more importantly, Walter and I had crossed the threshold of being a crew: A fine day's work. We never heard another transmission on that frequency all the way to the coast. For just one day, it truly was fun being the fastest guys out there.

More on Shul's website: http://www.sleddriver.com/

You have never been lost until you have been lost above Mach 3.

HELICOPTER COMMANDMENTS

I'm not a Rotorhead, although I have had my hands on them 'way in the distant past for a few brief turns at the controls. I know many who are, however, and they walk about with 'that look' in their eyes – like something bad is about to happen. I include this for those poor souls who look for their emergency landing area through the chin bubble of their aircraft.

1. He who inspecteth not his aircraft giveth his Angel cause to concern him.

2. Hallowed is thy airflow across thy rotor disc thus restoring thy translational lift.

3. Let infinite discretion govern thy movement near the ground for vast is the area of destruction.

4. Blessed is the pilot who strives to maintain his standards, for without them shall he surely perish.

5. Thou shalt maintain thy speed between 10' and 400' lest the earth rise up and smite thee.

6. Thou shalt not make a trial of thy center of gravity lest thou dash thy foot against the stone.

7. Thou shalt not thy confidence exceed thy ability, for broad is the path to destruction.

8. He that doeth an approach and alloweth the wind to turn behind him shall surely make restitution.

9. He who alloweth the tail rotor to catch up the thorns behind curses his children's children.

10. Observe these commandments lest on the morrow thy friends mourn thee.

United States Army Air Corps - Bombardier
1941 – 1947

Hovering is for pilots who love to fly but have no-where to go.

HIGH FLIGHT: FAA SUPPLEMENT

"High Flight" is a famous poem by John Gillespie Magee, Jr. (1922-1941). A Royal Canadian Air Force pilot, he died at age 19 ...in a mid-air collision during World War II. Here's his brief, classic poem -- with a few notes now required by the Federal Aviation Administration.

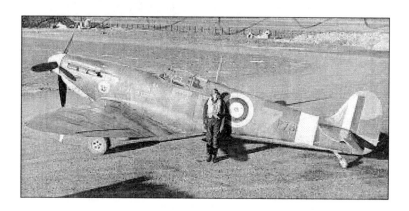

Oh, I have slipped the surly bonds of Earth (1),
And danced (2) the skies on laughter silvered wings;
Sunward I've climbed (3) and joined the tumbling mirth (4)
Of sun-split clouds (5) and done a hundred things (6)
You have not dreamed of wheeled and soared and swung (7)
High in the sunlit silence (8). Hov'ring there (9),

I've chased the shouting wind (10) along, and flung (11)
My eager craft through footless halls of air.
Up, up the long, delirious (12), burning blue
I've topped the wind-swept heights (13) with easy grace.
Where never lark, or even eagle (14) flew.
And, while with silent, lifting mind I've trod
The high untrespassed sanctity of space (15),
Put out my hand (16), and touched the face of God (17).

1. Flight crews must insure that all surly bonds have been slipped entirely before aircraft taxi or flight is attempted.

2. During periods of severe sky dancing, crew and passengers must keep seatbelts fastened. Crew should also wear shoulder belts as provided. The FASTEN SEAT BELT sign must be constantly illuminated.

3. Sunward climbs must not exceed the maximum permitted aircraft ceiling.

4. Passenger aircraft are prohibited from joining the tumbling mirth.

5. Pilots flying through sun-split clouds under VFR conditions must comply with all applicable visibility and cloud clearance minimums.

6. Do not perform these hundred things in front of Federal Aviation Administration inspectors.

7. Wheeling, soaring, and swinging will not be attempted except in aircraft rated for such activities and within utility or aerobatic class weight limits.

8. Be advised that sunlit silence will occur only when a major engine malfunction has occurred.

9. "Hov'ring there" constitutes a highly reliable signal that a flight emergency is imminent.

10. Forecasts of shouting winds are available from the local FSS. Encounters with unexpected shouting winds should be reported by pilots.

11. Pilots flinging eager craft through footless halls of air are reminded that they alone are responsible for maintaining separation from other eager craft. Such aircraft flinging is also a major cause of passenger discomfort and/or airsickness (See rule #4)

12. Should any crew member or passenger experience delirium while in the burning blue, submit an irregularity report immediately upon flight termination. Pilots and aircrew are reminded to abide by FAR 61.53 operating an aircraft during a medical deficiency, of which delirium is included.

13. Windswept heights will be topped by a minimum of 1,000 feet to maintain VFR minimum cloud clearances.

14. Aircraft engine ingestion of, or impact with, larks or eagles should be reported to the FAA using FAA Form 5200-7, Bird/Other Wildlife Strike Report [available at http://wildlife-mitigation.tc.faa.gov].

15. Aircraft operating in the high un-trespassed sanctity of space must remain in IFR flight regardless of meteorological conditions and visibility. ATC must issue a special clearance for such high-altitude treading.

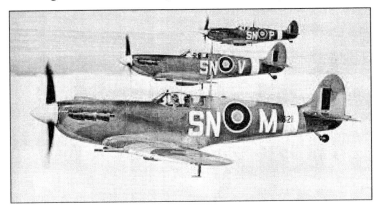

16. Pilots and passengers are reminded that opening doors or windows in order to touch the face of God may result in loss of cabin pressure. Military pilots shall avoid touching face of God to maintain separation of church and state as required by law.

17.Neither the FAA, nor any other branch of the Federal Government, will make, or cause to make, any official statement concerning the existence, or non-existence, of God or any other Supreme Being.

Asking a pilot what they think of the FAA is like asking a fire hydrant what it thinks of a dog.

HIGH FLIGHT: MILITARY SUPPLEMENT

Some T-38 students out at Williams AFB [Now Phoenix-Mesa Gateway: KIWA] came up with these. ATC is not Air Traffic Control, but Air Training Command.

Oh, I have slipped the surly bonds of Earth (1),
And danced (2) the skies on laughter silvered wings;
Sunward I've climbed (3) and joined the tumbling mirth (4)
Of sun-split clouds (5) and done a hundred things
You have not dreamed of wheeled and soared and swung (6)
High in the sunlit silence (7). Hov'ring there,
I've chased the shouting wind (8) along, and flung (9)
My eager craft through footless halls of air.
Up, up the long, delirious (10), burning blue
I've topped the wind-swept heights (11) with easy grace.
Where never lark, or even eagle (12) flew.
And, while with silent, lifting mind I've trod
The high untrespassed sanctity of space, (13)
Put out my hand and touched the face of God (14).

ATC Supp – 1, C2 to C4, High Flight

1. Surly bond slipping is performed dual or PIT team only. This does not preclude solo studs crabbing.

2. Dancing the skies on the wing will be performed Dual – Dual two ship only.

3. Aircraft cleared sunward will climb within the horizontal boundaries of their assigned area of operation.

4. When joining the tumbling mirth, apply the techniques described in ATCM 51-38, Rejoins, T-38 only.

5. T-38 aircrews may disregard the use of position lights when entering clouds forecast to be sunsplit.

6. When wheeling and swinging are combined in one maneuver, T-38 aircraft are limited to 4.1 symmetrical G's.

7. High in the sunlit silence is defined as the airspace above FL 290 from 1 hour prior to official sunrise to 1 hour past official sunset.

8. Chasing the shouting wind along is restricted to WX ships under specific DO approval.

9. Aircraft on exceptional release will be flung subsonic only.

10. Should any aircrew experience delirium while in the burning blue, proceed immediately with oxygen system emergency operations.

11. If windswept heights cannot be topped prior to JODEY, advise ABQ Center prior to 30 DME.

12. When Larks and/or Eagles are flying, the SOF will coordinate with PHX TRACON to insure adequate separation.

13. Nothing prevents civil or military VFR traffic from transiting the WAFB high untrespassed sanctity of space while operating under Visual Flight rules.

14. Pilots will not sacrifice aircraft control or exceed canopy ops limits to touch God's face.

Romania Field Pilot
1940 – 1947
King Michael of Romania (6 September 1940 to 30 December 1947), one of the last surviving monarchs ante bellum, was ousted when the Communists took over in 1947.

NEVER trust a fuel gauge.

HOW "POLICY" HAPPENS

I'm not all that convinced this wasn't an actual experiment somewhere, sometime. It sure has the ring of truth to it. I'm not going to question it because, frankly, I don't want to be sprayed with cold water. Read on...

Start with a cage of five monkeys. In the cage, hang a banana on a string and place some stairs under the banana. Before long, one of the monkeys will climb the stairs and reach for the banana. As soon as that happens, spray all the monkeys with cold water.

After a while, another monkey will try the stairs to get to the banana. Do the same thing; spray all the monkeys with cold water. Continue this until, when a monkey tries for the banana, the other monkeys stop him. Now, turn off the cold water and replace one of the original five monkeys with a new one. The new monkey sees the banana and wants to climb the stairs. To his horror, the other monkeys attack him. After another attempt and another attack, he knows that if he climbs the stairs he will be assaulted.

Next, remove the second of the original monkeys and replace him with a new one. The newcomer goes to the stairs and is attacked; the previous newcomer with enthusiasm takes part in the punishment meted out. Again, replace another of the original monkeys with a third replacement; the new one makes it to the stairs and is then attacked as well. Two of the monkeys that beat him have no idea why they were not permitted to climb the stairs or why they participated in the beating of the newest monkey.

After replacing the fourth and fifth original monkeys, all the monkeys that have experienced being sprayed with cold water have been replaced. Nevertheless, no monkey ever again approaches the stairs in an attempt to get the banana for fear of a beating. Why not?

"Because that's the way it's always been done around here."

That's how "Policy" happens…

If you must make a mistake, try to make it a new one.

HOW SHIT HAPPENS

All of us who have worked in a corporate environment have, at one time or another had to deal with the decisions of 'management'. As all line pilots know, the head office often has little-to-no idea what occurs out there in the 'wild blue yonder'. We can only shake our heads in wonder and befuddlement as to the pronouncements, policies, rules & regulations sent forth from on high. Other such bindings and shackles are placed on those who must slip the surly bonds every day; unending pursuit of corporate profits and the attainment of golden parachutes for those who inhabit the ivory towers. Here then, for the first time in print (well, sorta) and submitted for your consideration, is the explanation of...

In the beginning was THE PLAN. Thence thereafter came forth the ASSUMPTIONS, and they were without form. And thus THE PLAN was without substance.

Darkness fell upon the face of the Workers as they muttered amongst themselves, saying: "It is a crock of shit and it stinketh."

So then the Workers went unto their Supervisors, crying:

"It is a pail of dung and none may abide the odor thereof."

Thus informed did then the Supervisors approacheth their Managers, exclaiming: "It is a container of excrement and it is very strong, such that none may abide by it."

It then came to pass the Managers entreated their Directors, pronouncing:

"It is a vessel of fertilizer and none may resist its strength."

In due time did the Directors then consult amongst themselves, saying to each one: "It contains matter that fosters growth, and thus is very powerful."

The Directors, thus encouraged, approached the Vice-Presidents, saying unto them: "It promotes expansion and vitality, with highly potent effect."

And so it came to pass the Vice-Presidents all arose, gaining audience with the President, beseeching: "This will actively promote expansion and vigor of the company and so must be spread unto every corner of the firmament."

And thus did the President gaze upon THE PLAN and saw that it was good.

And so did THE PLAN become POLICY *[see: How Policy Happens]*.

Yea, verily, all ye who hearken unto these words take comfort that the truth is now with you as to HOW [and why] SHIT HAPPENS.

Everything in the Company Manual – policy, warnings, procedures, instructions, the works – can be summed up in one simple sentence:

"Captain, it's your baby."

FAR's are worded either by the most brilliant lawyers in Washington – or the most stupid.

HOW TO TELL IF YOUR PILOT IS OVER 60

One of the more recent changes to come along in commercial aviation is raising the retirement age from 60 to 65, assuming a First Class medical can be maintained. I know many pilots – those with years and years of experience in the cockpit – who could maintain that to [and past] age 70. Write your congressman... [As if that does any good]. Also changed was the length of validity for medical certification [which just <u>might</u> be a question during a flightcheck!]

10. Orders a "Geritol Frappuccino" at Starbucks.

9. Layover clothes consist of black shoes, white knee socks, Bermuda shorts and yellow golf shirt.

8. Yells "I've landed and can't get up", then laughs uncontrollably.

7. Uses his AARP card as a second form of I.D. to get a jump seat.

6. Medic alert bracelet keeps setting off the metal detector.

5. Uses the aircraft power outlet to charge up his wheel chair batteries.

4. Carries a Commodore 64 computer in his flight bag.

3. Thinks the flight attendants in Narita are "hot".

2. Bids the Wilmington, NC layovers, but doesn't remember why.

And the number one way to tell if you're flying with someone over 60:

1. Flies across the country with the left landing light blinking all of the way.

FAR 61.23 Medical Certificates: Requirement & Duration

What is presented in this regulation is too extensive to be paraphrased here; suffice to say:

(a) Operations Requiring a Medical Certificate

This section details when a medical certificate – and what grade of certificate – is required for the various operating privileges. Particulars for 1st, 2nd and 3rd class medical certification are presented; also –

(b) Operations Not Requiring a Medical certificate

In this section are listed the nine situations whereby a medical certificate is not required when exercising pilot privileges.

(c) Operations Requiring Either a Medical Certificate or U.S. Driver's License

Lists the four examples when either a medical certificate or driver's license is required to exercise pilot privileges.

(d) Duration of a Medical Certificate

THIS is the section which might – I say just might – be tested during a flightcheck. Certainly the grade and duration of medical certificate required for the pilot certificate and/or rating you're going for. It behooves the wise application to know them all, even if you're a long way below age 40. If you're over 40, I might give you a pass on all the 'under 40' requirements.

An airplane flies because of a principle discovered by Bernoulli, not Marconi.

HUNG UP ABOUT FLYING

There was recently a photo circulating the internet that depicted a plane caught in power lines, hanging right above buildings. I thought about it for quite some time in an attempt to analyze just what happened. Usually, they don't allow power lines that close to a runway - unless it's a private strip – and the building is too close to any approved airport approach paths. I can only conclude this hapless pilot was attempting an off-airport landing somewhere, perhaps after an engine failure, and wound up hanging around waiting for assistance.

FAR 91.119: Minimum Safe Altitudes

Except when necessary for takeoff and landing, no person may operate an aircraft below the following:

(a) Anywhere: An altitude allowing, if a power unit fails, an emergency landing without undue hazard to persons or property on the ground.

As a DPE, I ask about this regulation during the flight portion of a checkride to determine whether or not the applicant is aware of this section of the regulation. Many can spout off the numbers and altitudes in this regulation (go ahead and look them up if you do not know them), but many 'forget' (or didn't know) this little 'gotcha' exists.

Anyone who has flown over any large metropolitan area certainly realizes there are minimal places to land without creating "undue hazard to persons or property on the ground." Anyone who has flown over desolate territory, heavily forested and/or mountainous terrain knows a good (heck, even a not-so-good but it'll do) emergency landing area is worth its weight in whatever is valuable these days.

TRY THIS EXERCISE:

The next time you are flying, 'surprise' yourself and pull the power to idle simulating the proverbial engine failure [assuming you're flying ASEL]. Accomplish the recommended cockpit procedures. Select a suitable emergency landing area and then tell yourself "Everything else is forest."

Can you make the field –THAT CHOSEN FIELD - on target, on altitude and most importantly, on proper airspeed – without the possibility of over- or under-shooting? If you can, good on ya!

If not, you need to practice this more. The key to this exercise is to remember what one does with precious things: Keep them close! Do the same for your emergency landing area: Keep it close. Circle above it and (you know what pattern altitude looks like, don't you?) when you are at the proper altitude, break out of the circle, do a close-in downwind, base and final and prove to yourself you can land on a dime and get nine cents change.

Do not violate the other portions of this – or any other – regulation, but see what happens. You may surprise yourself – one way or the other.

Military Pilot
Spain
1939 – 1963

Good judgment comes from experience: Experience comes from bad judgment.

IF A DOG WAS YOUR INSTRUCTOR

We have all known airport dogs; those friendly, loyal, sometimes mangy, sack-lunch stealing, warmest-place-in-the-line-shack hogs who consider the pilots' lounge sofa as their personal domain. I recall Rufus, a very black Black Labrador who would mooch food from everybody and then wolf it down as if he had been starved for weeks. Skipper was the consort of a retired Navy pilot, who would lie patiently by the pilots' lounge door until his master returned in his single-seat Mooney Mite. Then there were Wilbur and Orville, a couple of [not-so] Great Danes who always bounded out to greet their owner when he returned in his J-3 Cub. One day Wilbur got too close as the engine was shutting down and he got clipped by the wood prop right across his skull...sent him flying and shattered the prop. He was taken to the dog hospital where he received many stitches, returning to the airport a week later. He never would get close to the airplane again, though.

When loved ones come home, always run to greet them.
Wait 'til the prop stops, of course.

Never pass up the opportunity to go for a joyride.
My dog Frodo had over 200 hours of flight time; 199 of those asleep.

Allow the experience of fresh air and wind in your face to refresh yourself.
Fly open-cockpit whenever you can. All my automobiles have been rag-tops.

When it's in your best interest – practice obedience.
Sit. Stay. Lie down.

Warn your people when others have invaded your territory.
Welcome those who need welcoming.

Take naps and stretch before arising.
If you can't bring yourself to take a 'nap', try a Siesta instead.

Run, romp and take some time each day for play.
Early to rise and early to bed makes Jack healthy, wealthy and dead.

Avoid biting when a simple growl will suffice.

And occasionally, the same effect can be had by a scathing glare.

On warm days, take time to lie on your back in the grass.

Or at the very least, take off your shoes and go barefoot [remember the novelty song 'Tip-toe Through the Tulips'? Who sang that?*]

On hot days, drink lots of water and find a shady spot.

Remember what bad things a high density altitude does to aircraft performance? The same thing happens to pilots.

No matter if you're scolded, don't buy into the guilt trip and pout – run right back and make friends.

A good IP never yells, scolds or makes the student feel inadequate. They instruct, lead by example and encourage.

Eat with gusto, enthusiasm. Stop when you've had enough.

There's more to 'fine dining' than a candy bar and a Coke.

Be loyal.

People come and go, but a good friend is forever. And sadly, there are so few of them.

If what you want lies buried, dig until you find it.

Persistence and determination are omnipotent.

When someone is having a bad day, be silent, sit close by and nuzzle them gently.

Follow this one with a modicum of discretion, okay?

* Tiny Tim: A 6'4" 130 lb., ukulele-strumming long-hair falsetto singer circa 1967

You hear about the dyslexic aetheist? He doesn't belive in Dog.

IF AIRLINES SOLD PAINT

This came from an airline Captain with close to three decades in the airline industry. He said "I never really understood how airline ticket pricing worked until I read this analogy. Perhaps those of you who still fly on airlines (Hostage Class) will appreciate it."

Customer: Hi. How much is your paint?

Clerk: Well, sir, that all depends on quite a lot of things.

Customer: Can you give me a guess? Is there an average price?

Clerk: Our lowest price is $12 a gallon, and we have 60 different prices up to $200 a gallon.

Customer: What's the difference in the paint?

Clerk: Oh, there isn't any difference; it's all the same paint.

Customer: Well, then I'd like some of that $12 paint.

Clerk: When do you intend to use the paint?

Customer: I want to paint tomorrow. It's my day off.

Clerk: Sir, the paint for tomorrow is the $200 paint.

Customer: When would I have to paint to get the $12 paint?

Clerk: You would have to start very late at night in 21 days, or about 3 weeks. But you will have to agree to start painting before Friday of that week and continue painting until at least Sunday.

Customer: You've got to be *&%^#@* kidding!

Clerk: I'll check and see if we have any paint available.

Customer: You have shelves FULL of paint! I can see it!

Clerk: But it doesn't mean that we have paint available. We sell only a certain number of gallons on any given weekend. Oh, and by the way, the price per gallon just went to $16. We don't have any more $12 paint.

Customer: The price went up as we were talking?

Clerk: Yes, sir. We change the prices and rules hundreds of times a day, and since you haven't actually walked out of the store with your paint yet, we just decided to change. I suggest you purchase your paint as soon as possible. How many gallons do you want?

Customer: Oh, give me 10, maybe 12 gallons; that way I'll have a little extra if I need it.

Clerk: Oh no, sir, you can't do that. If you buy paint and don't use it, there are penalties and possible confiscation of the paint you already have. If you change any colors there is a $50.00 change fee, even if it is the same brand. Also, no refunds.

Customer: WHAT?

Clerk: We can sell enough paint to do your kitchen, bathroom, hall and north bedroom, but if you stop painting before you do the bedroom, you will lose your remaining gallons of paint.

Customer: What does it matter whether I use all the paint? I already paid you for it!

Clerk: We make plans based upon the idea that all our paint   is used, every drop. If you don't, it causes us all sorts of problems.

Customer: This is crazy!! I suppose something terrible happens if I don't keep painting until after Saturday night!

Clerk: Oh yes! Every gallon you bought automatically becomes the $200 paint.

Customer: But what are all these, "Paint on sale from $12 a gallon", signs?

Clerk: Well that's for our budget paint. It only comes in half-gallons. The first half-gallon is $6 and will cover half a room. The second half-gallon to complete the room is $20. None of the cans have labels, some are empty and there are no refunds, even on the empty cans.

Customer: To hell with this! I'll buy what I need somewhere else!

Clerk: I don't think so, sir. You may be able to buy paint for your bathroom and bedrooms, and your kitchen and dining room from someone else, but you won't be able to paint your connecting hall and stairway from anyone but us. And I should point out, sir, that if you paint in only one direction, it will be $300 a gallon.

Customer: I thought your most expensive paint was $200!

Clerk: That's if you paint around the room to the point at which you started. A hallway is different.

Customer: And if I buy $200 paint for the hall, but only paint in one direction, you'll confiscate the remaining paint.

Clerk: Yes, and we'll charge you an extra use fee plus the difference on your next gallon of paint. But I believe you're getting it now, sir.

Customer: You're insane!

Clerk: Thanks for painting with us!

Forget all that stuff about Lift, Weight, Thrust & Drag - an airplane flies because of money.

I FLEW

I will reminisce of the days I once knew,
I will not remember the 3 AM alerts...
But only that I flew!
I will not remember the crew rest in tents
Nor recall how cold Arctic winds blew,
But only that I flew!
I will never forget when nature became angry
And challenged my intrepid crew,
And I'll always remember the fear that I felt
And the pride in knowing that I flew!
I will remember the sights my mortal eyes have seen
Colored by multitudes of hues,
Those beautiful lights on cold winter's nights
Seen only by those who flew.
God was extremely good to me,
And let me touch his face,
He saw my crew through war and peace
And blessed us with His grace.
So when I stand at Saint Peter's Gate
And tell him that I'm new.
I know He'll smile and welcome me,
Because he knows I FLEW

- Brad Baker

INCIDENT REPORT

Either the archer was very, very good – or this pilot might, just might, have been a little low somewhere...out there...

```
*****************************************************
**    Report    created    6/22/2005    Record    3
*****************************************************
**IDENTIFICATION Regis#: 7752L Make/Model: C172
Description: 172, P172, R172, Skyhawk, Hawk XP, Cutla Date:
06/21/2005 Time: 1930 Event Type: Incident Highest Injury:
None Mid Air: N Missing: N Damage: Unknown LOCATION
City: COLORADO SPRINGS State: CO Country: US
DESCRIPTION ACFT ON LANDING, FOUND AN ARROW
STUCK IN THE RIGHT WING, COLORADO SPRINGS, CO
INJURY DATA Total Fatal: 0 # Crew: 2 Fat: 0 Ser: 0 Min: 0
Unk: # Pass: 0 Fat: 0 Ser: 0 Min: 0 Unk: # Grnd: Fat: 0 Ser: 0
Min: 0 Unk: WEATHER: UNK OTHER DATA Departed: Dep
Date: Dep. Time: Destination: Flt Plan: Wx Briefing: Last Radio
Cont: Last Clearance: FAA FSDO: DENVER, CO (NM03)
Entry date: 06/22/2005
```

NTSB Part 830.5 Immediate Notification

The operator of any civil aircraft…shall immediately, and by the most expeditious means available, notify the nearest NTSB office when:

(a) An aircraft accident or any of the following listed serious incidents occur:

The regulation proceeds to list 12 situations whereby notification is required. There are several sub-parts listed in a few of the situations, so it would be prudent to know the when's, where's and what-if's of this regulation.

NTSB Part 830.6 details the information required to be given in the report.

NTSB Part 830.15 mentions when a written report is required if requested. That report must be submitted within 10 days after the event.

BTW – after reading all the situations requiring immediate notification – and assuming no flight controls were damaged or caused to malfunction – this was not an event required to be reported. Now…insurance requirements might be a different matter.

This, however, will require notification…after they climb down…and change their underwear.

The Law of Gravity is not a generalized rule.

INEVITABLE PRANG

During "The Big One" [WWII] our noble allies 'the Brits' put out a directive to all RAF [Royal Air Force] pilots:

"If a 'prang' appears inevitable. Endeavor to strike the softest object around as slowly as possible."

In all my years of aviation, I have found no-where [save the website mentioned below] whereby instruction is offered as to 'how to' crash an airplane and live through the event. We have all countless times practiced the proverbial engine fail drill ["Set best glide and trim, choose and circle a suitable landing area, attempt to restart and/or diagnose the problem if there's time, transponder to 7700 and comm radio to 121.5 and make a call, prepare the airplane and occupants for an off-airport landing"] only to commence a recovery at a suitable altitude. But what about those last 500 feet and the landing? No-one practices that.

On the 41st anniversary of my first solo, while administering a flightcheck in a Light Sport airplane, two of the three propeller blades departed the airplane and the applicant and I had to crew an actual emergency off-airport landing. I'm here to tell you that all my training kicked right in and it turned out to be a relatively calm experience.

[See http://blog.aopa.org/flighttraining/?p=1852]

A local FAA inspector named Mick Wilson had for years investigated aircraft accidents, also wondering why apparently survivable events resulted in fatalities and why an accident where no-one should have lived through it had survivors. He did his research and put out a book [and now a CD and DVD] on his findings.   Go to **www.Crashandsurvive.com** to check these items out.   I strongly recommend pilots have an idea what to do when having to land in a forested area or other inhospitable terrain or environments.   It will open your eyes.   And carrying emergency equipment and survival gear suitable for the terrain and conditions you're flying over/through is the first place to begin.   If for nothing else than to prove to that nasty old DPE you've read completely the PTS and have considered what is being addressed therein.

In thrust I trust
[put another way: I feel the need for speed]

INFLIGHT MALFUNCTION FLOW CHART

The humor detailed on the next page notwithstanding, dealing with inflight MALF's is a serious business. It is here where the true professional [and professionally-minded] pilot must shine. NOW is the time where all the nightly study and memorization pays off. Your systems knowledge and familiarity with the notes, cautions, warnings and boldface items in the AFM/POH and emergency checklist(s) must immediately come to the front of your brain.

The FIRST RULE in dealing with MALF's is: **ALWAYS FLY THE PLANE**, first and foremost. If you're a crew of one; fly first, then deal with the problem on a workload-permitting basis. If you're a flightcrew member, first decide who is flying and who will deal with the problem.

If you're flying military, corporate or airlines you no doubt have gone through the required training for these events [see 'IPC']. Follow those procedures and if you experience an 'Event', you may use the 'Nuremburg Defense', not that it will do any good.

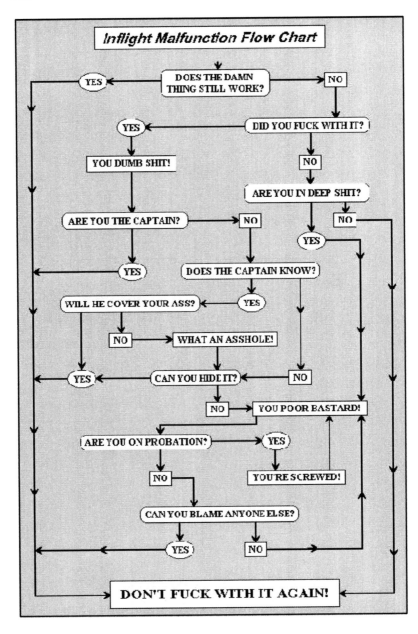

To order an 8" x 10" copy of this chart suitable for framing - resistant to 100LL, Jet A, JP-9, lubricating & smoke oil and printed on a paper stock that will outlast your aviation career - go to www.Coloradoskymaster.com and click on 'Products'.

For you General Aviation types, it's another matter: If you're blessed with another pilot in the family, have them fly while you go through the AFM/POH section 3 [Emergency Procedures] and refamiliarize yourself with the contents thereof. A little role-playing and simulated problem-solving when things aren't going Tango-Uniform goes a long way towards preparing for when they do. If you do not have a flying spouse and/or fly alone, DON'T do this while flying. Take the manual home and study there. Better yet, do some 'dry flying' while the airplane is tied down.

If the emergency is drastic, revert to:

Practice the procedure – "Segment Your Secondary Tasks".

Fly the plane; find the checklist. Fly the plane; find the emergency section. Fly the plane; find the correct checklist. Fly the plane; confirm it's the correct checklist. You can see where this is going: After performing each item on the checklist, return to command and control of the plane. No sense flying a checklist and losing control of the aircraft.

The 4 F's of Emergencies:

1. FLY the plane.

2. FLY TO and get over your emergency FIELD.

3. Try to FIX the issue.

4. FONE for help [121.5 on comm and 7700 on the transponder]

And now some words to Student Pilots and low-time aviators. Could an electrical failure be deemed an 'emergency' at this stage in your aviation career? Could a landing gear MALF be called an 'emergency'? If you were unsure of your position during a cross-country, could a 100-hour pilot call that an 'emergency'? The answer to all these questions is "YES!"

The very first 'real' regulation in 14 CFR Part 91 is:

FAR 91.3 Responsibility and Authority of the Pilot in Command

(a)The Pilot in Command of an aircraft is directly responsible for, and the final authority as to,

the operation of that aircraft.

(b)In an in-flight emergency requiring immediate

action, the pilot in command may deviate from

any rule of this part to the extent required to

meet that emergency.

What this means is that in the event of any emergency – and YOU are the one who determines that - YOU, as PIC, have the authority to do whatever you deem prudent, safe and legal [in that order] to ensure safety of yourself and passengers. Do not EVER be 'afraid' to declare an emergency if you think you are in trouble or need help. There are any number of resources out there ready, willing and able to assist you. Do not EVER be afraid to call for help and use the 'E'-word if you think you're in trouble. What little paperwork there <u>might</u> be sure beats that created by an accident or worse, a fatality. There is another gouge available to help deal with any emergency if it isn't forcing you to make an 'off-airport' landing:

The 3 'C's' for inflight problems:

1.CLIMB to a higher altitude [your radio has a much farther range]

2.CONFESS your problem so they can help solve your exact issue

3.COMPLY with directions

I have been fortunate (?) in needing to use the 'E' word on a number of occasions; from a landing gear MALF where all the firemen and fire trucks in the county appeared at the airport expecting to see my plane do a belly-flop on the runway [must have been a slow day at the fire station] to experiencing smoke in the cockpit of a fabric-covered classic [I was really happy all those trucks showed up then]. After equalizing my adrenaline to red blood-cell ratio the only paperwork was basic name, rank & serial number for the airport ops report. Simple as that.

One last consideration: If you think you need to be on the ground NOW, it's better to do a "Precautionary Landing" – meaning one where you may still have engine power available and have complete control over the aircraft – than having to perform a "Forced Landing" – meaning having to land on whatever terrain is below you. Landing on ground of your own choosing sure beats landing on, shall we say, less conducive terrain.

It is better to be on the ground wishing you were flying, than flying wishing you were on the ground.

IN PRAISE OF THE ROUND ENGINE

I've had the responsibility, honor and pleasure of flying a number of planes powered by round engines. Learned a few new words from my IP during training and invented a few more colorful combinations thereof while PIC in them as well. I once was piloting a plane-load of jumpers in an old – and all too decrepit – Beech 18 when at 200' AGL the bottom two cylinders separated from the case - on the left engine – in a left turn. We were too low for the jumpers to get out (as I was yelling at them to do) and so I made the most gradual "Turn Around an Airport" maneuver I have ever done. Reports from the ground said it was spectacular, what with a great trail of white smoke behind the airplane. I had taken off with a full load many a time; I had never landed with one. Made the best partial-power one-engine landing ever. Two cylinders gone T.U. but the other seven kept firing: God bless the Wright R-985!

IN PRAISE OF THE ROUND ENGINE:

We gotta get rid of those turbines, they're ruining aviation and our hearing...

A turbine is too simple minded, it has no mystery. The air travels through it in a straight line and doesn't pick up any of the pungent fragrance of engine oil or pilot sweat.

Anybody can start a turbine. You just need to move a switch from "OFF" to "START" and then remember to move it back to "ON" after a while. My PC is harder to start.

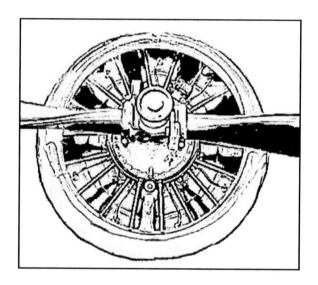

Cranking a round engine requires skill, finesse and style. You have to seduce it into starting. It's like waking up a horny mistress. On some planes, the pilots aren't even allowed to do it...

Turbines start by whining for a while, then give a lady-like poof and start whining a little louder.

Round engines give a satisfying rattle-rattle, click-click, BANG, more rattles, another BANG, a big macho FART or two, more clicks, a lot more smoke and finally a serious low pitched roar. We like that. It's a GUY thing...

When you start a round engine, your mind is engaged and you can concentrate on the flight ahead. Starting a turbine is like flicking on a ceiling fan: Useful, but hardly exciting.

When you have started his round engine successfully your crew chief looks up at you like he'd let you kiss his daughter!

Turbines don't break or catch fire often enough, leading to aircrew boredom, complacency and inattention.

A round engine at speed looks and sounds like it's going to blow up any minute. This helps concentrate the mind!

Turbines don't have enough control levers or gauges to keep a pilot's attention. There's nothing to fiddle with during long flights.

Turbines smell like a Boy Scout camp full of Coleman Lanterns.

Round engines smell like God intended machines to smell.

For you multi-engine [recip] pilots, can you still repeat the drill and immediate actions required when one engine decides to give up and quit?

Counter the yaw with opposite rudder!

Counter the roll with opposite aileron!

Maintain directional control!

Mixtures, props, throttles forward!

Confirm gear up, flaps up!

Stabilize, slow down and remember to breathe!

Identify, Verify & Feather!

Fly the plane!

Secure the INOP engine via checklist.

Proceed directly to the nearest airport

[Or if unable, pick the softest field close by in which to land]

Notify ATC.

Poland Bombardier
1919 – 1939
Poland's Air Force, already obsolescent by 1935, was wiped out while still on the ground during the opening days of the Nazi Blitzkrieg ("Lightning War") in September 1939.

A light twin defined is that airplane when one engine fails the other gets you to the scene of the crash.

IT WASN'T ON THE CHECKLIST

I've collected numerous reports – all unverified, thank you – of some of the strange, unfathomable and dumb things pilots have done. I've not checked the NTSB files for accuracy of any of these but they still have a lesson.

Make sure the airplane is aligned with the runway before applying takeoff power.

According to the Board's files, a C-172 was substantially damaged when, after receiving clearance for takeoff, the pilot "...applied full power from his Hold Short position without making a right turn onto the runway. The airplane traveled across the runway and adjacent grassy area and contacted two chain-link fences prior to coming to a stop." None of the four occupants was injured.

Retired Pilot
Prussia
1916 – 1918
(Retired from front-line duty due to wounds yet still on flight status)

It is always better to have C-sub-t greater than C-sub-d. Simply put, thrust should always exceed drag.

I WANT TO BE A PILOT

On my copy of this is printed "Barbara Darland – December 13, 1975" and "Written by a fifth grader". I can only assume she was a grade-school teacher who handed out an assignment to her class asking them what they would like to be when they grow up. Barbara surely is retired by now [thanks for sharing this!] and the fifth grader is probably now a 757/767 Captain. This is priceless...

"I want to be a pilot when I grow up because it's a fun job and easy to do.

That's why there are so many pilots flying today. Pilots don't need much school; they just have to know numbers so they can read the instruments.

I guess they should be able to read road maps so they can find their way if they get lost. Pilots have to be brave so they won't be scared if it's foggy and they can't see, or if a wing or motor falls off they can stay calm so they'll know what to do.

Pilots have to have good eyes so they can see through clouds and they shouldn't be afraid of lightning or thunder because they are close to where all that happens.

The salary pilots make is another thing I like. They make more than they can spend. This is because most people think flying is dangerous except that pilots know how easy it really is.

There isn't much about being a pilot I don't like, except that girls like pilots and all the stewardesses want to marry pilots so they always have to chase them away so they don't bother them.

I hope I don't get airsick because I get carsick and if I get airsick I couldn't be a pilot and then I'd have to go to work."

Passengers prefer old captains and young flight attendants.

LAWS OF AVIATION

The more I read these little 'gems', the more apropos they seem to be.

A baggage compartment will be fully loaded to capacity immediately upon becoming available.

- Corollary: Stuff expands to fill the available space.

The harder you try to please your IP, the less satisfied he/she is with your performance.

- This is as it should be; and even moreso the closer you get to the flightcheck.

When you are in the process of stuffing a large passenger into the rear seat of your airplane, remember all 'hefty' persons lie about their weight by a factor of at least 15%.

The overall weight of the airplane you are trying to fly out of some tight, short airstrip will seem to increase during the takeoff roll as the far end of the runway draws rapidly nearer.

- You have run the numbers for runway length vs. takeoff distance, haven't you?

Once a pilot realizes he/she is lost, everything they do will only seem to make matters worse.

    - That sounds like the 'Law of Decreasing Returns' to me.

It is easier to get off-course than it is to stay exactly on-course.

A passenger will only get airsick when there are no barf-bags on board.

When the art of radio communication between pilots and ATC is improved, the result will be vastly increased areas of significant misunderstandings.

Legibility of notes, flight plans and ATC clearances is inversely proportional to the importance of the information.

The length of briefing on a maneuver is always inversely proportional to the complexity of the maneuver. Therefore, if a task is simple enough, discussion approaches infinity.

The farther a pilot is from the home field, the more difficult and challenging the flight navigation.

The power-off glide into a partially wooded area is always one tree-stump short of the only clearing around.

    - Something to practice: Power-off glides into the precise chosen field.

The time required for a cross-country flight is nearly always – to a critical degree – at the endurance limit of the human bladder. The proof of this is, when one thinks one can 'hold it' no more, the destination appears off the nose, as if by magic.

Given the choice of two compass headings, the wrong one inevitably is chosen.

Winds aloft are always headwinds, of a velocity proportional to the need to cover the ground.

The pilot who teaches himself has a fool for a student.

> - I recall hearing of a pilot who went out in a Citabria [aerobatic trainer], would read about a maneuver in a text [in flight!] and then try it. The last time I heard of him, he wasn't dead...yet.

Slovakia Night Fighter-Bomber Pilot
1939 – 1944
Slovakia became a Nazi-ruled state with the breakup of Czechoslovakia in 1939. Fighting on the German side without enthusiasm resulted in their decimation on the Russian Front.

A fool and his money are soon flying more airplane than he can handle.

EVERYTHING I NEED TO KNOW I LEARNED AS A DOOR GUNNER

I include this list for everyone who has passed through the Valley of Death and come out the other side – Vietnam, Iraq, Afghanistan and all points in-between. Passed on to me by a high school buddy who went there, did that, got the t-shirt, was in the video, and came back with every part he left with. These were his wings...

US Army 1965 – 1973
Helicopter Door Gunner
(unauthorized)

- Once you are in the fight, it is way too late to wonder if this is a good idea.

- It is a fact that helicopter tail rotors are instinctively drawn toward trees, stumps, rocks, etc. While it may be possible to ward off this natural event some of the time, it cannot, despite the best efforts of the crew, always be prevented. It's just what they do.

- NEVER get into a fight without more ammunition than the other guy.

- The engine RPM and the rotor RPM must BOTH be kept in the GREEN. Failure to heed this commandment can affect the morale of the crew.

- Cover your Buddy, so he can be around to cover for you.

- Decisions made by someone above you in the chain-of-command will seldom be in your best interest.

- The terms Protective Armor and Helicopter are mutually exclusive.
- Sometimes, being good and lucky still is not enough.

- "Chicken Plates" are not something you order in a restaurant.

- If everything is as clear as a bell, and everything is going exactly as planned, you're about to be surprised.

- Loud, sudden noises in a helicopter WILL get your undivided attention.

- The BSR (Bang Stare Red) Theory states that the louder the sudden bang in the helicopter, the quicker your eyes will be drawn to the gauges.

- The longer you stare at the gauges the less time it takes them to move from green to red.

- No matter what you do, the bullet with your name on it will get you. So too, can the ones addressed "To Whom It May Concern".

- If the rear echelon troops are really happy, the front line troops probably do not have what they need.

- If you are wearing body armor, they will probably miss that part.

- Happiness is a belt-fed weapon.

- Having all your body parts intact and functioning at the end of the day beats the alternative.

- If you are allergic to lead, it is best to avoid a war zone.

- It is a bad thing to run out of airspeed, altitude, and ideas all at the same time.

- Hot garrison chow is better than hot C-rations which, in turn, are better than cold C-rations, which are better than no food at all. All of these, however, are preferable to cold rice balls, even if they do have the little pieces of fish in them.

- Everybody's a hero ... on the ground ... in the club ... after the fourth drink.

- A free fire zone has nothing to do with economics.

- The further you fly into the mountains, the louder the strange engine noises become.

- Medals are OK, but having your body and all your friends in one piece at the end of the day is better.

- Being shot hurts.

- "Pucker Factor" is the formal name of the equation that states the more hairy the situation is, the more of the seat cushion will be sucked up your ass. It can be expressed in its mathematical formula of: S(suction)+H(height) above ground) + I (interest in staying alive) + T (# of tracers coming your way) = Pucker Factor

- Thus the term 'SHIT!' can also be used to denote a situation where very high Pucker Factor is being encountered.

- Running out of pedal, fore or aft cyclic, or collective are all bad ideas. Any combination of these can be deadly.

- There is only one rule in war: When you win, you get to make up the rules.

- C-4 can make a dull day fun.

- There is no such thing as a fair fight, only ones where you win or lose.

- If you win the battle you are entitled to the spoils. If you lose you don't care.

- Nobody cares what you did yesterday or what you are going to do tomorrow. What is important is what you are doing-NOW-to solve our problem.

- Always make sure someone has a P-38. (That's a can opener for those of you who aren't military.)

- Prayer never hurts.

- Flying is better than walking. Walking is better than running. Running is better than crawling. All of these, however, are better than extraction by a Med-Evac, even if it is, technically, a form of flying.

- If everyone does not come home, none of the rest of us can ever fully come home either.

- If you have not been there and done that . . . you probably will not understand most of these.

A helicopter is a collection of rotating, oscillating & reciprocating parts going 'round and 'round & up and down – all of them attempting to become simultaneously random in motion.

McDONNELL-DOUGLAS SURVEY

This — allegedly - was posted briefly on the McDonnell Douglas Website by an employee who obviously had a sense of humor. The company, of course, did not and made the web department take it down immediately. (For once, the "IMPORTANT" note at the end is worth a read too.)

Thank you for purchasing a McDonnell Douglas military aircraft. In order to protect your new investment, please take a few moments to fill out the warranty registration card below. Answering the survey questions is not required, but the information will help us to develop new products that best meet your needs and desires.

1. [_] Mr.[_] Mrs.[_] Ms.[_] Miss
[_] Lt.[_] Gen.[_] Comrade
[_] Classified[_] Other

First Name:

_____

Initial: _____

Last Name:

_____

Password:

_____(max. 8 char)

Code Name:

_____

Latitude – Longitude:

_____

Altitude: _____ Meters or Feet (circle one)

2. Which model of aircraft did you purchase?
[_] F-14 Tomcat[_] F-15 Eagle
[_] F-16 Falcon[_] F-117A Stealth
[_] Classified

3. Date of purchase (DD/MM/YYYY: ____/____/_____

4. Serial Number:

_____

5. Please indicate where this product was purchased:
[_] Received as gift / aid package
[_] Catalogue / showroom
[_] Independent arms broker
[_] Mail order
[_] Discount store
[_] Government surplus
[_] Classified

6. Please indicate how you became aware of the McDonnell Douglas product you have just purchased:
[_] Heard loud noise, looked up

[_] Store display
[_] Espionage
[_] Recommended by friend / relative / ally
[_] Political lobbying by manufacturer
[_] Was attacked by one

7. Please indicate the three (3) factors that most influenced your decision to purchase this McDonnell Douglas product:
[_] Style / appearance
[_] Speed / maneuverability
[_] Price / value
[_] Comfort / convenience
[_] Kickback / bribe
[_] Recommended by salesperson
[_] McDonnell Douglas reputation
[_] Advanced Weapons Systems
[_] Backroom politics
[_] Negative experience opposing one in combat

8. Please indicate the location(s) where this product will be used:
[_] North America[_] Afghanistan
[_] Iraq[_] Aircraft carrier
[_] Iran[_] Europe
[_] Iraq[_] Middle East (not Iraq/Iran)
[_] Iran[_] Africa
[_] Iraq[_] Asia / Far East
[_] Iran[_] Misc. Third World countries
[_] Iraq[_] Classified
[_] Iran[_] Other: _____

9. Please indicate the products that you currently own or intend to purchase in the near future:
[_] Color TV[_] VCR
[_] ICBM[_] Killer Satellite

[_] CD player[_] Air-to-Air Missiles
[_] Space Shuttle[_] Home Computer
[_] Nuclear Weapon[_] HummVee

10. How would you describe yourself or your organization?
(Indicate all that apply)
[_] Communist / Socialist[_] Terrorist
[_] Crazed[_] Neutral
[_] Democratic[_] Dictatorship
[_] Corrupt[_] Primitive / Tribal

11. How did you pay for your McDonnell Douglas product?
[_] Deficit spending[_] Cash
[_] Suitcases of cocaine[_] Oil revenues
[_] Personal check[_] Credit card
[_] Ransom money[_] Traveler's check

12. Your occupation:
[_] Homemaker[_] Sales / marketing
[_] Revolutionary[_] Clerical
[_] Mercenary[_] Tyrant
[_] Middle management[_] Eccentric billionaire
[_] Defense Minister / General[_] Retired
[_] Student

13. To help us better understand our customers, please indicate
the interests and activities in which you and your spouse enjoy
participating on a regular basis:
[_] Golf[_] Boating / sailing
[_] Sabotage[_] Running / jogging
[_] Propaganda / misinformation [_] Destabilization / overthrow
[_] Default on loans[_] Gardening
[_] Crafts[_] Black market / smuggling
[_] Collectibles / collections[_] Watching sports on TV

[_] Wines[_] Interrogation / torture
[_] Household pets[_] Crushing rebellions
[_] Espionage / reconnaissance[_] Fashion clothing
[_] Border disputes[_] Mutually Assured Destruction

Thank you for taking the time to fill out this questionnaire. Your answers will be used in market studies that will help McDonnell Douglas serve you better in the future -- as well as allowing you to receive mailings and special offers from other companies, governments, extremist groups, and mysterious consortia. As a bonus for responding to this survey, you will be registered to win a brand new F-117A in our Desert Thunder Sweepstakes!

Comments or suggestions about our fighter planes? Please write to:

McDONNELL - DOUGLAS CORPORATION
Marketing Department
Military, Aerospace Division

IMPORTANT: This email is intended for the use of the individual addressee(s) named above and may contain information that is confidential privileged or unsuitable for overly sensitive persons with low self-esteem, no sense of humor or irrational religious beliefs. If you are not the intended recipient, any dissemination, distribution or copying of this email is not authorized (either explicitly or implicitly) and constitutes an irritating social faux pas.

Unless the word absquatulation has been used in its correct context somewhere other than in this warning, it has no legal or grammatical use and may be ignored. No animals were harmed in the transmission of this email, although the kelpie next door is living on borrowed time, let me tell you. Those of you with an overwhelming fear of the unknown will be gratified to learn there is no hidden message revealed by reading this backwards, so just ignore that Alert Notice from Microsoft.

However, by pouring a complete circle of salt around yourself and your computer you can ensure that no harm befalls you and your pets. If you have received this email in error, please add some nutmeg and egg whites, whisk, and place in a warm oven for 40 minutes.

Imperial Russia Pilot
1912 – 1917
Never a potent force, the Russian Air Service split after the October 1917 revolution into pro-Communist (Red) and pro-monarchy (white) factions. This badge has Cyrillic inscriptions and the 1914 date inscribed on the reverse.

Fighter pilots make movies; attack pilots make history.

MECHANICAL TRUISMS OF AVIATION

*Anyone who has been around airplanes, aircraft &
aerospace vehicles – and especially those who
perform their own maintenance thereupon – will see
and understand the truth in these, well, truisms.
Truisms occur because they are true, hence the
name...*

When a misbehaving radio is removed from the aircraft – with
no little difficulty – and taken to the shop, the problem will not
be able to be duplicated on the ground.

When a plane must be worked on out-of-doors, it will be in a
remote location with no artificial lighting available. The repair
work will then reach its most critical phase right at the onset of
night.

The vacuum pump is certified to fail at either 500 hours' time-in-
service or whenever you are in the clag, whichever comes first.

A tire will blow out only during the most critical part of the landing – or after you have taxied several miles to reach the departure runway.

The exhaust manifold gasket that fails first will always be on the one most inaccessible.

After your hands become coated with grease, your nose will itch and you have to pee.

When you try to prove to someone that some machine or piece of equipment won't work, it will.

Any object dropped during repairs will always find its way to the least accessible area, requiring complex dismantling to retrieve it. The smaller the lost item, the further away it goes.

Brakes will fail just as the plane is being taxied towards a closed hangar door with no room to slow down or maneuver away from the building.

Only brand-new propellers pick up rocks.

A ten-cent fuse will protect itself by destroying the $2,000 radio to which it is connected.

Delivery of a part which normally takes two days will take five when you specify AOG.

All warranty and guarantee clauses become null and void upon payment or just prior to failure, whichever comes first.

FAR 43, Appendix A (c) details the 31 preventative maintenance items a non-A&P mechanic owner/operator may perform. "Preventative Maintenance" is defined in FAR 1.1 as "simple or minor preservation operations and the

replacement of small standard parts not involving complex assembly operations.

If it ain't broke, don't fix it. If it ain't fixed, don't fly it.

MECHANICS TOOL GUIDE: Part I

"You gotta use the right tool for the job!" was the mantra of many a crew chief, plane captain, senior mechanic and A&P/IA. When working on planes I made a promise that if I needed a tool twice I would get one for myself – which I have. AND I keep a list of who borrows what; can't have those things growing legs, y'know.

AIR COMPRESSOR	A machine that takes energy produced in a coal-burning power plant 200 miles away and transforms it into compressed air that travels by hose to a Chicago Pneumatic impact wrench that grips rusty bolts last tightened 60 years ago by someone in Springfield, and rounds them off.

BAND SAW 	A large stationary power saw used primarily by most workshops to cut good aluminum sheeting into smaller pieces which fit more easily into the trash bin since you cut on the inside of the line and not the outside edge.
BATTERY ELECTROLYTE TESTER 	A handy tool for transferring sulfuric acid from a car battery to the inside of your toolbox after determining that your battery is dead as a doornail, just as you thought.
BELT SANDER 	An electrical abrasion machine commonly used to convert minor touch-up jobs to major refinishing ones.
CIRCULAR (SKILSAW) 	A portable cutting device for making wood studs too short.

DRILL PRESS 	A tall upright machine useful for suddenly snatching flat metal bar stock out of your hands so that it smacks you in the chest and flings your beer across the room, denting the freshly-painted project which you had so carefully set in the far corner so nothing could get to it.
ELECTRIC HAND DRILL 	Normally used for spinning steel Pop rivets in their holes until you die of old age, but it also works great for drilling mounting holes in sheet metal just above the hydraulic line that goes to the landing gear.
E-Z OUT BOLT AND STUD EXTRACTOR 	A tool that snaps off in bolt holes and is ten times harder than any known drill bit.

GASKET SCRAPER (SNAP-ON)	Theoretically useful as a sandwich tool for spreading mayonnaise; used mainly for getting dog-doo off your boot.
HACKSAW	One of a family of cutting tools built on the Ouija board principle. It transforms human energy into a crooked, unpredictable motion, and the more you attempt to influence its course, the more dismal your future becomes.
HAMMER	Originally employed as a weapon of war, the hammer nowadays is used as a kind of divining rod to locate expensive parts not far from the object we are trying to hit.
HOSE CUTTER:	A tool used to cut hoses 1/2 inch too short.

HYDRAULIC FLOOR JACK: 	Used for lowering a motorcycle to the ground after you have installed your new front disk brake setup, trapping the jack handle firmly under the front fender. (For youse guys what works on yu Harley's when there's no other aviation work to do).
MECHANIC'S KNIFE 	Used to open and slice through the contents of cardboard cartons delivered to your front door; works particularly well on boxes containing plastic panels and upholstery.
METAL SNIPS 	See hacksaw.
OXYACETYLENE TORCH 	Used almost entirely for lighting various flammable objects in your hangar on fire. Also handy for igniting the grease inside a wheel assembly out of which you're trying to get the bearing race

PHONE	Tool for calling your neighbor to see if he has another hydraulic floor jack.
PLIERS	Used to round off bolt heads; sometimes used for the creation of blood blisters.
PRY BAR:	A tool used to crumple the metal surrounding that clip or bracket you needed to remove in order to replace a 50 cent part.
1/2 x 16-INCH SCREWDRIVER	A large motor mount prying tool that inexplicably has an accurately machined tip on the end of the screwdriver without the handle.
STRAIGHT SCREWDRIVER	A tool for opening paint cans and other prying jobs, sometimes used to convert common slotted screws into non-removable screws.

TABLE SAW: 	A large stationary power tool used to launch wood projectiles to test wall structural integrity.
TROUBLE LIGHT 	The mechanic's own tanning booth. Sometimes called a drop light, it is a good source of vitamin D, "the sunshine vitamin," which is not otherwise found inside aircraft or under motorcycles. Health benefits aside, its main purpose is to consume 40-watt light bulbs at about the same rate that 105-mm howitzer shells might be used during, say, the first few hours of the Battle of the Bulge. More often dark than light, its name is somewhat misleading.
TWEEZERS 	A tool for removing wood splinters.

TWO X FOUR 8' LONG DOUGLAS FIR 	Used for levering a motorcycle upward off a hydraulic jack.
TWO-TON HYDRAULIC ENGINE HOIST 	A handy tool for testing the tensile strength of ground straps, wires and hydraulic lines you may have forgotten to disconnect.
UTILITY KNIFE 	Used to slice open the contents of cardboard cartons; works particularly well on boxes holding seat upholstery, vinyl records, liquids in plastic bottles, collector magazines and sundry rubber or plastic parts: Especially good for slicing work clothes, but only when being worn.
VISE GRIPS 	Generally used after pliers to completely round off bolt heads. If nothing else is available, they can also be used to transfer intense welding heat to the palm of your hand.

WHITWORTH SOCKETS	Once used for working on older British cars and motorcycles, they are now used mainly for impersonating that 9/16 or 1/2 socket you've been searching for the last 15 minutes.
WIRE WHEEL	Cleans rust off old bolts and then throws them somewhere under the workbench with the speed of light. Also removes fingerprint whorls and hard-earned guitar calluses in about the time it takes you to say, "Ouc...."
SONUVABITCH TOOL $$#!!%!!#	Any handy tool that can be grabbed and thrown across the hangar while yelling "Son of a Bitch!" at the top of your voice -often, it is the very next tool you will need.

A mechanic's favorite: "It's not a leek...it's a seep."

MEMORANDUM: SPECIAL HIGH INTENSITY TRAINING

Everyone's knowledge and skill levels tend to deteriorate over time; it's the old "Use it or lose it" syndrome. Management [see: HOW SHIT HAPPENS] has therefore issued the following...

To: All Employees
From: Boss in General
Subject: Special High Intensity Training

In order to assure the shareholders and the public who utilize our services that our employees may continue providing the highest quality work possible, it will be our policy to keep all employees current and abreast of the latest developments through our program of Special High Intensity Training. Henceforth, we will give our employees more S.H.I.T. than our competitors.

If any employee feels they are not receiving their full measure of S.H.I.T. on the job, please see your Supervisor or Chief Pilot. You will then be placed at the top of their S.H.I.T. list. All Supervisors and/or Chief Pilots are particularly well-qualified to make sure you receive all the S.H.I.T. you can handle.

If you consider yourself well-trained and up on all the company's S.H.I.T., you may be interested in assisting in the training of those who's S.H.I.T. is weak. We will add your name to our Basic Understanding Lecture List – Special High Intensity Training [B.U.L.L.S.H.I.T.] program.

To assist your efforts in this endeavor, we have created a liaison between Management, staff and the workers to whom you will give all your S.H.I.T. You will report to the Special Administrator of Computer Keypunching – Special High Intensity Training [S.A.C.K. of S.H.I.T.]

Failure to meet the requirements of this memorandum will force Management to place non-complying employees on the Departmental Employee Egress Program – Special High Intensity Training [D.E.E.P.S.H.I.T.]. Those who do not take their S.H.I.T. seriously must attend an Employee Attitude Timeout – Special High Intensity Training [E.A.T.S.H.I.T.] seminar.

If you have any questions, please address them to the company's Head Of Training – Special High Intensity Training [H.O.T.S.H.I.T.]. The entire program will be managed by the Head Of Resource Specialty Education – Special High Intensity Training [H.O.R.S.E.S.H.I.T.] who will report directly to the Oversight Head – Special High Intensity Training [O.H.S.H.I.T.]

Since our managers, supervisors, Chief Pilot(s) and Line Check

Airmen took a lot of S.H.I.T. prior to promotion, they do not have to do S.H.I.T anymore.

Thank you,

Boss In General – Special High Intensity Training [B.I.G.S.H.I.T.]

P.S. Displaying the proper attitude while complying with this Special High Intensity Training – Tutelage Indoctrination of Everyone [S.H.I.T.T.I.E.] program could result in your promotion to the Director of Intensity Programming – Special High Intensity Training [D.I.P.S.H.I.T.]

Be nice to your first officer – he just might be your captain at the next airline.

MILITARY PLACEMENT TEST

One of the questions from the career placement test given applicants for a military commission:

"Rearrange the letters P N E S I to spell out an important part of human body that is more useful when erect."

Those who spell SPINE will become doctors…

…the rest will go to flight school and become pilots.

For those who don't care, fly Military Air.

MISS JUNE: TSA PLAYMATE

When someone sent me this, there were the obligatory 12 cheesecake poses which would have constituted a traditional 12-month calendar. But after all – how many times can a man open the centerfold and see something not seen before? So I include just this – Miss June TSA – in a demure setting...X-ray room Bravo on the B-concourse at Denver International airport (DIA). Ain't she a sweetheart? Just the kind you wanna take home to meet your mother.

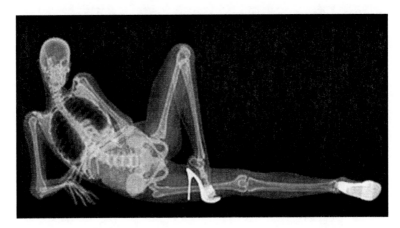

Is that a fuel tester in your pocket or are you just happy to see me?

MORE ABOUT FIGHTER PILOTS

Fighter Pilots – and for that matter all forms of front line flyers – can be recognized here. For this I take no responsibility – I'm just passing it on.

Please don't shoot the piano player…

A fighter pilot is one of those elite men who have been selected to fly sleek, sexy, supersonic aircraft in dazzling aerial combat, as well as put on cool Air Shows and pose for photographs. Only the best pilots in the world get to be fighter pilots. The rest fly slow, heavy, ugly aircraft used to haul rubber dog shit out of Hong Kong --- or worse --- Detroit.

Typically, fighter pilots wear elaborate uniforms which they claim are specially designed to be fireproof to protect them in case of an emergency: Actually, the uniforms are made of a special type of cloth which repels beer stains. Note: You can tell the really 'shit hot' fighter pilots by the zipper on their beer repelling uniform. The lower it is, the more skilled the aviator. These "flight suits" also allow a fighter pilot to be able to get dressed and undressed in less than ten seconds flat and also perform various skills that might otherwise be impossible or painful in normal attire.

Fighter pilots have been a part of every major conflict, making notable appearances in World Wars I, II, Korea, Vietnam, the Gulf wars and other associated events.

Facts about Fighter Pilots:

Fighter pilots are absolutely irresistible to women, who will drop their panties if a fighter pilot so much as enters the room.

Fighter pilots are highly skilled and take pride in their ability to consume massive quantities of alcohol, and can speak in complete sentences consisting entirely of swear words.

How do you tell if a fighter pilot is in the room? Just wait a minute... He'll tell you!

Fighter pilots always wear large dark sunglasses.

Fighter pilots drive the fastest, most flashy cars money can buy, and they always have the speedometer on the peg.

Fighter pilots wear a bigger watch than you. It's an easier target when they practice aerial combat with their hands.

Fighter pilots do not high-five.

Fighter pilots do not carry briefcases or umbrellas or babies.

Most fighter pilots chase women with cute asses. A-10 fighter pilots chase women with cute purses.

Fighter pilots subsist on a diet consisting entirely of coffee, cigars, chewing tobacco, beer, and whiskey.

Fighter pilots are better and cooler than you.

Fighter pilots usually are given testosterone-ridden call signs like 'Jockstrap' or 'Whiplash'.

Fighter pilots can fly ANYTHING and do it better than anyone else, but why would they want to.

Fighter pilots are often seen as exceedingly arrogant and full of themselves. However, they have earned it, so do not scoff at them; remember that YOU will never get to fly that fighter jet! If you wish to take down a fighter pilot, don't even think about it when he's anywhere within a hundred miles of his flying metal monster. Wait till he's on the ground and you have an M1 Abrams at your disposal, unless he's flying an A-10, in which case you're screwed.

The Thunderbirds and Blue Angels are NOT fighter pilots. They are Movie Stars. They are usually re-admitted to the role of the fighter pilot when they move on to their next assignments.

Fighter pilots have secret hand gestures and handshakes. They will never tell you what they are, and you will never see them do them in public (unless you are a hot, slightly drunk, 25-year old nymphomaniac stripper attending the O-Club on a Friday night.)

Fighter pilots are a dying breed: The last fighter pilot has been born. In 20 Years, all fighters will be unmanned.

The world will be a sadder place.

And another thing, guys…

Women make damn good fighter pilots, too!

Never, ever think they can't hose your ass in a dogfight -

'Cause they will…without a second glance!

Manfred Freiheer von Richthofen
"The Red Baron"
WWI highest scoring ace – 80 victories

The next time war is decided on how well you can land on a carrier, the Navy will clean up. Until then, I'll worry about who spends their training time flying and fighting.

MORE COMMANDMENTS

Okay, okay – I know…any more than two rules and/or regulations get you all glassy-eyed and squirming in your seat. Deal with it, okay?!?

1. I am thy aircraft which will lead thee from bondage with the earth. Thou shalt preflight me thoroughly with both thine eyes and all thy heart.

2. Thou shalt not make getting home a graven image to be worshipped. Often exists weather in the heavens above which would easily put thee beneath the earth.

3. Thou shalt make secure thy seat and seatbelts before arising from the firmament, lest during takeoff thee shalt back-slide into eternity.

4. Thou shalt always maintain thy airspeed that neither the ground rise up and smite thee nor thy ox or thy ass be lost.

5. Thou shalt keep eternal vigilance about thine aircraft during flight lest ye meet thy brother or sister unexpectedly.

6. Thou shalt not fear the scorn of thy fellows in the name of safety for lo, 'tis better to be a live chicken than a dead duck.

7. Thou shalt have no other thoughts before flying of thine aircraft lest distraction lead thee unto perdition.

8. Thou shalt not covet thy neighbor's aircraft which demandeth skills beyond thy ability.

9. Thou shalt not bear false pride, for 'tis better to seek aid and comfort from thy air traffic control servant or thy fellow pilot, appearing dumb for but a brief moment, than to burden thine heirs with eternal defense of thy stupidity.

10. Honor these commandments and surely goodness and safe flying shall follow thee all the rest of thy days.

Experience is the knowledge that enables you to recognize a mistake when you make it again.

NEW SAFETY DEVICE FOR AIRCRAFT

There is an old aviation adage truer than most: "Lose not thy airspeed lest the earth rise up and smite thee". It's so true – those wings – and rotors, too – need airflow over them to keep your sorry behind up there in the sky. The recent Asiana Airlines crash at SFO is a prime example of this (NTSB cause of accident yet to be established, btw) when whoever is supposed to be flying the airplane allows it to get too low and/or too slow. Only bad things can happen then...unless you have tons and tons of thrust available – and even then, that might not be enough.

"Better higher than lower; better faster than slower." A little extra altitude and/or airspeed you can always give up close to or over the runway. If you're running out of altitude, airspeed and ideas all at the same time, let's hope your insurance policy is all paid up.

BOEING PROPOSES NEW FLIGHT DECK EQUIPMENT

EVERETT, WA (AP) Boeing Commercial Airplane Company Vice President of Engineering, Bill Alum, today announced the company's development of a new, high technology transport jet flight deck warning system designed to help pilots avoid the sort of incident that Asiana Airlines flight 214 experienced recently while attempting to land in San Francisco. The new device utilizes measurements of air pressure taken at different points on the aircraft's airframe to calculate how fast the airplane is traveling through the air. The actual technology involved in the inputs and how they are processed is still considered proprietary technological information by Boeing, as well as by the U.S. Department of Defense.

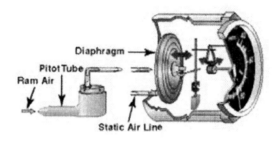

Mr. Alum said that this device, if installed in all new aircraft, as well as being retrofitted into the existing commercial aircraft fleet, "has the potential to save hundreds of lives each year". It is engineered to provide the pilots of these mammoth, high performance aircraft with continuous, real-time updates of how fast the airplane is moving. This will allow them to always make sure that the aircraft's speed remains within a safe operating envelope. "Information is power", said Mr. Alum. The full name of the device is yet to be determined, but the current working name is *"airspeed indicator"*. Reaction within the aviation industry has ranged from skepticism to enthusiasm. Dr. Phillip Head, chairman of the Department of Aeronautical Engineering at M.I.T. stated that his department has been recommending something such as an *airspeed indicator* for many years, but that their advocacy for it has "fallen on deaf ears".

In Toulouse, France, AirBus Chief Engineer Pierre Le Fou said that, due to AirBus' advanced flight guidance systems, such a device would be an unnecessary addition to their flight decks. "The technical advancement of our flight decks is such that pilots have no need for this type of information. Our guidance systems are constantly aware of all pertinent parameters while in flight, and will automatically keep them within the normal range. The pilots of our aircraft have no use for such a device as an *airspeed indicator*".

In Seoul, Korean Pilots Association (KPA) spokesman Lee Bang-wan stated that a device such as this proposed *airspeed indicator* would only serve to be a distraction in the flight deck, and that KPA pilots would probably just ignore it. Additionally, he stated that such a complex system was unneeded considering that the KPA pilots have a safety record that is "equal to that of any air carrier that is currently based in Korea".

ASIANA FLIGHT 214
PILOTS' NAMES

- Captain Sum Ting Wong
- Wi Tu Lo
- Ho Lee Fuk
- Bang Ding Ow

These fictitious names were spread all over creation by the 'news' media for at least 1 day until the hoax was revealed.

In Washington, D.C., R. N. Mowth, a spokesman for the U.S. Air Transport Association, stated that "oppressive federal regulation, such as any requirement to have so-called *airspeed indicators* installed in transport aircraft, is just one more sign of a government run amok with too much power, and its stifling of the free enterprise system."

Skepticism notwithstanding, Boeing seems to be determined to proceed with the development of this new flight deck technology. Mr. Alum stated that "we feel that, once pilots reach the point that they understand the value of the heretofore unavailable information that our proposed *airspeed indicator* gives them, they will embrace this new device and will learn to keep a close eye on it."

When Boeing is finished developing the *"AIRSPEED INDICATOR"*, rumor has it that they are going to begin developing an instrument that tells the pilot how high he's flying and they're going to call it an **"ALTIMETER"**. It will also be an important instrument for the pilot to keep his eyes on, especially during an IFR or VFR approach.

One of the things I look for during a flightcheck is how stabilized the airplane is during the various maneuvers and phases of flight.

I might ask, for the 'Slow Flight' portion of say a Private Pilot flightcheck, for the applicant to fly at an altitude of his/her choice, at a heading of his/her choice, but at a speed less than cruise and above minimum controllable airspeed (Vmca); perhaps 70 or even just 60 KIAS. I will then watch as the Carburetor Heat is pulled on, power reduced to idle, flaps extended to 30 degrees (below the Vfe limitation if they don't want to fail right then), airspeed decreases to well below the target airspeed, they finally realize they're too slow and apply full power (forgetting the have 30 degrees flaps extended) and then, with a deer in the headlights look, admit to me they can't hold the speed requested. All I can think of at that point is "Have you never just flown straight-and-level at 70 knots before?"

The applicant has never been taught to fly the airplane in a stabilized, by-the-numbers fashion. And while the applicant may take the hit, I sorely wish on many occasions I could have failed the instructor at that point.

Try this: Go out with another pilot friend and develop the following chart. Take your time while doing this and keep in mind – SOMEBODY MUST BE FLYING THE AIRPLANE AND LOOKING AROUND FOR TRAFFIC AT ALL TIMES!

Pick two or three speeds appropriate to your airplane and note them along the left side of the chart.

Then do some 'flight testing' to figure out what all has to occur or be set to fly LEVEL & STABILIZED at that speed.

Then perform the same 'flight tests' to figure out what the airplane needs to maintain that particular airspeed while in a 500 feet-per-minute descent. That descent rate at those chosen speeds will result in a stabilized visual descent AND will also define the airplane configuration for a stabilized ILS or LNAV approach as well. No hunting around for power settings, pitch attitudes, gear & flaps positions – it's ALL THERE! You'll be flying stabilized not only during 'Slow Flight' but during your visual and instrument approaches as well – a SURE way to impress the examiner (and get him out of your airplane as soon as possible!).

LEVEL

	MP	RPM	CH	Gear	Flaps
100					
90					
80					
70					
60					

500 fpm descent

	MP	RPM	CH	Gear	Flaps
100					
90					
80					
70					
60					

(MP = Manifold Pressure,   RPM = RPM,   CH = Carb Heat)

Of course you may add any other factor unique to the particular airplane you fly (boost pump on/off, cowl flap(s) open/closed, air conditioning on/off etc.) to this chart. You have my permission to customize it as much as you want. If this helps in creating knowledgeable, skilled, competent and confident pilots, then my work here is done (I'll just leave a silver bullet where someone can find it).

The airlines fly "by the numbers"; the military flies "by the numbers."

So can we in General Aviation.

Never let an airplane take you anywhere your brain hasn't been to at least 5 minutes prior.

NICOLA'S LETTER

I just adore the wide-eyed, take-it-all in, innocent view of things by children. This one kinda brings a tear to your eye.

an actual drawing, handed to a flight attendant on a Quantas flight by an 8 yr old girl

dear Captain
My name is Nicola im 8
years. old, this is my first
flight but im not scared. I
like to watch the clouds go
by. My mum says the crew is
nice. I think your plane is
good. thanks for a nice flight
don't fuck up the landing
LuV Nicola
xx x x

Always remember: You fly with your head, not just your hands.

NIGHTMARE AT FL350

You'd think with all the ~~crap~~ *ahhh...negatives...elucidated below, no-one would want to go there...but they do. Bless 'em all for having a dream and a goal. There's the story about a young pilot flying a Cub envying the pilot flying a cargo Baron: "That's real flying." The baron pilot is looking up at the commuter plane overhead saying "There's where I want to be; that's real flying." The commuter pilot is staring at the airliner on high, thinking "Someday...that's real flying." And the bored airline captain is looking down at the Cub thousands of feet below: "Now, there's real flying."*

I had a bad dream last night. In it was the FAA, a Chief Pilot, crew scheduling, bad schedules, bad management, unserviceable aircraft equipment, no extra holding fuel, ever-changing procedures, endless flight manual amendments, dead-heading in the middle seat, broken luggage, lost luggage, nasty passenger agents, crabby old 170 lb. flight attendants an axe-handle wide, all-nighters, foreign countries, sleep deprivation, mergers, seniority squabbles, company threats, food poisoning, no food, bad coffee, bidding, pulled away from my family for weeks at a time, fleabag hotels, late cabs and maniac cab drivers, bidding vacation, waiting for gates, weather, low visibility approaches, aircraft de-icing, PCs, Gestapo check airman, medicals, commuting to and from work in unspeakable weather, the parking lot from Hell, parking lot buses, inter-terminal busses, spring break, Christmas rush, Easter rush, PA announcements, insurance, drug and alcohol testing, noise violations, customs lineups, dry cleaning, terrorism, security passes, rude security personnel, high gas/oil prices, pay cuts, rush hour traffic, that infernal alarm clock, crash pads, catching cold away from home, lackadaisical crew members, blatant homosexuality, sexual harassment threats, flight attendants and co-pilots implying that they are a gift to aviation after being there three years, back-biting, gossip, cell phones, aircraft cram courses, plus laying my job on the line several times a year with simulators, endless procedural memorization and Annual Recurrent Training days.

Then I woke up and joyously found myself still retired.

United States Army Air Corps – Aerial Gunner
1941 – 1947

If it doesn't work, rename it. If it still doesn't work,
the new name isn't long enough.

NORTH POLE APPROACH

Along with "The Aviator's Night Before Christmas" this is a fun holiday item to review. Some friends and I determined that if the field were below minimums and you had to fly on to your alternate, all you would have to do is fly heading 180° to return to London. Or New Dehli. Or Tokyo. Or New York. Or...

To see the video covering Santa's flightcheck. An oldie but goodie, go to:

https://www.youtube.com/watch?v=50vE47DGEy4

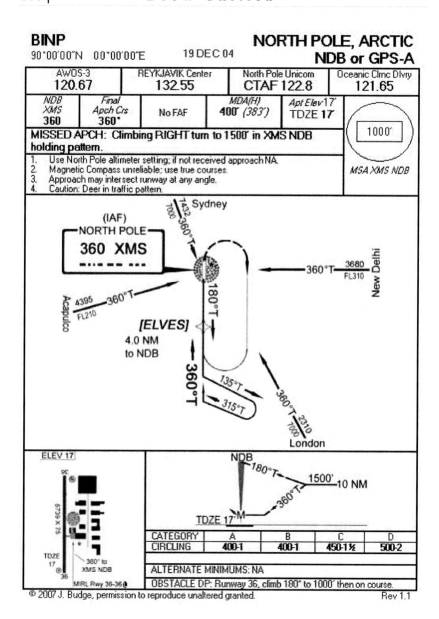

BINP
90°00'00"N 00°00'00"E   19 DEC 04

NORTH POLE, ARCTIC
NDB or GPS-A

AWOS-3	REYKJAVIK Center	North Pole Unicom	Oceanic Clmc Dlvry
120.67	132.55	CTAF 122.8	121.65

NDB XMS 360	Final Apch Crs 360°	No FAF	MDA(H) 400' (383')	Apt Elev 17' TDZE 17'	

MISSED APCH: Climbing RIGHT turn to 1500' in XMS NDB holding pattern.

1. Use North Pole altimeter setting; if not received approach NA.
2. Magnetic Compass unreliable; use true courses.
3. Approach may intersect runway at any angle.
4. Caution: Deer in traffic pattern.

1000'

MSA XMS NDB

(IAF)
NORTH POLE

360 XMS
---·· --·· ···

Sydney
1432 360°T 7000

360°T — 3680 FL310

New Delhi

180°T

Acapulco 4395 360°T FL210

[ELVES]
4.0 NM
to NDB

360°T

135°T
315°T

360°T 2310 7000
London

ELEV 17

NDB
180°T
1500' 10 NM
360°T

TDZE 17 M

CATEGORY	A	B	C	D
CIRCLING	400-1	400-1	450-1½	500-2

TDZE 17
360° to XMS NDB
35
MIRL Rwy 36-36

ALTERNATE MINIMUMS: NA

OBSTACLE DP: Runway 36, climb 180° to 1000' then on course.

One of the most important skills a pilot must master is ignoring those things in an aircraft which were put there by non-pilots to get the pilots' attention.

NPRM: FEDERAL AIR REGULATIONS COMPREHENSION ACT [FARCA]

1.000 – A No pilot or pilots, or person or persons acting on the suggestion or supervision of a pilot or pilots may try, attempt, endeavor, strive, aim, seek, undertake or make an or any effort to comprehend and/or understand any or all, in whole or in part, of the herein mentioned Federal Air Regulations [FAR's], except as authorized by the Administrator and/or an agent appointed by the Administrator.

1.000 – B If the pilot or pilots, or group of associated pilots become aware of, or realizes, or detects, or discovers, or finds out that he and/or she, or they, are, or have been, beginning to understand, comprehend, fathom the intent thereof, of the afore-mentioned Federal Air Regulations [FAR's], they must, within three [3] days notify, in writing, the Administrator or authorized agent thereof, using FAA form 8710-12 (NIC), Notice of Impending Comprehension.

1.000 – C Upon receipt of any above-mentioned Notice of Impending Comprehension [NIC], the Administrator shall immediately cause to be revised, amended, rewritten and/or otherwise change the afore-mentioned FAR's in such a manner as to eliminate any further comprehension hazards [FCH].

1.000 – D The Administrator may, at his or her option, require the offending person or persons, pilot or pilots, to attend remedial instruction classes, at the discretion of the Administrator, concerning the FAR's until such time as the Administrator has determined the person or persons, pilot or pilots, has become confused to such a degree as to be incapable of understanding anything contained in the afore-mentioned FAR's.

If you are looking for a cure for insomnia, just settle down in your comfy chair, open the FAR/AIM [or FOM for you airline types] and begin quietly reading to yourself. I guarantee you'll be dozing off within minutes.

HOWEVER, if you want to maximize your learning, read the regs out loud. Better yet, read them to your pet. I used to share quarters with a Labrador/Shepard mix who absolutely LOVED regulations, technical manuals, field manuals and the Dash-One's [POH]; she could sit there and listen for hours. Reading the regs out loud brings to that feeble pilot brain of ours multiple layers of comprehension. We read the words [symbols of knowledge], interpret those words into knowledge, change that knowledge back into words and then verbalize those words. We then hear the words, interpret them back into knowledge and then visually compare what we have just said with what we have just read. If you've followed me so far, the result is about 6 layers of knowledge reinforcement as opposed to just reading the words quietly to oneself and letting it go at that. Reading aloud also allows you to become aware of the little 'gotcha's' found in said FAR's.

Beyond that – KMAG YOYO

NPRM: MILE HIGH CLUB OPERATIONS

I seem to recall an accident report out of the Las Vegas area where one sentence in the report pretty much summed up the entire sequence of events:

"Peculiar injuries to the pilot indicated he was receiving oral sex at the time of the crash."

DEPARTMENT OF TRANSPORTATION
Federal Aviation Administration
14 CFR Part 61
(Docket No. 75487345, Notice No. 88-523040306)

NPRM: "Mile High Club" Operations

ACTION: Notice of Proposed Rulemaking (NPRM)

SUMMARY: This notice proposes to require additional qualifications and testing before a certificated pilot may engage or continue to engage in "Mile High Club" Operations (MHCO) while also exercising the privileges of a pilot certificate.

DATES: Comments should be received before December 31, 1999.

ADDRESSES: Comments may be mailed or delivered in sextuplicate to: Federal Aviation Administration, Office of Chief Counsel, Attention: Rules Docket (AGC-204), Docket No. 75487345, 800 Independence Avenue SW, Washington DC 20591. Comments may be examined in the Rules Docket weekdays, except Federal holidays, between 8:00 a.m. and 5:00 p.m.

SUPPLEMENTARY INFORMATION

Need for Rulemaking:

Under the provisions of the Wheat Silo Subsidy Act (P.L. 100-872398-A), Congress has mandated the FAA to regulate the activities of the formerly unregulated "Mile High Club" (MHC). Under present rules, anything accomplished at an altitude of one statute mile (5,280 feet) above ground level (AGL), regardless of the degree of difficulty or the level of expertise demanded, earns a certificate good for membership in the "Mile High Club."

Through a procedure of self-regulation, the organization has set forth requirements that activities take place at an altitude of at least 5,280 feet above ground level to prevent Denver pilots from messing around on the ramp. Although the organization has adopted rigid admission requirements for its pilot members, a recent National Transportation Safety Board (NTSB) report disclosed an accident in a light training aircraft (LTA) caused by pilot error in the form of disorientation of a student pilot [sex unknown) after the Certified Flight Instructor (CFI) (sex unknown) attempted to introduce the student to a maneuver not included in the MHC syllabus.

Similarly, the crash of a corporate-owned Learjet in western

Pennsylvania was thought to have been caused by the absence of the crew from the cockpit at the time the aircraft arrived in Pittsburgh. Further, evidence suggests that some hitherto unexplained accidents may have been due to pilot fatigue following Mile High Club Operations (MHCO) activities. These accidents have amply demonstrated that there is a compelling need for regulation of MHCO activities for the protection of the public and property under the flight paths of such aircraft.

The FAA is proposing to expand the scope of Part 61 of the FARs by the addition of paragraphs 61.300 through 61.305 to prohibit the propositioning of any occupant of a certificated aircraft by any licensed and current pilot who has not first demonstrated the ability to execute the duties of pilot-in-command and/or co-pilot to the satisfaction of an Operations Inspector or a designated Pilot Examiner. It is further proposed to establish minimum experience, age, and skill levels for the issuance of MCHO ratings to pilots' certificates. To ensure that a satisfactory level of proficiency is maintained by certificated pilots possessing MHCO ratings, it is proposed that biennial proficiency reviews be mandated.

Environmental Impact Statement:

The adoption of these regulations is not anticipated to have a significant impact upon the environment including an impact upon population pressures.

Economic Impact Statement:

The proposed rules would not materially impact the economics of MHCO activities, including those conducted for hire under Part 135.

Definitions:

For the purposes of this NPRM, the following Definitions are established:

PILOT: An applicant for or possessor of a MCHO rating regardless of sex, creed, color, political affiliation, proclivities, or physical dimensions.

CO-PILOT: Any person regardless of sex, creed, color, political affiliation, proclivities, or physical dimensions assisting a certificated, MHCO-rated pilot in carrying out MHCO activities.

PASSENGER: Any reliable witness to an MHCO flight test who does not actively participate.

FLIGHT ENGINEER: Anyone other than a co-pilot who assists the pilot in establishing the proper conditions for accomplishing the minimum requirements of MHCO activities.

AIRCRAFT: Any vehicle aloft suitable for MHCO activities. Does not include automobiles or parachutists falling from high places.

GLIDER: Anyone performing an MHCO activity entirely in mid-air such as during the free-fall period of a parachute jump.

HANG GLIDER: Glider with above-average equipment.

SOLO FLIGHT: A practice session where the pilot is the sole manipulator of the controls.

DUAL FLIGHT: An MHCO activity during which the pilot uses both hands.

AUTOPILOT AUTHORIZATION: An authorization from the FAA permitting someone else to do it for a shy pilot.

The Proposed Rule:

For reasons set forth above, the FAA is proposing to amend Part 61 of the Federal Aviation Regulations as follows:

PART 61 - [AMENDED]

1. The authority citation for Part 61 continues to read as follows:

Authority: Secs. 313(a), 314, 601, 602, Federal Aviation Act of 1958, 49 U.S.C. 1354(a), 1355, 1421, 1422; sec. 6(c), Department of Transportation Act, 49 U.S.S. 1655(2), unless otherwise noted.

2. Section 61 would be amended by adding the following:

61.300
An applicant for a Mile High Club Operations (MHCO) rating on a pilot certificate must meet the following minimum qualifications:

(a) The applicant must have reached his/her sixteenth birthday..

(b) The applicant must present a high school diploma or equivalent indicating a grade of failing or better, or a notarized statement proving the applicant has compromised at least one substitute teacher.

61.301

An applicant for an MHCO rating must pass a written examination on the following applicable aviation subjects:

(a) Care, operation, a periodic maintenance of articulating seats in certificated U.S. civil aircraft.

(b) Basic anatomy and other considerations in selecting a co-pilot.

(c) Dangers associated with the destruction of aircraft panel instruments by bare feet.

61.302

An applicant for an MHCO rating will be tested on the following maneuvers:

(a) Takeoffs. Applicant will prepare the co-pilot for MHCO activities.

(b) Stalls. Applicant will demonstrate any acceptable and workable method of delay maneuvering to avoid premature results.

(c) Approaches. Applicant will demonstrate at least six (6) precision or three (3) non-precision approaches to a co-pilot who does not suspect the purpose of the flight.

(d) Soft Field Landings. Applicant will show proficiency in selecting procedures to be utilized under soft conditions.

(e) Short Field Landings. Applicant will show proficiency in utilizing the proper procedures under short conditions.

(f) Forced Landings. Applicant will will accomplish the minimum MHCO activities despite co-pilot's objections.

(g) On-pylon Eights. Applicant will select two prominent landmarks and maneuver between them. If the co-pilot is not endowed with sufficiently prominent landmarks, the activity may be performed in a light simulator approved by the Administrator.

(h) In-flight Emergencies. Applicant will conduct a suitable approach with the zipper jammed in the "up" position and will demonstrate the smooth emergency extension of gear before contact.

(i) Holding Patterns. The Applicant will show proficiency in covering all points of interest with only two hands.

(j) Radio Navigation. Applicant will insert the radial into the omnibearing selector and achieve station passage before the "off" flag appears.

(k) Back Course Approach. Not an approved procedure.

(l) Diverting to an Alternate. Applicant will make an approach to a passenger when it becomes obvious that the original destination has gone below minimums because of a cold front.

(m) Maneuvering with an Inoperative Engine. Self- explanatory.

(n) Weather Recognition. Applicant will readily identify cold fronts and warm fronts with the cockpit lights inoperative.

(o) Lost Communications Procedures. Applicant will show

proficiency in blocking the co-pilot's voice channel using a broad-band antenna with great frequency.

61.3 03 Proficiency Review

(a) No person may conduct MHCO activities unless, within the preceding 24 months, that person has:

1. Accomplished a proficiency review given to him, in an aircraft for which the person is rated, by an appropriately certificated flight instructor or other person designated by the Administrator who possesses a valid MHCO Inspection Authorization.

2. Had his/her log book endorsed by the person conducting the review certifying that the person has satisfactorily accomplished all the required activities of the review.

3. However, a person who has, within the preceding 24 months, satisfactorily completed an MHCO proficiency check conducted by the FAA or otherwise been satisfactorily screwed by the FAA need not accomplish the flight review required by this section.

61.304 General Experience

No person may engage in MHCO activities as pilot-in-command of an aircraft carrying passengers, nor of an aircraft certificated for more than one required pilot flight crewmember unless within the preceding 90 days that person has satisfactorily carried out MHCO activities and has made suitable log book entries attesting the fact. This requirement does not apply to persons holding an airline transport pilot certificate or to activities conducted while operating under part 135 of this chapter.

61.3 05 Instrument Experience

No person may engage in MHCO activities unless, during the
preceding 6 months, that person has conducted MHCO
operations in the immediate vicinity of cold fronts and
successfully logged at least 6 hours under actual or simulated
conditions which involved at least six approaches.

Yugoslavia Observer-Navigator
1944 – 1949

Out on the line, all the girls are looking for
husbands...and all the husbands are looking for girls.

ODE TO A 6-MONTH CHECK

I lifted this from the QB <u>Beam</u> of August 2012: Says quite a lot, doesn't it? 'Stub' was born 29 February 1912, learning to fly in biplanes during the 1930's. He flew with a number of airlines and served during WWII as a test pilot for Douglas Aircraft in Santa Monica, CA. where he was known as a consummate pilot. R.I.P.

ODE TO A 6-MONTH CHECK
By Captain Claude Harding Ferguson
Who went west 24 July, 2004
at 92 years.

You've flown a lot through snow and ice and often when it's raining,
But the time has come again, my friend, to bust your ass while "training".
First there comes the 'Oral' and, like I told my Pard,
The questions all are easy; it's the answers that are hard.

They've simplified the mental quiz and they've plugged a lot of leaks,
So if you hit the books real hard you can get it in two weeks.
Now, if you pass the 'Oral' you've gained a little ground.
But you get another chance to flunk when you do the 'walk-around'.

What is that? What's in there? How much air is in those tires?
Makes a person long again to hear the wind sing through the wires.
What's behind? What's up front? You nearly almost guessed.
This is the one that's standardized; it's different from the rest.

Now if you pass the walk-around, try to conceal your fright;
You now have won the golden chance to go up for your flight.
The time has come to do your best and to keep from getting fired;
You may have to demonstrate your skills to someone that you hired.

The flight is always lots of fun, there really is no heat;
The reason that you sweat so much is just what you had to eat.
You have to do the stalls while clean and then again while dirty;
Which is just about like is was 'way back in nineteen-thirty.

Watch your heading! Hold it straight! Don't you know the proper powers?
How the hell did you slip by for twenty-thousand hours?
Your past is all forgotten and your future ain't too bright,
If you should flub the contest on the ground or up in flight.

But, if you're full of answers then you allay your fears
And you're allowed to carry on
What you've done for thirty years.

Zeppelin Service – Officer
Prussia
Commemorative badge issued throughout the 1920's

A good simulator checkride is like successful surgery
on a cadaver.

ODE TO AVIATORS

Anyone who has passed a flightcheck is entitled to wear wings. Naval Aviators have their "Wings of Gold", USAF pilots wear "Silver Wings" and then there are all the variations and different versions in-between. Just don't wear them on your pajamas when you go to bed.

Once the wings go on, they never come off whether they can be seen or not.

It fuses to the soul through adversity, fear and adrenaline and no one who has ever worn them with pride, integrity and guts can ever sleep through the `call of the sky` that wafts through bedroom windows in the deep of the night.

When a good pilot leaves the `job' and retires, many are jealous, some are pleased and yet others, who may have already retired, wonder.

We wonder if they know what is being left behind, because we already know.

We know, for example, that after a lifetime of camaraderie that few experience, it will remain as a longing for those past times.

We know in the world of flying, there is a kinship which lasts long after the flight suits are hung up in the back of the closet.

We know even if he throws them away, the wings will be on him with every step and breath for the rest of his life.

We also know how the very bearing of the man speaks of what he was and in his heart still is.

Because we fly, we envy no-one on earth.

- Author Unknown

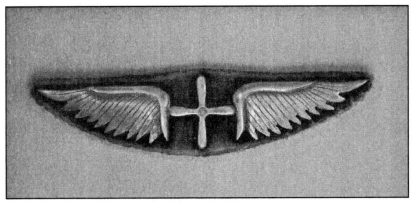

Enlisted Pilot
US Army Air Service
1917 – 1918

Please don't tell Mother I'm a pilot – she thinks I play piano in a whorehouse.

ONCE A KNIGHT IS ENOUGH

I got my copy of this tale directly from the hands of J.W. Duff [Gone west 2013], of Duff's Aircraft Company in Denver, Colorado. J.W.'s business was recovering aircraft wrecks from anywhere and once the insurance dust settled, parting out the remains. I'd love to investigate his various hangars and secret bases to see what treasures lie within: Sadly, his Doberman's keep the riff-raff out.

"Forsooth" sayeth the knight as he riseth from yon round table, "This is my offeth day so shall I mount my iron bird and soar forth." Thus spoke the knight who then entered his wheeled carriage and traveleth far to the place of the roaring birds. Striding around the winged monster, he pulleth here and proddeth there in a manner to checketh the firmness of the fowl's feathers.

Seemingly pleased with the condition of said bird, the knight then did mounteth and doeth various things to the bird's interior which then causeth it to roar and shake. It then waddeleth off to a stretch of black firmament, did then take a running leap and so did soar upward with a mighty rush of wind.*

* 'Tis better to break ground and fly into the wind than the other way 'round.

Thus there cometh a feeling of great joy to the knight; he zoometh around yon sky with great abandon until verily, more than an hour had passeth. The knight so did decendeth from the high places and flyeth beside the black earth, causing the wind to cease its roar. The knight turneth the bird towards yon alighting path. As the bird approacheth the firmament it was seen that one wing flyeth lower than its mate. Some say this is because the wind bloweth across the black earth.

The bird did thence alight on one foot whereupon it launcheth itself into the heavens again, turneth its nose into the wind and so then hitteth hard upon the firmament – such as to the extent as its legs then did spreadeth on the ground.

Its whirling nose did thence biteth angrily into the black earth and so did the bird casteth one wing down and thence did slide along the black earth upon its belly. The knight did thence dismounteth and woefully regard the crumpled bird.

And yea, there cometh a troop of rolling cavalry calling themselves 'Investigators' and thence did they doeth all sorts of mysterious manner of things to the broken bird.

Then he, of the gray beard, addresseth the knight in this manner: "Verily I say unto thee that thou hast lost all directional control when attempting to alight upon the firmament. T'would have been much better had thou regained occupancy in the sky and goeth around again to attempt another alightment. 'Tis far better to push forward yon throttle than boot ye rudder, for thy spur is quicker than thy rein."

"However, thy book of logs revealeth no bird time within the past half-year. For this transgression, next time thou contemplateth taking to the heavens again, thou must beseech the

Senior Knight that he may instruct thee as to how to alight thy bird with safety."

This little fable covers much of which we who fly must be aware. First of all is:

FAR 91.103 Preflight Action

Each pilot in command shall, before beginning a flight, become familiar with all available information concerning that flight.

It then goes on in detail about what to check. I assume they mean all available information from the fact that Venus and Mars are aligning with Jupiter and Saturn all the way down to, fuel requirements, weather reports and so forth. I have my applicants begin with a weight-and-balance, get a weather briefing, combine that with predicting take-off and landing distances, then comparing those with the runway lengths at intended airports. It a matter of P-7.

FAR 61.57(a)(1) Recent Flight Experience: Pilot in Command

No person may act as pilot in command of an aircraft carrying passengers...unless that person has made at least three takeoffs and three landings within the preceding 90 days.

While in this fable the pilot was not carrying passengers, he would have had to log at least three takeoffs and landings before carrying passengers. However, the mishap seemingly occurred during his first landing attempt and so "There's the rub." Most likely the FAA would require some remedial training by an authorized instructor followed by a 709 ride – that is, a recheck of his landing skills with an FAA inspector.

Moral: Stay current or get some instruction from an authorized instructor before committing aviation after a long hiatus.

Observer – Pilot
US Army Air Corps
1920 – 1926
(Veteran pilots who could no longer pass the physical for pilots but were re-rated to serve as observers to remain on flight status)

You know you've landed gear up when it takes max power to taxi.

ONE OF THE
TRUSTED

Found in several places within this book are paeans to the 'Dark Side' of working for the airlines. Granted, there are many hurdles to attaining job 'security' in a volatile industry. And granted too, are the challenges which must be met and overcome on the day-to-day operational treadmill. But then, there ARE rewards...

Captain Dennis Koontz, Continental Air Lines (ret.)
(Although he will tell you "The 'old' Frontier Air Lines")

You are cruising at altitude.

The western sun is pink on the disc.

Your eyes flicker across the gauges.

The engines are contented.

Another day, another dollar.

You look down at your hands on the yoke.

They are veined and hard and browned.

Tonight you notice they look a little old.

And, by George, they are old.

How can this be?

Only yesterday you were in flight training.

Time is a thief.

You have been robbed and what do you have to show for it?

A pilot. Forty years a pilot.

A senior pilot.

And what of it?

Just a pilot.

A voice breaks your reverie –

The flight is full and the FA's want to begin serving the passengers.

Oh, yes, the passengers…

You noticed the line of them coming aboard;

The businessmen, the young mothers with children in tow,

The older couples, the two priests

And four soldiers going to who-knows-where.

A thousand times you have watched them file on board

and a thousand times disembark.

They always seem a little happier after the landing

than before the takeoff.

Beyond doubt, they are all a little apprehensive when aloft.

But why do they keep coming up?

Up here in the bright blue sky?

Up here in the dark cold sky?

Up here in the sky?

Captain Larry Camden, Continental Air Lines (ret.)
Now Chief Pilot of Executive Flight Training, Englewood, Colorado
(Still giving back to aviation)

Despite their fears, they keep coming up into the sky.

You have often wondered about that.

*You look down at your hands again and softly, gently it comes to
you –*

They come because they trust you.

You – the pilot.

They turn over to you their lives and their loved ones

and their hopes and their dreams to you:

For safekeeping.

To be a pilot means to be one of the trusted.

In their seats they pray that you are skillful

And strong

And wise.

To be a pilot is to hold their lives in your hands

and be worthy of their faith.

In you.

No, you have not been robbed.

You aren't 'just' a pilot.

There is no such thing as "just a pilot."

You and your job is one of trust.

The years you have spent on this have been a trust.

You have been all these years -

One of the trusted.

Who could hope to be more?

-Author Unknown

Trust in your Captain...but keep your seatbelt
securely fastened.

ORIGIN OF THE CHECKLIST

It's something today that is taken for granted and sad to say, I've seen some pilots never use. Yes, we may fly every day; perform the same tasks every day, in the same order every day. But that does not relieve us of the necessity, the obligation to do things correctly each and every time. All it takes is a minor distraction [cell phone call, friend coming by, bathroom break, etc.] while doing a preflight inspection to miss something critical; in Major Hill's case [described below], control locks. Most all the FAR's and procedures we now use were written because blood was spilled. But good can come about out of disaster – in this case the checklist.

Every PTS mentions performing the preflight while referring to the checklist ["Checklist in hand"], NOT performing the preflight then afterwards referring to the checklist to "make sure everything was covered." The PTS's also state that while in flight using a checklist during a critical phase of flight may likely be a distraction from safe flight. In that case, it is acceptable to use reminders, gouges, flows, mnemonics [GUMPS checks, etc.] then referring to the appropriate checklist when it is safe and prudent to do so.

On October 30, 1935, at Wright Air Field in Dayton, Ohio, the U.S. Army Air Corps held a flight competition for airplane manufacturers vying to build its next-generation long-range bomber. It wasn't supposed to be much of a competition. In early evaluations, the Boeing Corporation's gleaming aluminum-alloy Model 299 had trounced the designs of Martin and Douglas. Boeing's plane could carry five times as many bombs as the Army had requested; it could fly faster than previous bombers, and almost twice as far.

A Seattle newspaperman who had glimpsed the plane called it the "flying fortress," and the name stuck. The flight "competition," according to the military historian Phillip Meilinger, was regarded as a mere formality. The Army planned to order at least sixty-five of the aircraft.

A small crowd of Army brass and manufacturing executives watched as the Model 299 test plane taxied onto the runway. It was sleek and impressive, with a hundred-and-three-foot wingspan and four engines jutting out from the wings, rather than the usual two. The plane roared down the tarmac, lifted off smoothly and climbed sharply to three hundred feet. Then it stalled, turned on one wing and crashed in a fiery explosion. Two of the five crew members died, including the pilot, Major Ployer P. Hill (thus Hill AFB, Ogden, UT.).

An investigation revealed that nothing mechanical had gone wrong. The crash had been due to "pilot error," the report said. Substantially more complex than previous aircraft, the new plane required the pilot to attend to the four engines, a retractable landing gear, new wing flaps, electric trim tabs that needed adjustment to maintain control at different airspeeds, and constant-speed propellers whose pitch had to be regulated with hydraulic controls, among other features.

While doing all this, Hill had forgotten to release a new locking mechanism on the elevator and rudder controls. The Boeing model was deemed, as a newspaper put it, "too much airplane for one man to fly." The Army Air Corps declared Douglas's smaller design the winner. Boeing nearly went bankrupt.

Still, the Army purchased a few aircraft from Boeing as test planes, and some insiders remained convinced that the aircraft was flyable. So a group of test pilots got together and considered what to do.

They could have required Model 299 pilots to undergo more training. But it was hard to imagine having more experience and expertise than Major Hill, who had been the U.S. Army Air Corps' Chief of Flight Testing. Instead, they came up with an ingeniously simple approach: they created a pilot's checklist, with step-by-step checks for takeoff, flight, landing, and taxiing. Its mere existence indicated how far aeronautics had advanced.

In the early years of flight, getting an aircraft into the air might have been nerve-racking, but it was hardly complex. Using a checklist for takeoff would no more have occurred to a pilot than to a driver backing a car out of the garage... But this new plane was too complicated to be left to the memory of any pilot, however expert.

With the checklist in hand, the pilots went on to fly the Model 299 a total of 18 million miles without one accident. The Army ultimately ordered almost thirteen thousand of the aircraft, which it dubbed the B-17. And, because flying the behemoth was now possible, the Army gained a decisive air advantage in the Second World War which enabled its devastating bombing campaign across Nazi Germany.

Boeing B-17G

The owners' guide that comes with a $1,000 refrigerator makes more sense than the one that comes with a $100 million dollar airliner.

'OUR AIRLINE' SLOGANS

Okay, okay...it's not the traditional 'top ten' list, but so what? Back in 1987 there occurred to a major airline a series of 'boo-boo's' that got the aviation community considering new slogans for the hapless company. Around that time this airline had managed to experience an airplane landing at the wrong airport, several near-misses, failed the good engine when the other one went Tango-Uniform, had passengers hurt when using the emergency evacuation slide [not really their fault] and almost landed in the ocean when approaching a sea-side runway. The types who had way too much time on their hands came up with a whole new set of slogans.

[Hell, no, I'm not gonna name the airline!]

15. We get you close.

14. You think it's so damn easy? Get your own plane!

13. We might be landing right in front of your house.

12. Our pilots have nothing to lose.

11. Complimentary Champagne in free-fall.

10. Bring your bathing suit to our in-the-cabin pool.

9. The kids will love our inflatable slides.

8. Enjoy the in-flight movie on the plane next to you.

7. Ask about our great out-of-court settlements.

6. Engines too noisy? We'll turn 'em off just for you.

5. Join our Frequent Near-miss Program.

4. We're AMTRAK with wings.

3. Terrorists are afraid to fly with us.

2. A real pilot lands whenever and where-ever he wants.

1. We never make the same mistake three times.

A 'greaser' landing is 50% luck, two in a row is 100% luck, and three in a row means someone's lying.

PERFORMANCE APPRAISAL

I've seen a number of these tongue-in-cheek performance reviews [Fitness Reports, Efficiency Reports, etc.], this one just happened to be at hand when it came time to insert one. Feel free to use this for the next FITREP you administer.

"Under the Freedom of Information and the Federal Privacy Act of 1974" I understand my work performance is being evaluated and documented. I have the right to examine and copy any such documentation. I have the right to review and appeal any such documentation to resolve differences. I have the right to request amendments to and/or modifications of any document in my file."

Name _____

Position _____

Date_____

Organization _____

Knowledge:

[ ] The SOB really knows his shit
[ ] The SOB knows just enough to be dangerous
[ ] The SOB has half-a-brain and doesn't use it
[ ] The SOB's coffee cup has a higher I.Q.

Accuracy

[ ] Does excellent work when not preoccupied with the opposite sex
[ ] Pretty good, only occasionally has head up ass
[ ] Must take off shoes to count higher than 10
[ ] Couldn't count their balls/tits twice and come up with the same number

Attitude

[ ] Extremely co-operative when ass repeatedly kissed
[ ] Brown-noser in good standing
[ ] Often P.O.s fellow workers
[ ] Doesn't give a shit; never did, never will

Reliability

[ ] A really dependable little jerk
[ ] Can rely on him/her at EVAL time
[ ] Can rely on him/her to be first out the door
[ ] Absolutely fricking worthless

Appearance

[ ] Extremely neat; combs his/her underarm hair
[ ] Looks great at EVAL time
[ ] Flies leave old turds behind to follow him/her
[ ] Dirty, filthy, smelly SOB

Performance

[ ] Goes like a sonovabitch when there is something in it for him/her
[ ] Does all kinds of good shit at EVAL time
[ ] Works only when kicked in the ass every few minutes or so
[ ] Couldn't do less work if they were in a coma

Leadership

[ ] Carries a whip, pistol, chainsaw and gets good results
[ ] Better leader than MacArthur (at EVAL time)
[ ] Only occasionally is told to go screw him/herself
[ ] Mother Theresa told him to F.O.

Evaluator's Signature _____

I understand I have been counseled and know my rights under the FOI & Privacy Act of 1974. I further acknowledge I am FUBAR'ed and will exert efforts to correct my deficiencies.

Evaluated's Signature _____

"Come see me" notes from the Chief Pilot are always distributed on Friday afternoons...after office hours.

PERSISTENCE & DETERMINATION

I include this in conjunction with "Don't Quit" also found in this book. There are sadly many people who try to dissuade others from going for their dreams. They will say these aspirations are 'unrealistic', 'unattainable', 'beyond your capabilities' or you are 'trying to be something you're not' or worse – 'You think you're better than us?' Those kind of people cannot abide someone from their midst rising to a position of prominence and importance; so they try to drag them down to wallow in their collective misery.

DO NOT LET THIS HAPPEN!

Few enough people in this life have a dream, fewer still do anything about it. If you are striving towards your dreams, you are already far and away above 90% of the world's population. Don't Quit! You may be beat, but you'll never surrender!

"Nothing in this world can take the place of persistence. Talent will not; nothing is more common than unsuccessful people with talent. Genius will not; unrewarded genius is almost a proverb. Education will not; the world is full of educated failures. Persistence and determination alone are omnipotent."

Calvin Coolidge
4 July 1872 – 5 January 1933
30th President of the United States (1923 – 1929)

To order an 8" x 10" copy of this quote printed on museum-grade art stock, go to www.Coloradoskymaster.com and click on 'Products'.

PICKING THE WRONG FLIGHT

You gotta admire the attitude of the F/A-18 jock...and the discretion of Iranian ADR.

Iranian Air Defense Radar:

'Unknown aircraft you are in Iranian airspace. Identify yourself.'

Aircraft: 'This is a United States aircraft. I am in Iraqi airspace.'

ADR: 'You are in Iranian airspace. If you do not depart our airspace we will launch interceptor aircraft!'

Aircraft: 'This is a United States Marine Corps F/A-18 fighter...Send 'em up, I'll wait!'

ADR: (no response .... total silence)

God bless our troops!

A kill is a kill.

PILOT COMMANDMENTS

Yeah, yeah...more 'Commandments': But each with more than a grain of truth.

I Beware the intersection takeoff, for verily the runway behind thee may be sorely missed.

II Be aware thy altitude, foresaketh it none too soon lest thou regret the need of it.

III Tarry not on active runways, for mad confusion may erupteth causing thee to regret thy folly and causeth also thy brethren to curse thee.

IV Ignore not thy checklist, for many are the switches, valves, handles and gizmos awaiting to take vengeance on thee for thy lack of attention to detail. [See: Origin of the Checklist]

V Gaze intently to thy left and right, up and down as thou journeyeth through the heavens lest another skyfarer happen upon thee unawares at the same time, place and altitude.

VI Buzz not, lest thee incur the wrath of the ground-dwellers and focus the fury of the FAA upon thy noggin.

VII Take always the measure of thy fuel prior to flight, for verily a tank full of air is an embarrassment at any altitude

VIII Push not through the scud lest the Angel Gabriel be awaiting thee on yon far side.

IX Trifle not with the thunderstorm, forsooth it is quite possible thy wings and tailfeathers will be shorn from thy fuselage and so ye be cast down upon the earth.

X Be wary of the words of the weather prophets, for the truth is not always with them. Many are the horrible tempests awaiting thy passing on thy journey.

XI Mind thy airspeed, especially when preparing to alight upon the firmament, lest the earth riseth up and smite thee.

XII Thou shalt conform to the Standard Operating Procedures for thy craft, lest trouble and rebuke be awaiting thee in strange and secret places.

XIII Recall, the FAA speaketh with scornful tongue. Obeying the rules shalt keep you from their house of bondage; for evil doth dwelleth therein and from those who findeth themselves trapped within is heard the gnashing of teeth and the woeful wails of the damned.

XIV Finding thou hast, of course unwittingly, transgressed an FAR, thou shalt immediately file a NASA report, lest the wrath of the FAA be focused on thy unprotected backside and woe be upon you. Said report doth relive thee of punishment and many are thy brethren who shall keep from following thee down the roads of inequity, sin and transgression.

The NASA report mentioned in XIV above is actually the report a pilot should submit under:

FAR 91.25 Aviation Safety Reporting Program: Prohibition against use of reports for enforcement actions.

The Administrator of the FAA will not use reports submitted to the National Aeronautics and Space Administration [NASA] under the Aviation Safety and Reporting Program (or information derived there from) in any enforcement action except information concerning accidents or criminal offenses which are wholly excluded from the program.

AC 00-46E available at www.FAA.gov more fully explains the program and its benefits to pilots and aviation personnel.

Visit http://asrs.arc.nasa.gov/ to view the program and electronically submit a report. You may also sign up for monthly e-newsletters reviewing topics and subjects in submitted reports. Remember, learn from the mistakes of others for you will never live long enough to make them all yourself.

Experience is a tough teacher: First comes the test, then the lesson.

PILOTS 3 FAVORITE THINGS

Right – If I have to explain this to you, you have no business being a pilot...

A pilot was driving down the road after a long flight and saw a sign in front of a restaurant:

> **HAPPY HOUR SPECIAL**
>
> **Lobster Tail and Beer**

"Lord Almighty," he said to himself. "My three favorite things."

Pilots believe in clean living...they never drink whisky from a dirty glass.

PILOTS ARE ~~CHEAP~~ FRUGAL

This is a long read, yet many of those who personified these examples of...ahhh...'thriftiness' might argue that since this stuff is 'free for the taking', no social faux pas had occurred. I can attest to that fact since one of my bathroom drawers is still half-full of little soap bars and bottles of shampoo.

When my company hired me, one of the first things I noticed about many of my fellow pilots was that they were cheap bastards. I consider this to be a compliment to my fellow aviators. Hotels offer a plethora of freebies that end up in the homes of pilots. There are soaps, shampoos, lotions, sewing kits, and other things of strategic value. On the nightstands in hotel rooms, there usually is a pad of stationary and a cheap pen. The stationary pads are commonly found in the cockpits on the built-in clipboards, but the pens are too valuable to leave behind. If there are free newspapers at the front desk, we are certain to take one. At some of the better hotels you can find a newspaper and a Wall Street Journal at the same time [major score!].

There is the story of the pilot who finally sends his first child off to college. The young adult returns for the holidays and proceeds to tell the parents everything they have learned. The parents are told many things, but their child was most impressed by learning that most bars of soap are actually very big and shampoo comes in bottles that are bigger than their thumb. Being raised on hotel toiletries brought home by the student's father, the young person was ignorant to this important part of life, only because the father, a pilot, was a cheap bastard.

Discounts and deals abound in the pilot world. Almost every airport eatery and hotel restaurant offers a percentage off of whatever we purchase to eat. There are coupons for free drinks or buffets. I have seen 50% off in some places, which none of us can pass up. I was at a coffee shop in a layover hotel recently, getting ready to head to the airport. The young woman working the counter got me my coffee and handed me two big chocolate chip cookies for free. Of course I shyly refused, but she insisted that I take the cookies. 'You never know when you might get hungry', She said. I was trying to smile and not drool at the same time. This treatment is not unusual. I was walking through the Cincinnati airport once, when Mrs. Fields Cookies employee waved me over and said, "'You can have all the left over cookies for five dollars." I walked away with three bags of cookies and boasted about my good deal for weeks after. I had realized that the cookies kiosk was closing and instead of throwing the cookies away, they would offer them all at a price no pilot could refuse. I scored those bags of cookies several times but got so sick of them, that I eventually refused the good deal.

The same thing happened in Buffalo New York one night. We were doing a turn around, so we were there for about an hour. I ran down to the cafeteria and ordered some wings. The man working the counter asked if I wanted extra wings. I said, 'Sure, sounds good'. He brought out three large to go boxes of wings, mild, medium, and hot. We stuffed ourselves. When ordering a meal where the food is scooped up in a predetermined amount, the generous workers dishing out the food usually add a partial scoop more, smiling at us while they do it. I have never seen a pilot tell them to take it back.

There is a good chain of communication amongst pilots, allowing us to share the free things or good deals in our layover cities. A fellow pilot told me about free coffee at the hotel coffee shop in Boston. He said, 'You have to be in uniform to get the free coffee'. I mentioned this to my copilot the evening we arrived at that hotel. The next morning I was in the lobby of the hotel studying the subway map. We had the entire day off and I was interested in visiting a museum. I was surprised to see the copilot walk by in his uniform, seven hours before we were to be picked up. He marched over to the coffee shop and picked up a free cup of coffee, saving himself about $2.50. "You make me proud", I said. He smiled, held up the free cup of Joe in a salute, and then proceeded to pick up a newspaper someone left on a chair. He went back to his room, drank free coffee and read a free paper. It doesn't get much better than that.

I worked the Hawaiian operation for several years. Our layover hotel was at a gargantuan hotel complex with three, forty story towers. Through the grapevine, I had found out that the rooftop of every tower had a hot tub on it with an ice chest of soda next to it. Access to the rooftop was limited to the expensive business rooms on the upper floors. This was by no means a deterrent to us pilots. I discovered that if I took the elevator as high as I could go without using a room key, I could then take the stairwell up the remaining floors, to the rooftop. I was not interested in the hot tub, but drinking a free soda and taking in the incredible view from forty stories up, was great. I spent many hours up there over those years and never saw another person on that roof. On my way down one day I decided to take the elevator from the highest floor. As I walked towards the elevator I saw a door open to what looked like a lounge. I walked into the room and realized this was a suite converted into the business club lounge.

The suite was gorgeous, fronting the ocean, filled with food, drinks, newspapers, and a self-serve bar. The best part of this situation was realizing that there were no hotel employees in the room. I was alone with platters of food, free drinks, and 24 hours off. I settled in like I owned the joint. I left two hours later, only when another hotel guest entered the room. I went back many times, but one day, when I walked in, I saw a woman sitting behind a desk. 'Good afternoon sir, can I assist you?' she said. I wanted to say, 'Yeah, can you just go away from this good deal I have?' I remained calm and said, 'I am trying to find my boss, and I was told to meet him here.'

"Oh, no problem, what is his name? I can look him up and contact him," she said. I was digging myself into a hole. I politely refused her help and left quickly. I could tell she was eyeing me suspiciously. When I got to the elevators, I turned around to smile at her. Next to every elevator was a big bowl of tropical fruit and a stack of newspapers. In an act of defiance, I picked up a papaya, a mango, and a Wall Street Journal while smiling. The elevator arrived quickly and I left. I called the front desk and asked when the business lounge was staffed. I was told that at 4:30 every afternoon, the business lounge was staffed. I had my answer. From then on I made sure I never spent time in that room after 3:00.

I spread the word about the rooftop and lounge to my fellow pilots. One of my fellow pilots brought his wife with him on a trip to Honolulu. He convinced the wife to go to the rooftop with him and sit in the hot tub. It was a beautiful night and they ended up having sex, then more sex, then running around the rooftop naked. Just as they were getting back to putting their clothes on, a security team came out onto the roof. Both parties were surprised as hell to see each other. The pilot apologized to the security team as he was putting his clothes on, grabbed a couple of free sodas and left with his humiliated and unhappy wife.

There was a time when most airlines served good food, especially in first class. I am allowed to sit in first class when I travel off duty. The pass system at my company allows me to travel unlimited times a year. Some years ago a pilot told me that over the weekend he took his wife and children on a flight that was a round trip flight to another city. He flew out on the first leg enjoying a nice lunch and free drinks in first class. They were on the ground for an hour before the same aircraft with the pilot and his family still on it, returned to its point of origin. He and his family enjoyed a first class dinner on the way back, the children enjoying a few ice cream sundaes. That was how they spent their day and evening, enjoying free food, drinks, desserts, and movies. The monthly food bills were less than normal because the pilot was uncanny in his ability to be a cheap bastard.

Not that long ago I was riding to a hotel for a layover. Across the street from my hotel I saw a sign on the marquee of another hotel advertising free wireless Internet. My monthly schedule requests were due the next day and I needed Internet access to send my requests in. Instead of paying for the service in my hotel, I walked across the street that next morning to use the free Internet at the other hotel. I walked past the lobby and sat in a public area near a fireplace that had couches and coffee tables. As I was booting up my computer I saw a large urn of coffee across the room. 'What the heck' I thought. 'it's just a cup of coffee.' I got up and fixed myself a large cup of coffee, just the way I like it. I was working on my computer with a solid Internet connection, drinking my coffee, when a hotel employee approached me. "Sir, the breakfast buffet is now open, would you like me to show you what we have this morning?" she said. Without the slightest hesitation, I said, "Why that would be great, thank you."

I proceeded to make myself a waffle, gather a plate of eggs and bacon, a glass of juice, and a container of strawberry banana yogurt. I was still there three hours later when they closed down the breakfast area. I was asked if I would like anything else, so I asked if I could take a snack to go. I have shared this nugget with many of the pilots I fly with and they too have enjoyed a scrumptious morning buffet, across the street.

This story could go on and on as there are endless examples of pilots being cheap bastards, but there is one last example I would like to share with you: About 16 years ago, I was an engineer on the Boeing 727. The captain brought a bag onboard at the beginning of our trip. He handed me the paper bag and told me to put it in a safe place. When we got to our destination that night, he asked me for the bag. During our four-day trip, each day would start out the same, he would hand me the bag, I would put it out of harm's way, and he would ask for it at the end of the day. On the last day he handed as he handed me the bag, I heard the clinking of glass. 'Be careful with that,' he said. I asked him what was in the bag. He told me there were about ten light bulbs in the bag. I asked him why he carried all of these light bulbs around. He said to me, 'I take the burned out light bulbs from home and exchange them with the working light bulbs in our hotel rooms.' I was at a loss for words, but I remember thinking that this guy is one cheap bastard.

Okay - Here's a true story I've told some of you but not all. I flew with a guy that turned in his dirty uniform shirts [this was before 9/11] to a charity. He would come back a few days later when they were hanging on a rack & buy them back for .50-.75 cents.

He said it was cheaper than sending them to the laundry and he'd get credit for a Tax deduction for his charitable donation.

Now that that guy is cunningly cheap!

Military Sea Pilot
Imperial Russia
1915 – 1917

Flying is the perfect vocation for a man who wants to feel like a boy – but not for one who still is.

PILOTS DEFINED #1

PILOTS

The average pilot, despite the somewhat swaggering exterior, is very much capable of such feelings as love, affection, intimacy, and caring.

These feelings just don't involve anyone else.

PILOTS DEFINED #2

PILOT'S NEW YEAR'S EVE STORY

I went out with some friends on New Year's Eve and tied one on. I got really hammered. Knowing that I was wasted, I did something that I have never done before.

I took the bus home.

We went right through the police roadblocks; no troubles at all.

I arrived safe and warm, which seemed really surprising as I have never driven a bus before.

If you ever get convicted for a Motor Vehicle Action [MVA] you MUST report it per **FAR 61.15(e)** to the address listed therein not more than 60 days after the MVA. I know some pilots who, 30 years (!!!) after their conviction for driving under the influence were hauled before a judge: Before this regulation existed, even. Do NOT mess around with this one. The FAA views lack of a report as more of an offense than the original DUI! Do NOT take this lightly!

What are my reporting responsibilities under the FARs regarding drug/alcohol related offenses?

In addition to reporting the offense on your next FAA Application for Airman Medical Certification, you must report to FAA Civil Aviation Security Division as outlined in the following regulation:

FAR Part 61.15 ? Offenses involving alcohol or drugs.

a. A conviction for the violation of any Federal or State statute relating to the growing, processing, manufacture, sale, disposition, possession, transportation, or importation of narcotic drugs, marijuana, or depressant or stimulant drugs or substances is grounds for:

1. Denial of an application for any certificate, rating, or authorization issued under this part for a period of up to 1 year after the date of final conviction; or

2. Suspension or revocation of any certificate, rating, or authorization issued under this part.

b. Committing an act prohibited by Sec. 91.17(a) or Sec. 91.19(a) of this chapter is grounds for:

1. Denial of an application for a certificate, rating, or authorization issued under this part for a period of up to 1 year after the date of that act; or

2. Suspension or revocation of any certificate, rating, or authorization issued under this part.

c. For the purposes of paragraphs (d), (e), and (f) of this section, a motor vehicle action means:

A conviction after November 29, 1990, for the violation of any Federal or State statute relating to the operation of a motor vehicle while intoxicated by alcohol or a drug, while impaired by alcohol or a drug, or while under the influence of alcohol or a drug;

The cancellation, suspension, or revocation of a license to operate a motor vehicle after November 29, 1990, for a cause related to the operation of a motor vehicle while intoxicated by alcohol or a drug, while impaired by alcohol or a drug, or while under the influence of alcohol or a drug; or the denial after November 29, 1990, of an application for a license to operate a motor vehicle for a cause related to the operation of a motor vehicle while intoxicated by alcohol or a drug, while impaired by alcohol or a drug, or while under the influence of alcohol or a drug.

d. Except for a motor vehicle action that results from the same incident or arises out of the same factual circumstances, a motor vehicle action occurring within 3 years of a previous motor vehicle action is grounds for:

Denial of an application for any certificate, rating, or authorization issued under this part for a period of up to 1 year after the date of the last motor vehicle action; or

Suspension or revocation of any certificate, rating, or authorization issued under this part.

e. Each person holding a certificate issued under this part shall provide a written report of each motor vehicle action to the;

FAA, Civil Aviation Security Division (AMC-700)
P.O. Box 25810
Oklahoma City, OK 73125

no later than 60 days after the motor vehicle action. The report must include:

1. The person's name, address, date of birth, and airman certificate number;

2. The type of violation that resulted in the conviction or the administrative action;

3. The date of the conviction or administrative action;

4. The State that holds the record of conviction or administrative action; and

5. A statement of whether the motor vehicle action resulted from the same incident or arose out of the same factual circumstances related to a previously reported motor vehicle action.

Download FAA DUI Reporting Form Letter at

http://www.aviationmedicine.com/resources/files/pdf/faa_protoc ols/fduiform.pdf

f. Failure to comply with paragraph (e) of this section is grounds for:

1. Denial of an application for any certificate, rating, or authorization issued under this part for a period of up to 1 year after the date of the motor vehicle action; or

2. Suspension or revocation of any certificate, rating, or authorization issued under this part.

Contact FAA directly for more info at FAA DUI/DWI
home page:

http://www.faa.gov/about/office_org/headquarters_offices/ash/ash_programs/investigations/airmen_duidwi/

Anyone involved with a driving offense related to alcohol/drug
may want to contact VFS assistance. We can assist in attempting
to prevent such delays at the time of the pilots' next FAA
medical exam. Remember every situation is different.

Nothing flies without fuel – so let's have some coffee.

PILOT'S POEM

I can't see all the old retired accountants, lawyers, school teachers, doctors and a hundred other professions having reunions to reminisce about the 'good old days' doing whatever it was they did. But pilots? We get to fly the same missions and – as the wife of a Colonel once said – "Shoot down the same airplanes and strafe the same trucks" over and over again, each retelling getting more hairy with each iteration. Hey...that right comes with the wings, right?

I hope there's a place way up in the sky,
where pilots can go on the day that they die.
A place where a guy can buy a cold beer
for a friend or comrade, whose memory is dear.
A place no doctor or lawyer can tread,
nor the FAA would ever be caught dead.
Just a quaint little place, dark, full of smoke,
where patrons sing loud, and love a good joke.
The kind of place a lady could go,
and feel safe and protected by the men she would know.
There must be this place where old pilots go,
when their flying is finished, and their airspeed gets low.
Where the whiskey is old and the women are young,

where songs about flying and dying are sung.
Where you see all the fellows who'd flown here before,
Who would call out your name as you came through the door.
Who would buy you a drink, if your thirst should be bad,
and relate to others, "He was a good lad."
And then through the mist, you'd spot this old guy,
you hadn't seen in years, though he taught you to fly.
He'd nod his old head, and grin ear to ear,
and say, "Welcome home son, I'm pleased that you're here.
For this is the place where true flyers come,
when their journey is over and their war has been won.
Here they feel safe and "at home"
from pundits, the bureaucrats, the management clones.
Where all hours are happy, enjoying a cold one,
maybe deal from a deck;
This is heaven, my son.....you've passed your last check!"

Eber Hamilton "Ham" Lee
QB #3135
1892 – 1994

Fuel in the tanks is limited – Gravity is forever.

PILOT'S RIDDLE

OK, let's see how good you guys are.

- You are on a horse, galloping at a constant speed.

- On your right side is a sharp drop-off.

- On your left side is an elephant traveling at the same speed as you.

- Directly in front of you is a galloping kangaroo and   your horse is unable to overtake it.

- Behind you is a lion running at the same speed a you and the kangaroo.

What must you do to get out of this highly dangerous situation?

Answer:

Get your drunken ass off the merry-go-round and go home!

Assumption is the mother of all screw-ups.

PILOT vs. PROFESSOR

I include this apocryphal story – true or not – despite it having no real bearing on aviation per sé. It does however have a bearing on how I feel about the liberal, anti-armed forces, anti-religious, anti-Second Amendment, anti-respect-for-anything, anti-American "teaching" going on in our establishments of 'higher learning' and how the young are being brainwashed and sold a bill of goods (meaning: a pig in a poke) regarding the country of their birth. Whether this story is true or not is immaterial: I render honors and a standing ovation to those who put their lives, their fortunes and their sacred honor (Do those words sound even remotely familiar?*) on the line every day for this country.

A left-coast university professor who was an atheist and very active with the ACLU was in class one day when he got the attention of the class. A student had entered late apologizing for her tardiness; she had stayed late at the chapel services. The prof began berating the student for believing in "medieval hokum" and then flatly stated he was going to prove there was no God.

Looking up at the ceiling, he shouted: "GOD! If you are real, knock me off this platform!" The room fell silent; you could hear a pin drop. Ten minutes of uncomfortable silence went by.

"I'm waiting, God. If you're real, come knock me off this platform."

Again some more uncomfortable minutes went by, the professor then said in a mocking, taunting tone "Here I am, God; I'm still waiting!"

It had been a long fifteen minutes when an Army Aviator, recently returned from parts unknown overseas and now going to school, rose from his chair and walked towards the professor. He then hit the professor full force in the face and sent him flying from the dais, knocked out cold. The pilot then quietly resumed his seat as the class began to babble in confusion.

Eventually, the professor came to and after regaining his senses, angrily addressed the man, still calmly seated at his desk. "What the hell did you do that for?" the professor yelled, "What the hell's the matter with you?"

The too-old-for-his-years aviator rose calmly from his place and in a voice that left no doubt as to his sincerity, he said:

"God is really busy right now looking out for American soldiers who are protecting your right to be an asshole and to say stupid shit like that...

...so he sent me."

* It's the last line in the Declaration of Independence.

There are NO atheists in the foxholes.

PORTSMOUTH, NH- IAP

Who says the FAA doesn't have a sense of humor? Anyone who grew up watching Warner Brothers cartoons on Saturday morning will see the humor in this. If you were born too late to enjoy them, they can be found on-line; sure beats the drivel that passes for 'entertainment' these days.

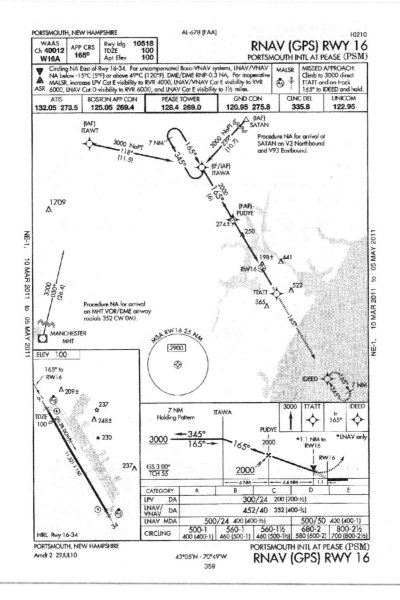

The three most common things heard on the CVR are "Was that for us?", "What did he say?" and "Oh, shit!" Since computers are now onboard airplanes, a fourth and fifth have been added: "What's it doing now?" and "Why's it doing that?"

THE PREACHER AND THE PILOT

*It's been said "There are no atheists in a foxhole."
The same argument could be said about the cockpit –
hours of boredom interrupted momentarily by
moments of stark terror. On the other hand, how
could we pilots be up there in the sky and not observe
the Creator's handiwork? I've seen sunrises and
sunsets which rival any cathedral's stained glass.
The hum of a finely tuned powerplant [think of a
Rolls-Royce engine in a P-51] has a harmony no
choir could ever hope to match. A mere half-mile into
the sky and vistas are laid before you matching any
painting by any artist. As pilots, we are blessed.*

A preacher dies and is waiting in line at the Pearly Gates. Ahead of him is a guy who's dressed in sunglasses, a loud shirt, leather jacket and jeans. Saint Peter addresses this cool guy, "Who are you, so that I may know whether or not to admit you to the Kingdom of Heaven?"

The guy replies, "I'm Peter Perfect, retired Airline Pilot from Miami."
Saint Peter consults his list. He smiles and says to the pilot, "Take this silken robe and golden staff and enter the Kingdom."

The pilot goes into Heaven with his robe and staff.

Next it's the preacher's turn. He stands erect and booms out, "I am Joseph Snow, pastor of Saint Mary's in Pasadena for the last 43 years." Saint Peter consults his list. He says to the preacher, "Take this cotton robe and wooden staff and enter the Kingdom."

"Just a minute," says the preacher. "That man was a pilot and he gets a silken robe and golden staff, and I get only cotton and wood? How can this be?"

"Up here, we work by results," says Saint Peter, "When you preached, people slept. When he flew, people prayed."

Observer
US Army Air Service
1917 – 1918

If God had meant for man to fly, He would have given him green, baggy Nomex skin and full wallets.

PRELIMINARY ACCIDENT REPORT – FLIGHT 1549

With all due respect for the entire crew of the "Miracle of the Hudson"...

PRELIMINAEY ACCIDENT REPORT – FLIGHT 1549:

"Captain held responsible for unauthorized actions which resulted in crash." says F.A.A.

Subject: NTSB Report on Flight 1549

US Airways violated Federal migratory bird regulations by hunting geese with an A-320 Airbus jetliner, claim anonymous government sources. The pilot of flight 1549, Air Force veteran and avid hunter Chesley B. Sullenberger, tried combining both of his interests by bagging a brace of geese over the wetlands near New York's LaGuardia airport after takeoff, on his way to Charlotte, North Carolina.

The imported European $77 million A-320 airliner is not certified for either waterfowl or upland bird hunting, so it was not surprising that the aircraft malfunctioned. When he realized that both New York and New Jersey State Game and Fish enforcement officers would soon be approaching, Captain Sullenberger unsuccessfully attempted to hide the plane in the Hudson River.

The crew and 150 passengers were chilled and shaken but unhurt. Most were simply grateful to avoid spending the weekend in Charlotte. National Transportation Safety Board inspectors rushed to the scene, and reportedly found no Duck Stamps on the downed aircraft's fuselage. Captain Sullenberger has not been charged, but is being held incommunicado at an undisclosed location.

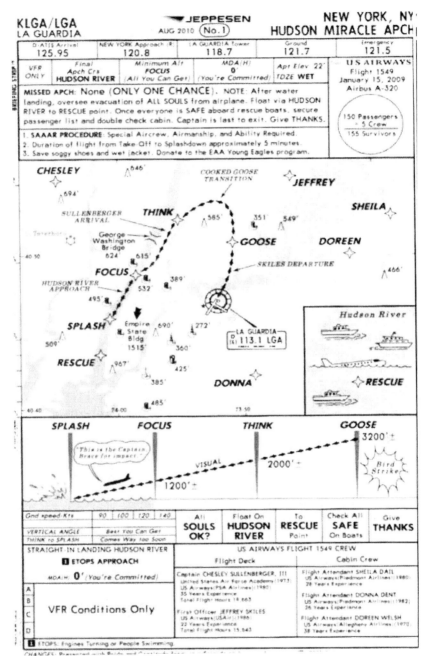

The good people at Jeppesen created this for Captain Sullenberger and F/O Skiles.

PETA is urging the government to prosecute the pilot for double honkercide and poaching, and the animal rights group is expected to file a civil suit on behalf of the flock. The victims were undocumented aliens, according to sources close to the investigation; Canada geese who had over-stayed their visas. Their goose gang scandalized the quiet Queens community by squatting in local cemeteries and golf courses, parking on the grass, cooking strange-smelling food, defecating in public and throwing wild parties late into the night. Neighbors say police dogs were called out on several occasions.

Such incidents have triggered a wave of anti-Canada goose sentiment, but at this time revenge or hate crime motives are not suspected in the US Airways bird bashings.

Forensic examination of the avian corpses continues, and technicians are analyzing the cadavers under heat with chestnuts, prunes, and Armagnac. NTSB inspectors have contributed a supply of testing fluid, a 2005 Zind-Humbrecht Merlot from Alsace. We will update this story as entrees details become available.

When you're sitting in the rubber raft looking up at where your airplane used to be, it's too late to check the flight plan or wonder where the emergency checklist is.

PRINCIPLES OF FLIGHT – ENGINE INOP

Engine-out procedures in twin-engine airplanes are a mandatory testing item and rightfully so. At a local airport a few years back a pilot took off in a B-55 Baron [260 hp per side] with three others on board – a plane I've flown which was very capable on one engine even at the higher field elevations and Density Altitudes here in Colorado. When the engine failed the pilot lost control and crashed, killing all on board. If you fly twins, you better have your shit together.

Those of us who fly General Aviation twin-engine airplanes have been trained [hopefully] in the exact timing and sequence of procedures which must be accomplished <u>immediately</u> following an engine failure in all phases of flight. These phases are:

1. The take-off roll

2. Post lift-off with the landing gear still extended, and

3. Post lift-off after the landing gear has been retracted.

These procedures <u>will</u> be tested and viewed critically by the Inspector, Check Airman or DPE as to your competency in flying such an airplane. Whether or not it's a V1 cut, an engine failure prior to Vmc or a failure in cruise, the pilot <u>must</u> be ready for this event at all times. I have flown all manner of twins from 150 hp per side 'twin-engine simulators' ["Which engine do you want to lose: The one with the only generator or the one with the only hydraulic pump? Doesn't matter – the single-engine service ceiling is 1,000 feet below where we're standing right now."] to corporate jets and most all principles of engine-out flight cover the range of planes with two engines.

Recommendation to all you who hope to fly twins, are training to fly twins or are flying twins now: BRIEF YOURSELF OUT LOUD prior to every take-off as to 'What would I do if...?'

MOVE YOUR HANDS and feet to get muscle memory with the program. THINK about what you're doing and why.

I suggest the following take-off brief after all pre-flight checks have been accomplished. What you should think about and SAY OUT LOUD before accepting the runway for take-off:

1. "If anything happens during the takeoff roll – an uncommanded yaw, a door or window pops open, a bird strike or something doesn't feel right...

> I will close the throttles, maintain directional control with rudders and use brakes to come to a stop." [Guess what? That's Accelerate-Stop!]

2. "If I have the same conditions after take-off and the landing gear is still down...

> I will close the throttles, maintain directional control with rudders, pitch down and land straight ahead". [Guess what? That's a take-off over a 50 foot obstacle combined with landing over a 50 foot obstacle!]

3. "If I have an uncommanded yaw during flight with the landing gear retracted, I will...

> - Maintain directional control using opposite rudder and aileron to the yaw & roll

> - Address the mixtures [Full rich may result in less-than max power depending on the induction system and Density Altitude]

> - Prop maximum RPM

- Throttles maximum power [Be careful not to overboost turbo-charged engines lest the   proverbial   'double-engine flame-out' occurs]

- Confirm landing gear up

- Confirm flaps up

- Remember to breathe

- Identify the failed/problem engine

- Verify the failed/problem engine [Remember, if your engine is sick – not 'dead' – and still producing some thrust, you must now decide if you can keep using that thrust or need to feather the propeller prior to complete engine failure when you can't feather the propeller.]

- Diagnose/Decide whether you can fix or restart the problem engine or need to shut it down.

- Feather the propeller on the failed engine

- Shut down and secure the failed engine

- Declare an emergency to ATC

- Determine if you can maintain altitude [Single-engine service ceiling] long enough to get to an airport or if you must choose a friendly-looking suitable landing area and land there.

Flying a twin doesn't make you twice as safe – it merely doubles the chances of suffering an engine failure.

PUSHING THE ENVELOPE

One factor which will result in a 'bust' on any flightcheck is "Exceeding aircraft limitations." I recall an applicant – after the simulated engine failure – diving for the emergency landing field and, at Vfe + 20 knots, extending the flaps to 30°! I immediately raised the flaps before they reached 10° and failed the flightcheck. The applicant was incredulous at first but when it was explained to him in such a way as he understood his sin, he acknowledged the error...and the failure which I HAD to announce. Limitations are there for a reason; if you research the "ARROW" gouge, the 'O' stands for "Operating Limitations" [which are contained in the AFM/POH], NOT 'Operating Manual' as some think. The FAA doesn't mandate the pilot 'knowing' anything else about the aircraft but the limitations. All the rest is for extra credit

"When it comes to testing new aircraft or determining maximum performance, pilots like to talk of "pushing the envelope." They're talking about a two-dimensional model: The bottom is zero altitude, the top is maximum altitude. The left side is zero speed and the right side is maximum velocity. So, pilots are always pushing that upper right-hand corner of the envelope. What everyone tries not to dwell on is, that's where the postage gets cancelled too."

- Attributed to Admiral Rick Hunter, USN.

The main thing is to take care of the main thing.

QUOTE FROM "AIRPLANE"

To this day a film that falls in my "Top 20" list of movies to watch when nothing is on [despite having cable and gazillions of channels], Airplane is the best aviation satire out there – beating Top Gun by a country mile – and edging out the Hot Shots series by a nose. "Surely you can't be serious!" you exclaim. "Yes, I am...and don't call me Shirley!"

"I know...but the guy doing the flying has no airline experience at all. He's a menace to himself and everything else in the air...yes, birds, too."

Air traffic controller in the movie "Airplane"

AIM Section 7-4 Bird Hazards & Flight Over National Refuges, Parks & Forests

Section 7-4-1 addresses migratory bird activity. While most bird strikes occur less than 3,000' agl, there are a number of birds known to fly higher. Knowledge of the primary flyways is especially relevant March – April and August – November as these are the primary months of migratory activity.

Section 7-4-2 details the ways to reduce the risk of bird strikes. If face-to-face with a flock of birds, climb immediately as a bird's natural tendency is to dive to avoid a threat.

Section 7-4-3 urges pilots to report any bird strikes using FAA form 5200-7 or they may download a form from the FAA website http://wildlife-mitigation.tc.faa.gov

You know the Feds would have a field day sorting out all the FAR violations seen in this film. FAR 61.56 deals with the requirements for Flight Reviews; FAR 61.57 covers Recent Flight Experience: Pilot in Command and although there are exceptions listed in paragraph (e) they pertain to persons employed by carriers; this poor Bozo couldn't be hired by Fly-by-Night Airways even on a good day. And then there were the night landing requirements, instrument currency, instrument proficiency checks, FAR 61.58 Pilot-in-Command Operation of aircraft requiring more than one flight crewmember. Hey, let's throw in FAR 91.13 Careless and Reckless Operation as well. Long story short – I wouldn't want to stand in front of the Review Board for this flight. It was a lot of fun, though…

Shortly after this film came out I was making a night approach into Buckley ANG base in Denver [now Buckley AFB] and the turbulence was so bad it was all I could do to keep the airplane more-or-less upright and pointy-end going forward. As I turned on to final – they had two operational runways then – just like in this movie the runway lights went out! One minute I'm trying to line up on a runway, the next I'm on final into a black hole! Just about the time my finger finds the transmit button, ATC comes on telling me the winds are slightly better aligned to the other runway. I ultimately was able to land and secure all the airplane parts I had departed with – a feat in itself – but I'll always remember those runway lights fading into nothingness and wondering "Whiskey Tango Foxtrot!"

Naval Aviator
US Navy
1920 – 1930's
(variation)

Every pilot knows the definition of a 'good landing' is one you can walk away from. A 'great' landing, however, is when the airplane can be used again without major maintenance.

QUOTES ABOUT DRINKING

More about drinking – one of a pilot's myriad activities while on terra firma. I don't need to quote the FAR about this, do I?

"Sometimes I think back on all the wine I've consumed and I feel ashamed. Then I look into the glass and think about all the workers who had a hand in producing this and all their hopes and dreams. If I didn't drink this wine they would all be unemployed and their hopes and dreams shattered. Then I say to myself "It is better that I drink this wine and let their dreams come true than be selfish and worry about my liver."

- Jack Handy

Warning: Drinking alcohol may find you wondering what you did with your bra and panties.

"I feel sorry for people who don't drink. When they wake up in the morning that's the best they're going to feel all day."

- Frank Sinatra

Warning: The consumption of alcohol may create the illusion you are tougher, faster, smarter and better-looking than most people.

"When I read about the evils of drinking, I gave up reading."

- Henny Youngman

Warning: The consumption of alcohol may create the illusion that people are laughing <u>with</u> you.

"24 hours in a day - 24 beers in a case. Coincidence? I think not."

- Stephen Wright

Warning: The consumption of alcohol may create the illusion that you can sing.

"When we drink, we get drunk. When we get drunk, we fall asleep. When we fall asleep, we commit no sin. When we commit no sin, we go to heaven. So – let's all get drunk and go to Heaven."

- Brian O'Rourke

Warning: The consumption of alcohol may cause those who are not pregnant to become pregnant.

FAR 61.16 Refusal to Submit to an Alcohol Test or to Furnish Test Results

A refusal to submit to a test to indicate the percentage by weight of alcohol in the blood...or...refusal to furnish or authorize the release of the test results...is grounds for:

(a) Denial of an application for any certificate, rating or authorization...for a period up to 1 year after the date of that refusal; or

(b) Suspension or revocation...of any certificate, rating or authorization issued under this part.

See FAR 91.17(c) Alcohol or Drugs regarding "a crewmember shall...on request of a law enforcement officer, submit to a test to indicate alcohol concentration in the blood or breath..."

It's bad enough to drive under the influence, it's worse if you're attempting to fly. It's even more terrible if you do not report the fact of your conviction to FAA security. Just be extra-extra discerning when and if you imbibe. No drink is worth your ticket.

"It was my ex-wife who drove me to drink. It's the only thing I'm grateful to her for." - W.C. Fields

REALIZATION

I include this mainly for the fact that we, as pilots, are blessed with the ability of being able to fly anytime and anywhere we wish. The greater majority of the world's population is relegated to the dreams of a caveman – you may look up and wish you could fly, but you'll never ever get to go there. No matter who – or what – you believe in as a Creator, Supreme Being or as the National Lampoon once pronounced – "Cosmic Thunderer or Hairy Muffin", each day I get to fly is a blessing – and I render thanks and homage to God that I was born who I am, where I am, when I am.

To realize the value of a family – ask someone who doesn't have one.

To realize the value of ten years – ask a newly divorced couple.

To realize the value of four years – ask a recent graduate.

To realize the value of one year – ask someone who failed their final exam.

To realize the value of nine months – ask a mother who gave birth to a stillborn.

To realize the value of one month – ask the mother of a premature child.

To realize the value of one week – ask the editor of a newspaper.

To realize the value of one minute – ask someone who missed a plane.

To realize the value of one second – ask the person who survived an accident.

Time waits for no-one…

Treasure every moment you have.

Latvia Pilot
Reverse of wings inscribed with maker's name and 'RIGA',
capitol of Latvia

There will be a day when you walk out of an airplane and one of two things will be true: You will either know it's your last flight in an airplane, or you won't.

SELF-MEDICATION FOR PILOTS

In the Aeromedical section of the AIM lies the key to medical self-certification for flying – the acronym "I'M SAFE". It stands for Illness, Medication, Stress, Alcohol, Fatigue, Eating/Emotions." If any of those are an issue, it's very likely NOT a good day to go flying.

"I ran out of altitude, airspeed and ideas all at the same time."
Attributed to just about every test pilot who ever survived a crash.

SERVICE ACADEMY QUESTIONS

Bob Norris is a former naval aviator who also did a 3 year exchange tour flying the F-15 Eagle. He is now an accomplished author of entertaining books about US Naval Aviation including "Check Six" and "Fly-Off". In response to a letter from an aspiring fighter pilot on which military academy to attend, Bob replied with the following.

Young Man:

Congratulations on your selection to both the Naval and Air Force Academies. Your goal of becoming a fighter pilot is impressive and a fine way to serve your country. As you requested, I'd be happy to share some insight into which service would be the best choice. Each service has a distinctly different culture. You need to ask yourself "Which one am I more likely to thrive in?"

USAF Snapshot:

The USAF is exceptionally well organized and well run. Their training programs are terrific. All pilots are groomed to meet high standards for knowledge and professionalism. Their aircraft are top-notch and extremely well maintained. Their facilities are excellent. Their enlisted personnel are the brightest and the best trained. The USAF is homogeneous and macro. No matter where you go, you'll know what to expect, what is expected of you, and you'll be given the training & tools you need to meet those expectations. You will never be put in a situation over your head. Over a 20-year career, you will be home for most important family events. Your Mom would want you to be an Air Force pilot...so would your wife. Your Dad would want your sister to marry one.

Navy Snapshot:

Aviators are part of the Navy, but so are Black Shoes (surface warfare) and bubble heads (submariners). Furthermore, the Navy is split into two distinctly different Fleets (West and East Coast). The Navy is heterogeneous and micro. Your squadron is your home; it may be great, average, or awful. A squadron can go from one extreme to the other before you know it. You will spend months preparing for cruise and months on cruise. The quality of the aircraft varies directly with the availability of parts. Senior Navy enlisted are salt of the earth; you'll be proud if you earn their respect. Junior enlisted vary from terrific to the troubled kid the judge made join the service. You will be given the opportunity to lead these people during your career; you will be humbled and get your hands dirty. The quality of your training will vary and sometimes you will be over your head. You will miss many important family events. There will be long stretches of tedious duty aboard ship. You will fly in very bad weather and/or at night and you will be scared many times. You will fly with legends in the Navy and they will kick your ass until you become a lethal force. And some days - when the scheduling Gods have smiled upon you - your jet will catapult into a glorious morning over a far-away sea and you will be drop-jawed amazed that someone would pay you to do it. The hottest girl in the bar wants to meet a Naval Aviator. That bar is in Singapore.

Bottom line, son, if you gotta ask - pack warm & good luck in Colorado.

Banzai

PS: Air Force pilots wear scarves and iron their flight suits.

P.S.S: And oh yes, there's the Army pilot program. Don't even think about it unless you got a pair bigger than basketballs. Those guys are completely crazy.

Yugoslavia Flight Mechanic
1944 – 1949
After Nazi occupation in 1941, scattered elements of the Yugoslavian Air force made it to Allied territory where they

---

Helicopters don't fly – they beat the air into
submission.
Sometimes the air wins.

SOUND

If that described below ever happens to you, just remember the "Four F's":

Fly the plane [Set up best glide and trim].

Fly to your emergency field [The closer the better].

Fix the problem [If there's time].

Phone it in [Call for help: 121.5 on the radio and 7700 on the transponder]

There are tunes that fill the heart with sadness; somber notes, depressing to the mind.

Rap music's modern style of madness is cacophony in rhythm intertwined.

The creaking of old hinges, ghastly, ominous in the ebon night when spirits roam the air,

Chill the marrow, while forebodings calamitous engulf self's composure with despair.

The city's din and tumult proves annoying; it rasps and grates upon jangled nerves

'Tho one ignores, by devious means employing, condoning for the purpose it serves.

Shock waves from construction detonations if perchance, a person stands too near,

Like thunder's mighty echoing reverberations are sorely sharp and painful to the ear.

And yet, of all the sounds produced in violence, there is none so fills the soul with dread

As the roaring, shattering, deafening silence – that awesome sound -

Of an engine just gone dead.

- Author Unknown

NOTE: The P-38 pictured in this section (P-38 is the USAAF twin-engine fighter of WWII) BOTH propellers rotated AWAY from the fuselage making it a twin-engine airplane with TWO 'critical engines'! Don't believe it? Go to:

https://www.youtube.com/watch?v=V0if-foCUIU

SO, YOU WANT TO BE AN AIRLINE PILOT?

While there is some humor in this, there is also a lot of sad truth. Many of my airline pilot friends lament the "old days" when being an airline pilot – especially a Captain – was the envy of all in aviation. Now-a-days it ain't necessarily so. Where are tomorrow's pilots going to come from when treated thusly? I dedicate this to DK who finished his career with Continental Airlines, still proudly saying he is "...retired from the 'Old Frontier' (RIP)."

I walked into the interview with a great deal of confidence and enthusiasm. Flying airplanes was my one true passion in life. This was my big chance to merge my occupation with my love. I was going to be an airline pilot.

"So, you want to become an airline pilot?" the interviewer asked.

"Yes sir. More than anything in the world." I was sounding like an anxious adolescent. "Well, great. Welcome aboard." The executive said.

"You mean I'm hired?" I asked incredulously.

"You bet, we're glad to have you. Actually, we've had trouble finding good pilots to hire," the exec explained. If I was surprised, it was overshadowed by my joy of reaching my dream.

"Let's just go over a few points before you sign on the dotted line," he continued. "We're going to send you to the world's most renowned medical center. They'll spend two days probing your body orifices, draining and analyzing your blood, and administering psychological exams. They'll literally take you apart and put you back together. If they find any hint of current or future problems, you're fired and can find your own ride home."

"Gee, I think my health is OK," I nervously choked out. The manager went on, "Good, next we'll evaluate your flying skills in an aircraft you've never been in before. If we don't like the way you perform, you're fired," I was confident with my flying, but this guy was making me nervous. He continued, "Next, if you're still here, we'll run you through our training program. If during any time in the next 10 years you decide to leave the company, you'll have to reimburse us $20,000, or we'll sue you. Also if you fail to measure up during training, you're fired."

The man who had just given me my dream job listed still more hurdles. "Each time, before we allow you near one of our multimillion dollar aircraft we'll X-ray your flight bag and luggage, because we don't trust you. Also we'll ask you to pass through a magnetometer each time. If you fail to do so, you'll be arrested and jailed."

"When you've completed your flight, we'll have you provide a urine sample, because we don't trust you to not take drugs. Very soon, we plan to take a blood sample to look for more drugs. "Also if you ever fly with another crew member who may have used drugs or alcohol, you must report to us immediately. If you fail to notice that anyone has used these substances, you'll be fired, have your licenses to fly revoked, and be fined $10,000."

"Every six months, we want you to go back to the medical center for another exam. If they ever find a hint of a problem, your license to fly will be revoked and we'll fire you. Anytime you see a medical person, you must tell us about it so we can see if you need to be grounded and terminated. Also, we need to examine your driving record, and you must tell us if you have even any minor infractions so we can remove you from the cockpit as soon as possible."

"At any time, without notice, a special branch of the government will send one of its inspectors to ride in your aircraft. The inspector will demand to see your papers and license; if your papers are not in order, you'll be removed, fined, terminated, and possibly jailed."

"If at any time you make an error in judgment or an honest human mistake, you will be terminated, be fined tens of thousands of dollars, and be dragged through months of court proceedings. The government will make sure you never fly again for any airline. You will be well out of town most holidays, weekends, and family events - half our pilots are always on the job at any point in time."

Smiling an evil smile now, the airline hirer went on. "Oh, and one last thing: Occasionally, we in management fail to see a trend and screw up royally or the country's economy falls flat on its face. If as a result of one of those events the corporation begins to lose money, you as an employee will be expected to make up the losses from your paycheck. Of course, management will not be held to the same standards. And, if we negotiate pay and work rule concessions from you in the in exchange for a better pension plan, we probably won't fund that pension plan agreement (unlike the management pension plan and golden parachutes) and will likely have yanked it away from you."

"Now sign here," he pointed, grinning as he handed me a pen.

I faked a sudden nosebleed. Holding my head back and pinching my nostrils, I hurried from his office. When I got to the hall, I began to run. I ran all the way to my car. I figured if I hurried I could still get to the county vocational school before 5:00 pm and enroll in the industrial welding career program!

United States Army Air Corps – Technical Observer
1941 – 1947
TO's served as manufacturer's flying representatives who
studied/evaluated the planes in combat and made
recommendations for improvements.

Tell someone you work for a different airline than
the one you really work for, and they'll tell you how
much better yours is.

SQUAWK THIS

Who says mechanics and/or ground crew are humorless wrench-turners who work in aviation only for the mere fact they can't find work in a reputable automobile repair shop?   Here is evidence they DO have a sense of humor!

Squawk: Unfamiliar noise coming from #2 engine.

Solution: Engine run for 4 hours. Noise now familiar.

Squawk: Noise coming from #2 engine; sounds like little man with a hammer.

Solution: Took hammer away from little man in #2 engine.

Squawk: Whining noise coming from #2 engine.

Solution: Returned hammer to little man.

Squawk: Flight attendants cold at altitude.

Solution: Ground checks OK.

Squawk: Left main tire almost needs replacement.

Solution: Almost replaced left main tire.

Squawk: Test flight OK except auto-land very rough.

Solution: Auto-land not installed on this aircraft.

Squawk: Something loose in cockpit.

Solution: Something tightened in cockpit.

Squawk: Dead bugs on windshield.

Solution: Live bugs on backorder.

Squawk: Auto-pilot in altitude hold mode produces 200 feet per minute descent.

Solution: Cannot duplicate problem on the ground.

Squawk: Evidence of a leak on right main landing gear.

Solution: Evidence removed.

Squawk: DME volume unbelievably loud.

Solution: Volume reset to more believable levels.

Squawk: Friction locks cause throttle levers to stick.

Solution: That's what they're there for.

Squawk: IFF inoperative in 'OFF' mode

Solution: EVERYTHING is inoperative in OFF mode.

Squawk: Suspected crack in FO's windscreen.

Solution: Suspect you're correct.

Squawk: #3 engine missing.

Solution:#3 engine found on right wing after very short search.

Squawk: Aircraft handles funny.

Solution: Aircraft warned to straighten up, fly right, and be serious.

Squawk: Target radar hums.

Solution: Target radar reprogrammed with lyrics.

Squawk: Mouse in cockpit.

Solution: Cat installed in cockpit.

One problem is a problem; two problems are a hazard, three problems create accidents.

STUDENT PILOT REALITY CHECK

TACTICAL AIRLIFT

This email apparently originated from a young kid who sent it to AETC (Air Education and Training Command) wanting to know how to prepare himself for a future career as a fighter jock. Can you imagine?

To LtCol Van Wickler:

Sir,
I am DJ Baker and I would appreciate it if you could tell me what it takes to be an F 16 fighter pilot of the USAF. What classes should I take in high school to help the career I want to take later in my life?
What could I do to get in the academy?

Sincerely;

DJ Baker

From: VanWickler Kenneth, Lt Col, HQ AETC
Anybody want to help this poor kid from Cyberspace?

Vee Dub

A worldly and jaded C-130 Pilot, Major Hunter Mills rose to the task!!

Dear DJ:

Obviously, through no fault of your own, your young, impressionable brain has been poisoned by the superfluous, hyped-up, "Top Gun" media portrayal of fighter pilots. Unfortunately, this portrayal could not be further from the truth. In my experience, I've found most fighter pilots pompous, back-stabbing, momma's boys with inferiority complexes, as well as being extremely overrated both sexually and aeronautically.

However, rather than dash your budding dreams of becoming a USAF pilot, I offer the following alternative: What you REALLY want to aspire to is the exciting, challenging, and rewarding world of TACTICAL AIRLIFT. And this, young DJ, means one thing....the venerable workhorse, THE C-130!

I can guarantee no fighter pilot can brag that he has led a 12-ship formation down a valley at 300 ft. above the ground, while trying to interpret a 9-line to a new DZ, avoiding pop-up threats, and coordinating with AWACS, all while eating a box lunch, with the engineer in the back taking a piss and the navigator puking in his trash can! I tell you, DJ, TAC Airlift is where it's at!

Where else is it legal to throw tanks, HMMWVs, and other crap out the back of an airplane, and not even worry about it when the chute doesn't open and it torpedoes the General's staff car! Nowhere else can you land on a 3000' dirt strip, kick a bunch of ammo and stuff off the ramp without even stopping, then take off again before range control can call to tell you you've landed on the wrong LZ!

And talk about exotic travel-when C-130s go somewhere, they GO somewhere (usually for 3 months, unfortunately). This gives you the opportunity to immerse yourself in the local culture enough to give any natives a bad taste in their mouths, re the USAF and Americans in general, not something those strato-lifter pilots can do from their airport hotel rooms!

As far as recommendations for your course of study, I offer these: Take a lot of math courses. You will need all the advanced math skills you can muster to enable you to calculate per diem rates around the world, when trying to split up the crew's bar tab so that the co-pilot really believes he owes 85% of the whole thing and the nav believing he owes the other 20.

Health sciences are important, too. You will need a thorough knowledge of biology to make those educated guesses of how much longer you can drink beer before the tremendous case of the shits catches up to you from that meal you ate at that place that had the belly dancers in some God-forsaken foreign country whose name you can't even pronounce!

Social studies are also beneficial. It is important for a good TAC Airlifter to have the cultural knowledge to be able to ascertain the exact location of the nearest titty bar in any country in the world, and then be able to persuade the local authorities to release the loadmaster after he offends every sensibility of the local religion and culture.

A foreign language is helpful, but not required. You will never be able to pronounce the names of the NAVAIDs in France, and it's much easier to ignore them and go where you want to anyway. As a rule of thumb: Waiters and bellhops in France are always called "Pierre," in Spain it's "Hey, Pedro" and in Italy, of course, it's "Mario." These terms of address also serve in other countries interchangeably, depending upon the level of swarth of the addressee.

A study of geography is also paramount. You will need to know the basic location of all the places you've been when you get back from your TDY and are ready to stick those little pins in that huge world map you've got taped to you living room wall, right next to that gigantic wooden giraffe statue and beer stein collection.

Well, DJ, I hope this little note inspires you. And by the way, forget about that Academy thing. All TAC Airlifters know that there are waaay too few women and too little alcohol there to provide a well-balanced education. A nice, big state college would be a much better choice.

Good luck and see you on the SKE scope!

Maj. Hunter Mills

Any attempt to stretch fuel is guaranteed to increase headwinds.

THE AEROPLANE

My Aunt sent me this poem she found in the children's book <u>Favorite Poems Old and New for Boys and Girls</u>, selected by Helen Ferris. She read these poems to her great-grandchildren (she's 96 as of 2013!) and finding the one below, she said she thought of me. The book was printed in the 1920's.

An Aeroplane has gigantic wings but not a feather upon her breast.

She only mutters when she sings, and builds a hangar for a nest.

I love to hear her stop and start; she has a motor for her heart.

That beats and throbs and then is still. She wears a fan upon her bill.

No eagle flies through sun and rain so swiftly as an Aeroplane.

I wish she would come swooping down between the steeples of the town;

And lift me right up off my feet and take me high above the street.

That all the other boys might see the little speck that would be me.

The nicer an airplane looks, the beter it flies.

THE AIRMAN'S WORLD

If you do not venture forth into sullen skies,

You will never come upon sun kissed valleys.

If your palms have never been moist,

Your heart has never been thrilled.

If you have never been afraid,

You have never been courageous.

- Gill Robb Wilson

When I was instructing civil aerobatics regularly, I would often be approached by someone who just obtained their Private Pilot certificate. "I want to learn aerobatics." was their plea and of course that pleased me for several reasons. First, they want to know more about flying and especially about taildraggers. Second, they had to go through my tailwheel course and become trustworthy, competent and safe in that machine (I used a Citabria and later a Super Decathlon). Thirdly, then their multi-dimensional orientation and training could begin. I loved sharing aerobatics with the aviation community and it was job security for me as well.

My policy for these young Nuggets was as follows: "Go get some seasoning as the Pilot in Command – go fly places you haven't been, land in crosswinds your instructor wouldn't allow you to as a Student Pilot – get some more experience in commanding and controlling your ship. Come to me when you have 50 hours of PIC time after your flightcheck OR after you have scared yourself mightily in an airplane, thought real hard about your commitment to flying and then come to the decision that the rewards were worth the risk. Come to me when either of those things occurs."

I'm proud to say in all the years I've been training tailwheel and aerobatics, no-one has as much as scratched my plane. I lay that record at the feet of good instruction and the good people with whom I've been fortunate to work.

The sharpest captains are the easiest to work with.

THE BEST FIGHTER PILOTS

This came from a gent who runs a 2,000 acre corn farm up around Barron, WI. Not far from Oshkosh. He used to fly F4-E's and F-16's for the Guard and participated in the first Gulf War... Submitted for your enjoyment, and as a reminder that there are other great, magnificent flyers around besides me us:

I went out to plant corn for a bit to finish a field before tomorrow morning and witnessed "The Great Battle". A golden eagle - big bastard, about six foot wingspan - flew right in front of the tractor. It was being chased by three crows that were continually dive-bombing it and pecking at it. The crows do this because the eagles rob their nests when they find them.

At any rate, the eagle banked hard right in one evasive maneuver, then landed in the field about 100 feet from the tractor. This eagle stood about 3 feet tall. The crows all landed and took up positions around the eagle, but kept their distance at about 20 feet from the big bird. The eagle would take a couple steps towards one of the crows and they'd hop backwards and forward to keep their distance. Then the reinforcements showed up.

I happened to spot the eagle's mate hurtling down out of the sky at what appeared to be approximately Mach 1.5. Just before impact the eagle on the ground took flight, and the three crows which were watching the grounded eagle, also took flight thinking they were going to get in some more pecking on the big bird.

The first crow being targeted by the diving eagle never stood a snowball's chance in hell. There was a mid-air explosion of black feathers and that crow was done. The diving eagle then banked hard left in what had to be a 9-G climbing turn, using the energy it had accumulated in the dive, and hit crow #2 less than two seconds later: Another crow dead.

The grounded eagle, which was now airborne and had an altitude advantage on the remaining crow, which was streaking eastward in full burner, made a short dive then banked hard right when the escaping crow tried to evade the hit. It didn't work - crow #3 bit the dust at about 20 feet altitude. This aerial battle was better than any airshow I've been to, including the warbirds show at Oshkosh!

The two eagles ripped the crows apart and ate them on the ground, and as I got closer and closer working my way across the field, I passed within 20 feet of one of them as it ate its catch. It stopped and looked at me as I went by and you could see in the look of that bird that it knew who was 'Boss of the Sky'. What a beautiful bird!

I love it. Not only did they kill their enemy, they ate them!!

Never ask a man if he's a fighter pilot. If he is, he'll let you know. If he isn't, don't embarrass him.

THE BICYCLE REPAIRMEN

This piece appeared in the Los Angeles Times' Calendar section years ago. I've kept the part I cut out for years. It was written by a very famous author known for interesting twists and turns in his short stories, novellas and books. A number of them were made into movies. An interesting fact about this man is that despite living in Los Angeles, where automobile transportation is virtually a necessity, this man did not drive. And yet he could pen something like this. I beg the indulgence of the author and the LA Times to allow including his work in this book.

My grandpa spoke of the rare fine shop they ran

Not far from the blowing shoals of sand,

Not far from that little stretch of land

They named for a Cat and a Bird.

Their dreams? Folks said they were 14 ounces to the pound absurd.

Their practical schemes? To fix bikes and tires at hardly more than a buck a head;

Then retread their sometimes dog-eared late noon

Nap-time snoozing revelations.

Their occupations when not so employed with wheels?

To peer off in the void or, that's to say,

Find clouds and follow them with their eyes,

Fall up in skies to drown with birds, build keels of wind

Half-whispering: "I wonder how that feels?"

Some people came right out and said: They're crazy.

No, just lazy to the point of being mad, some others said.

No mind. This time next year they'll both be dead

From barn-roof jumps with home-made wing.

Or running like chickens crazed with spring

Down the slopes to the sands

Where the one sound heard

Is the sound of a Cat and the sound of a Bird.

Try Hawk. Then Kitty. How's *that* sound?

…or is it the other way around…?

Ray Bradbury
20 August 1920 – 5 June 2012
R.I.P

I had the great pleasure of meeting and conversing for an hour or so with Mr. Bradbury when I was studying in Southern California years ago. Even got a nice inscription and his autograph in one of his books I still have to this day. He's a true gentleman...and a superb story teller – his books still a good read.
- Drew Chitiea

THE COMPLAINER

EVERY outfit, unit or company has one [and only one if you're lucky] of these types; there is just no way to shut them up. Everyone can be cold, hungry, tired, footsore, wet...you name it. And they think they have it the worst of everyone.

Note to those types: STFU!

You bring me cold coffee.

You serve me lousy food.

I cannot see the movie.

Not that it matters because you didn't bring me any headphones.

And my window doesn't even have a shade, so I can't sleep.

When he'd finally stopped whining, she said,

"Just shut up and fly the plane!"

How come every ground school class I've ever been in has one ass who, 5 minutes before the end of the day, asks a question requiring a 20-minute answer?

THE ENABLER

A real woman is man's best friend.
She will never stand him up and never let him down.
She will reassure him when he feels insecure
And comfort him when he feels blue.
She will inspire him to do things he never thought he could do;
To live without fear or regret.
She will enable him to express his deepest emotions and give in
to his most intimate desires.
She will make him sure he always feels as though
He's the most handsome person in the room and
Will enable him to be the most confident, sexy,
Seductive, invincible and…and, uh…

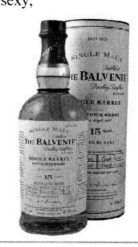

No, wait…SORRY!
I'm thinking of whiskey.
It's whiskey that does all that shit…
NEVER MIND.

Take note all ye who approacheth me : My alternate
brand.

THE MILITARY AVIATOR

This little treatise was sent to me courtesy of Colonel Ed Huber, USAF (ret.), a friend of years and a fellow pilot in the 69th Special Operations Group. All he said was: "I never fit this description. Or did I?" Yes, Ed, you did...

...As Seen By Himself:

An incredibly tall, intelligent, handsome, innovative and highly trained professional killer, idol to countless females, Gentleman Adventurer, who wears a star sapphire ring, carries a hair-trigger .45 Colt automatic in a specially-designed, hand-made, quick-draw holster along with his trusty survival knife, who is always on time thanks to his ability to always obtain immediate transportation and the reliability of his Rolex watch.

...As Seen By His Wife:

A disreputable member of the family who comes home once a year all bruised up, driving a stolen Jeep *(Okay...Hummer)* up to the back door carrying a torn B-4 bag full of dirty laundry, wearing a stained flight suit, smelling of stale booze and JP-4, wearing a huge watch, a fake ring, and that damn-ugly holster with that old beat-up pistol and stupid knife, who three months later will go out the front door, thankfully for another year.

...As Seen By His Commanding Officer:

A fine specimen of a drunken, brawling, Jeep-stealing *(Hummer absconding)*, woman-corrupting liar, with a star sapphire ring, fantastically accurate Rolex watch, and an unauthorized Colt .45 in a non-regulation holster and a rusty survival knife.

...As Seen By DoD:

An over-paid, rule-ignoring, over-ranked tax burden, who unfortunately is totally indispensable simply because he has volunteered to go anywhere, do anything, at any time, only so long as he can booze it up, brawl, steal Jeeps *(Yeah, yeah...that's sooo 20th century!)*, have his way with women, and wear a star sapphire ring, Rolex watch and carry an obsolete handgun and survival knife.

...As Seen By The Enemy:

The implacable Face of Doom!

Sure, the money is better in the private sector...
But then, you can't call in airstrikes.

THE OLD PILOT

Un-PC, but so what? It's my book, okay? Deal with it!

The old gentleman wearing a beat-up leather flying jacket with a squadron patch on the front sat down at the Starbucks and ordered a cup of coffee. As he sat sipping his coffee, a young woman sat down next to him... She turned to the man and asked, "Are you really a pilot?"

He replied, "Well, I've spent my whole life flying; biplanes, Cubs, Aeroncas, T-6s, flew F-100's in Vietnam and finished up in C-5's. I taught over 500 people to fly in Tweets and gave rides to hundreds, so yes, I guess I am a pilot."

She said, "I'm a lesbian. I spend my whole day thinking about naked women. As soon as I get up in the morning, I think about naked women. When I shower, I think about naked women. When I watch TV, I think about naked women. It seems everything makes me think of naked women."

The two sat sipping in silence. A little while later, a young man sat down on the other side of the old pilot and asked, "Are you really a pilot?"

The old man replied, "I always thought I was, but I just found out I'm a lesbian."

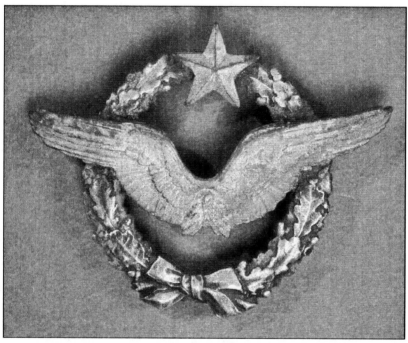

Military Pilot
France
1916

Everything in aviation is accomplished through teamwork until something goes wrong - then one pilot gets the blame.

THE PAYOFF

Professionalism, readiness, and knowledge can never be replaced by all the electronic gadgets in the world. Whether you drive a truck, 777 or a C-17, nothing beats knowing your capabilities and those of your machine, and knowing where you are at all times. It's hard to come up with options if you don't know what's going on.

Dedicated to Frank Crismon (1903-1990)
by Capt. G. C. Kehmeier (United Airlines, Ret.)

I ought to make you buy a ticket to ride this airline!" The chief pilot's words were scalding. I had just transferred from San Francisco to Denver. Frank Crismon, my new boss, was giving me a route check between Denver and Salt Lake City.

"Any man who flies for me will know this route," he continued. "'Fourteen thousand feet will clear Kings Peak' is not adequate. You had better know that Kings Peak is exactly 13,498 feet high. Bitter Creek is not 'about 7,000 feet.' It is exactly 7,185 feet, and the identifying code for the beacon is dash dot dash.

"I'm putting you on probation for one month, and then I'll ride with you again. If you want to work for me, you had better start studying!"

Wow! He wasn't kidding! For a month, I pored over sectional charts, auto road maps, Jeppesen approach charts, and topographic quadrangle maps. I learned the elevation and code for every airway beacon between the West Coast and Chicago. I learned the frequencies, runway lengths, and approach procedures for every airport. From city road maps, I plotted the streets that would funnel me to the various runways at each city.

A month later he was on my trip.

"What is the length of the north-south runway at Milford?" "Fifty-one fifty."

"How high is Antelope Island?" "Sixty-seven hundred feet."

"If your radio fails on an Ogden-Salt Lake approach, what should you do?" "Make a right turn to 290 degrees and climb to 13,000 feet."

"What is the elevation of the Upper Red Butte beacon?" "Seventy-three hundred."

"How high is the Laramie Field?" "Seventy-two fifty."

This lasted for the three hours from Denver to Salt Lake City.

"I'm going to turn you loose on your own. Remember what you have learned. I don't want to ever have to scrape you off some hillside with a book on your lap!"

Twenty years later, I was the Captain on a Boeing 720 from San Francisco to Chicago. We were cruising in the cold, clear air at 37,000 feet.

South of Grand Junction a deep low-pressure area fed moist air upslope into Denver, causing snow, low ceilings, and restricted visibility. The forecast for Chicago's O'Hare Field was 200 feet and one-half mile, barely minimums.

Over the Utah-Colorado border, the backbone of the continent showed white in the noonday sun. I switched on the intercom and gave the passengers the word.

"We are over Grand Junction at the confluence of the Gunnison and Colorado Rivers. On our right and a little ahead is the Switzerland of America--the rugged San Juan Mountains. In 14 minutes we will cross the Continental Divide west of Denver. We will arrive O'Hare at 3:30 Chicago time."

Over Glenwood Springs, the generator overheat light came on.

"Number 2 won't stay on the bus," the engineer advised.

He placed the essential power selector to number 3. The power failure light went out for a couple of seconds and then came on again, glowing ominously.

"Smoke is coming out of the main power shield," the engineer yelled.

"Hand me the goggles."

The engineer reached behind the observer's seat, unzipped a small container, and handed the copilot and me each a pair of ski goggles. The smoke was getting thick.

I slipped the oxygen mask that is stored above the left side of the pilot's seat over my nose and mouth. By pressing a button on the control wheel, I could talk to the copilot and the engineer through the battery-powered intercom. By flipping a switch, either of us could talk to the passengers.

"Emergency descent!" I closed the thrust levers. The engines that had been purring quietly like a giant vacuum cleaner since San Francisco spooled down to a quiet rumble. I established a turn to the left and pulled the speed brake lever to extend the flight spoilers.

"Gear down. Advise passengers to fasten seat belts and no smoking."

I held the nose forward, and the mountains along the Continental Divide came up rapidly. The smoke was thinning.

"Bring cabin altitude to 14,000 feet," I ordered.

At 14,000 feet over Fraser, we leveled and retracted the gear and speed brakes. The engineer opened the ram air switch and the smoke disappeared. We removed our goggles and masks. Fuel is vital to the life of a big jet, and electricity is almost as vital. The artificial horizon and other electronic instruments, with which I navigated and made approaches through the clouds, were now so much tin and brass.

All I had left was the altimeter, the airspeed, and the magnetic compass--simple instruments that guided airplanes 35 years earlier.

"Advise passengers we are making a Denver stop."

"The last Denver weather was 300 feet with visibility one-half mile in heavy snow. Wind was northeast at 15 knots with gusts to 20," the copilot volunteered.

"I know. I heard it."

The clouds merged against the mountains above Golden. Boulder was in the clear. To the northeast, the stratus clouds were thick like the wool on the back of a Rambouillet buck before shearing.

I dropped the nose and we moved over the red sandstone buildings of the University of Colorado. We headed southeast and picked up the Denver-Boulder turnpike.

"We will fly the turnpike to the Broomfield turnoff, then east on Broomfield Road to Colorado Boulevard, then south to 26th Avenue, then east to Runway 8." The copilot, a San Francisco reserve, gave me a doubtful look. One doesn't scud-run to the end of the runway under a 300-foot ceiling in a big jet.

Coming south on Colorado Boulevard, we were down to 100 feet above the highway. Lose it and I would have to pull up into the clouds and fly the gauges when I had no gauges. Hang onto it and I would get into Stapleton Field. I picked up the golf course and started a turn to the left.

"Gear down and 30 degrees."

The copilot moved a lever with a little wheel on it. He placed the flap lever in the 30-degree slot. I shoved the thrust levers forward.

"Don't let me get less than 150 knots. I'm outside."

I counted the avenues as they slid underneath . . . 30th, 29th, and 28th. I remembered that there was neither a 31st nor a 27th. I picked up 26th. The snow was slanting out of the northeast. The poplar trees and power lines showed starkly through the storm. With electrical power gone, we had no windshield heat. Fortunately, the snow was not sticking.

"Let me know when you see a school on your side and hack my time at five-second intervals from the east side of the school yard."

Ten seconds.

"There it is. The yard is full of kids. Starting time now!"

Good boy. Smiley faced Holly. From the east side of the school yard, I counted the streets; first Kearney, then Krameria, Leydon, Locust. Remember the double lane for Monaco Parkway. Then Magnolia, Niagara, Newport. Time the speed at 130 knots. Only eight blocks to the end of the runway. Oneida, Olive, Pontiac, Poplar. From Quebec to Syracuse, the cross streets disappear; figure eight seconds. Keep 26th Avenue under the right side of the nose.

"Full flaps."

Dead ahead, glowing dimly in the swirling snow, were the three green lights marking the east end of Runway 8. We crossed 20 feet above the center green light and touched down in a crab to the left. I aligned the nose to the runway with the right rudder, dropped the nose wheel, popped the speed brakes, and brought in reverse thrust.

It took us 10 minutes to find the terminal in the swirling whiteout. We saw the dim, flashing red light atop the building indicating the field was closed to all traffic. A mechanic materialized out of the snow carrying two wands. He waved me into the gate.

I set the parking brake.

"We have ground power," the engineer advised.

"Cut the engines."

The bagpipe skirl of sound spiraled down to silence.

"My hat is off to you, skipper. I don't know how you ever found this airport."

"I used to fly for an ornery old chief pilot who made me learn the route," I replied as I hung up my headset and scratched the top of my head where it itched.

Frank Crismon passed away at his home in Denver on 25 Jan 1990.

When in doubt, hold on to your altitude; no-one has
ever collided with the sky.
BUT – did you check about mountains along
your route at 'your' altitude?

THE TEST

Pretty much the way I remember it – except my father wasn't a Preacher. Dated a Preacher's daughter for a spell, though.

An old country preacher had a teenage son, and it was getting time the boy should give some thought to choosing a profession.

Like many young men his age, the boy didn't really know what he wanted to do, and he didn't seem too concerned about it.

One day, while the boy was away at school, his father decided to try an experiment. He went into the boy's room and placed on his study table four objects:

1. A Bible.

2. A silver dollar.

3. A bottle of whiskey.

4. A Playboy magazine.

'I'll just hide behind the door," the old preacher said to himself. "When he comes home from school today, I'll see which object he picks up."

"If it's the Bible, he's going to be a preacher like me, and what a blessing that would be!

"If he picks up the dollar, he's going to be a business man, and that would be okay, too.

"But if he picks up the bottle, he's going to be a no-good drunken bum, and Lord, what a shame that would be.

"And worst of all if he picks up that magazine he's going to be a skirt-chasing womanizer."

The old man waited anxiously, and soon heard his son's footsteps as he entered the house whistling and heading for his room. The boy tossed his books on the bed, and as he turned to leave the room he spotted the objects on the table. With curiosity in his eye, he walked over to inspect them. Finally, he picked up the Bible and placed it under his arm. He picked up the silver dollar and dropped into his pocket. He uncorked the bottle and took a big drink, while he admired the magazine's centerfold.

"Lord have mercy," the old preacher disgustedly whispered. "He's gonna be a pilot."

One who flies with fear encourages fate.

TICKET THIS

I've heard a few different versions of this, from various countries and various Air Forces. I include this one for the sole reason despite the fact we are "Two peoples separated by a common language", air defense speaks on a common frequency.

Two British traffic patrol officers from North Berwick were involved in an unusual incident while checking for speeding motorists on the A1 Great North Road. One of the officers used a hand-held radar device to check the speed of a vehicle approaching over the crest of a hill, and was surprised when the speed was recorded at over 300 mph. Their radar suddenly stopped working and the officers were not able to reset it.

Just then a deafening roar over the treetops revealed that the radar had in fact latched on to a NATO Tornado fighter jet which was engaged in a low-flying exercise over the Border district, approaching from the North Sea.

Back at police headquarters the chief constable fired off a stiff complaint to the RAF Liaison office.

Back came the reply in true laconic RAF style:

"Thank you for your message, which allows us to complete the file on this incident. You may be interested to know that the tactical computer in the Tornado had detected the presence of, and subsequently locked onto, your hostile radar equipment and automatically sent a jamming signal back to it. Furthermore, an air-to-ground missile aboard the fully-armed aircraft had also automatically locked onto your equipment. Fortunately the pilot flying the Tornado recognized the situation for what it was, quickly responded to the missile systems alert status, and was able to override the automated defense system before the missile was launched and your hostile radar installation was destroyed."

Czechoslovakia Pilot Training Graduation Badge
1930's – 1938
Given to pilot training graduates prior to actually being awarded their pilot badge - this one is numbered and has the graduate's initials inscribed on the reverse.

Any pilot who does not privately consider himself the best in the game is in the wrong game.

TO AVOID
CONFUSION

*There will be a test at the end of this training session,
so pay attention!*

Thought you would like to see the notice that British Airways sent to its pilots explaining what we in the US refer to as the "monitored approach" method where on an approach to very low visibility and ceiling one pilot flies the approach and when the other pilot sees the runway he takes the plane and lands. This removes the problem of the pilot having to make the transition from flying instruments and at the last minute looking outside and getting his bearings" as the other pilot is already "outside". If the pilot not flying says nothing by the time they reach "minimums", the pilot flying automatically starts the "go-around" procedure as he is still on the instruments. Now try this actual explanation of this procedure from the British Airways Manual.

British Airways Flight Operations Department Notice

"There appears to be some confusion over the new pilot role titles. This notice will hopefully clear up any misunderstandings. The titles P1, P2, and Co-Pilot will now cease to have any meaning, within the BA operations manuals. They are to be replaced by:

Handling Pilot,
Non-handling Pilot,
Handling Landing Pilot,
Non-Handling Landing Pilot,
Handling Non-Landing Pilot, and
Non Handling Non-Landing Pilot.

The Landing Pilot is initially the Handling Pilot and will handle the take-off and landing except in role reversal when he is the Non-Handling Pilot for taxi until the Handling Non-Landing Pilot, hands the handling to the Landing Pilot at eighty knots. The Non-Landing (Non-Handling, since the Landing Pilot is handling) Pilot reads the checklist to the Handling Pilot until after Before Descent Checklist completion, when the Handling Landing Pilot hands the handling to the Non-Handling Non-Landing Pilot who then becomes the Handling Non-Landing Pilot. The Landing Pilot is the Non-Handling Pilot until the "decision altitude" call, when the Handling Non-Landing Pilot hands the handling to the Non-Handling Landing Pilot, unless the latter calls "go-around", in which case the Handling Non-Landing Pilot, continues Handling and the Non-Handling Landing Pilot continues non-handling until the next call of "land" or "go-around", as appropriate.

In view of the recent confusion over these rules, it was deemed necessary to restate them clearly."

I hate to wake up and find my co-pilot asleep.

TURBULENCE PIREPs

My wife and I fly our Cessna P-210 all around the country in the mid- to upper teens as those altitudes are just about void of traffic. We can usually file direct after we accomplish the DP and, in most cases, we can either take advantage of the prevailing upper-level winds flying west-to-east or stay lower to avoid them (sometimes) flying east-to-west. I love to check in with Center when we're at 15,000 with "Cessna 12K, fifteen thousand, smooth ride." when all the heavy iron in the upper flight levels is reporting light-to-moderate at all altitudes and they can't find smooth air.

One day, while flying over the Rockies with a strong jet stream and many turbulence reports in the Denver airspace, I heard Denver Center ask for ride reports.

United 123:

"Good day, Denver, United 123 with you at FL 350."

Denver Center:

"Roger; United 123. How's your ride?"

United 123:

"Well, the captain is having his lunch, and he just jabbed himself with his fork; so we could call it as moderate turbulence."

Denver Center:

"Thanks; United 123. Break; Air Canada 456, how's your ride at FL350?"

Air Canada 456:

"Sorry, Denver, we can't tell. We haven't eaten yet."

I have been for years amused at what conditions pilots – especially the lesser experienced ones – will report as "moderate" and "severe". Just because you're getting bounced around a bit doesn't mean it's reportable as "moderate". And when I have heard "severe" turbulence reports from a C-172 I tend to scoff a little. "Moderate" reports from heavy iron and anything military will get my attention, though.

AIM 7-1-23, (table 7-1-9) PIREPs Relating to Turbulence:

| LIGHT | Turbulence that causes slight, erratic changes in altitude and/or attitude report as **Light Turbulence**. Slight, rapid & somewhat rhythmic | Occupants may feel slight strain against safety belts. Unsecured items may be displaced slightly. Food service may be | Occasional: Less than 1/3 of the time. Intermittent: 1/3 to 2/3 Continuous: More than |

	bumpiness without appreciable changes in altitude or airspeed report as **Light** Chop.	conducted with little or no difficulty walking.	2/3
MODERATE	Turbulence similar to Light but of greater intensity. Changes in attitude/altitude with variations in airspeed but the aircraft remains in positive control at all times, report as **Moderate Turbulence**. Rapid, rhythmic bumps and/or jolts without appreciable change in attitude or altitude report as Moderate Chop.	Occupants feel definite strains on safety belts. Unsecured objects are dislodged. Food service & walking are difficult.	Same
SEVERE	Turbulence that causes large, abrupt changes in altitude or attitude	Occupants are forced violently against	Same

	with large changes in airspeed. Aircraft may be momentarily out of control. Report as Severe Turbulence.	safety belts. Unsecured objects are tossed about. Food service & walking are mpossible.	
EXTREME	Turbulence in which the aircraft is violently tossed about & is practically impossible to control. It may result in structural damage or failure. Report as Extreme Turbulence.		

A thunderstorm is Nature's way of saying "Up Yours!"

ULTIMATE DARWIN AWARD WINNER

The following report, while technically not strictly aviation-related, nonetheless includes some aerospace technology and that brief, exhilarating moment of first lifting off the face of the planet before the realization sets in that you're in a world of trouble. The Mythbusters crew did a televised segment on this and disproved some of the premise of the story, but it's still too good not to include in this book. If you are unfamiliar with the Darwin Awards, they are given out annually to those individuals who perform the service of removing themselves from the gene pool in the most creative and/or extraordinarily stupid way. The prior year's winner was the man who was killed by a soda machine toppling over on him as he was trying to shake a free soft drink out of it. Now, for this years' [it doesn't matter which. – Ed.] winner...

The Arizona Highway Patrol came across a pile of smoldering metal embedded in the side of a cliff rising above the road, at the apex of a curve. The wreckage was at first thought to be an airplane but it turned out to be a car. The type of car was unidentifiable at the scene. It took the people in the lab to figure out what it was and what apparently transpired leading up to the crash.

It seems the driver somehow got possession of a JATO unit [Jet Assisted Take Off, actually a solid fuel rocket] used to give heavy military aircraft that extra push during takeoffs from short airfields. The driver had driven his mid-70's Chevy Impala out into the desert, finding a long, straight stretch of highway. He then attached the JATO unit to the roof of his trusty Impala, got up to speed and then ignited the rocket.

As best as the lab people could determine, this good ol' boy was doing somewhere between 250 and 300 mph [350 – 420 kph] when he came to the curve in the road. The brakes were completely burned away, indicating the driver was apparently trying to slow the car down when it became airborne prior to impacting the cliff face.

[Note to the readers: Solid-fuel rockets do not have an "off" switch. Once ignited they burn at 100% thrust until all the fuel is used up. Consider the JATO-assisted takeoffs of the Blue Angels' 'Fat Albert' support C-130. –Ed.]

FAR 91.403 Maintenance: General

(d) A person must not alter an aircraft based on a supplemental type certificate (STC) unless the owner or operator of the aircraft is the holder of the supplemental type certificate, or has written permission from the holder.

The lesson here is: When adding any after-market and/or non-standard equipment to an existing vehicle, ask lots and lots of questions before testing an unknown quantity. Indeed, your life could very likely depend on that.

Getting that Supplemental Type Certificate [STC] or making sure that part is Parts Manufacturer's Association [PMA] approved AND the proper aircraft logbook entries are made is crucial.

Balloon Pilot
US Army Air Service
1917 – 1918

Definition of 'Pilot': The first one to the scene of an aircraft accident.

USAAC DIRECTIVE

CONFIDENTIAL

ADDRESS REPLY TO
CHIEF OF THE AIR CORPS
WAR DEPARTMENT
WASHINGTON, D. C.

WAR DEPARTMENT

OFFICE OF THE CHIEF OF THE AIR CORPS

WASHINGTON

May 22, 1939

SUBJECT: Flying Status for Flying Safety.

TO: Brig. General Arnold N. Krogstad, A. C.,
Langley Field,
Hampton, Virginia.

1. The Chief of the Air Corps is deeply concerned that senior and older pilots take no unnecessary flying risks and thus jeopardize their valuable experience to the Air Corps.

2. To this end he has directed the classification of all pilots over forty-seven years of age into a group where they will not be required to pilot at night, to lead or drill with pursuit formations, to fly single seater aircraft, or to do any other types of particularly hazardous piloting where the natural and understandable depreciations coincident with age may render them less fit than men of younger years. He believes that there should be absolutely no evidence of any competition in piloting among men of higher rank and older age. There is no necessity and no justification for the feeling on the part of a senior officer that he must continue to pile up as much pilot time, or to pilot as skillfully as he did in his earlier years, or as well as younger pilots do.

3. Your particular attention is directed to the revision of War Department Circular 26 and to the minimum requirements set up in Circular 50-12, O.C.A.C. Every senior Air Corps Officer must use the soundest judgement at all times as to the types of flying performed and as to when, how, and where to fly, after a careful analysis of tactical situations and weather conditions. Officers in the command pilot group may fly as co-pilots or command pilots in meeting their flying requirements.

4. It is desired that you be accompanied by another pilot on all military flights.

H. H. Arnold,
Major General, Air Corps,
Chief of the Air Corps.

Sure makes you feel old, eh?

USAF AIRCRAFT IDENTIFICATION CHART

There are many persons of varying degrees of 'sanity' [and I do use that term as loosely as possible prior to everything just falling apart] who claim this planet has been, and is being, visited by...ahhh..."creatures from other worlds." Evidentally they are not referring to the denizens of coastal Southern California, the Peoples Republic of Boulder or Washington, DC, but of creatures from 'outer space'. Despite questions raised regarding their 'inner space' and the convincing "Men in Black" film trilogy, nothing extra-terrestrial as of the date of this book has been proven to exist. It is suggested these 'space cadets' place the poster below on their refridgerator – as did the 'plane spotters' of bygone years – to assist in the identifaction of "Unidentified Flying Objects" [UFOs]. It is also recommended they redirect the energies spent fearing alien rectal probing in favor of using their turn signals more often.

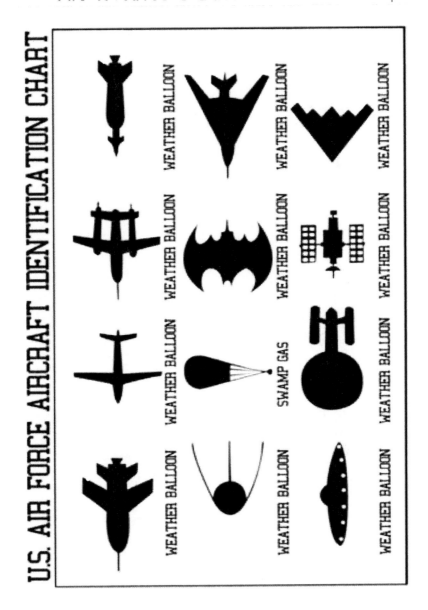

When a weather forecaster talks about yesterday's weather, he's a historian. When he talks of tomorrow's weather, he's reading tea leaves.

USS MIDWAY VA-25's TOILET BOMB

For those too young to remember, during the Vietnam conflict, carriers were so woefully short of ordinance that missions were often launched with only a half load just to keep the sortie rate up so that the REMF's in DC would not send out blistering messages about failure to support the war effort, etc.

Given that the loss rate approached, and sometime exceeded, one aircraft a day, all will understand that there was a degree of reticence to launch with less than a full load -- if I must dance with the elephant at least let's make it worthwhile. Nevertheless, the indomitable spirit of the carrier aviators and their squadron-mates prevailed in some rather perverse - and creative - ways.

I have every hope that today's successors to those who flew and fought then will persevere as well. "Kick the tires, light the fires, bolt for the blue and brief on guard -- last one up is lead." This story is true; it happened on the USS MIDWAY in Oct 1965. I thought you'd get a kick out of one squadron's ingenuity. Yes, this really happened. Once again history is stranger than fiction...and a lot funnier.

USS MIDWAY VA-25's TOILET BOMB:

In October 1965, CDR Clarence J. Stoddard, Executive Officer of VA-25 "Fist of the Fleet", flying an A-1H Skyraider, NE/572 "Paper Tiger II" from Carrier Air Wing Two aboard USS Midway carried a special bomb to the North Vietnamese in commemoration of the 6-millionth pound of ordnance dropped. This bomb was unique because of the type... it was a toilet!

The following is an account of this event, courtesy of Clint Johnson, Captain, USNR, Ret. Captain Johnson was one of the two VA-25 A-1 Skyraider pilots credited with shooting down a MiG-17 on June 20, 1965. 572 was flown by Commander C. W. "Bill" Stoddard. His wingman in 577 was Lieutenant Commander Robin Bacon, who had a wing station mounted movie camera (the only one remaining in the fleet from WWII).

The flight was a Dixie Station strike (off South Vietnam) going to the Delta. When they arrived in the target area and CDR Stoddard was reading the ordnance list to the FAC, he ended with "and one code name Sani-flush".

The FAC couldn't believe it and joined up to see it. It was dropped in a dive with LCDR Bacon flying tight wing position to film the drop. When it came off, it turned hole to the wind and almost struck his airplane.

It made a great ready room movie. The FAC said that it whistled all the way down. The toilet was a damaged toilet, which was going to be thrown overboard.

One of our plane captains rescued it and the ordnance crew made a rack, tailfins and nose fuse for it. The squadron flight deck checkers maintained a position to block the view of the Captain and Air Boss while the aircraft was taxiing onto the catapult. Just as it was being shot off we got a 1MC message from the bridge, "What the hell was on 572's right wing?"

FAR 91.15 Dropping Objects

No pilot in command of a civil aircraft may allow any object to be dropped from that aircraft in flight that creates a hazard to persons or property. However, this section does not prohibit the dropping of any object if reasonable precautions are taken to avoid any injury or damage to persons or property.

I love this regulation; mostly as the prime example of lawyers being able to say two [or more] things with the same breath. "Talking out of both sides of your mouth" is another apt and appropriate phrase.

What this regulation is saying is: You <u>may not</u> drop anything from an aircraft while in flight, however you <u>may</u> drop things from an aircraft while in flight. [Got it so far?] Now, even though it says you may not, if proper precautions are taken to avoid injury or damage then you may drop things from an aircraft in flight. However, even if you take these precautions yet still cause injury or damage by dropping something then you haven't taken the proper precautions to avoid injury or damage and so then have you not taken proper precautions and thus violated the intent of this regulation. BTW, you will most likely be charged with 91.13 Careless and Reckless Operation and a few more. I trust that clears up the intent of the regulation for my readers. – ed.

The things that do no good in aviation:

· Altitude above you

· Runway behind you

· Air in the fuel tanks

· Airspeed you don't have

· Approach plates in the car

· Half a second ago

Regarding engine power:
Lots is good, more is better & too much is just about
right.

WHATASTORE'S NEW GREETER

Retirement...what a word fraught with all kinds of meaning, inference and innuendo: I've known pilots who when they hung up their spurs never darkened the doorstep of an airport again. There are others who returned to their roots and are to this day giving back to the industry, guiding the young coming along with the same joy and wonder for the sky they entered it with 40 years earlier. In either case, these are the people some hard-hearted cynics may call 'has-beens'. I'd rather be a 'has-been' than a 'never-will-be'.

If you can cajole these wealth of information and experience persons back to the airport and get them involved, the things you'll learn and the stories you'll hear told.

Charley, a new retiree and greeter at Whatastore, just couldn't seem to get to work on time. Every day he was 10 or 15 minutes late. But he was a good worker, really tidy, clean-shaven, sharp minded and a real credit to the company and obviously demonstrating their "Older Person Friendly" policies.

One day the boss called him into the office for a talk. "Charley, I have to tell you, I like your work ethic, you do a bang up job, but your being late so often is quite bothersome."

"Yes, I know boss, and I am working on it."

"Well good, you are a team player. That's what I like to hear. It's odd though, your coming in late. I know you're retired from the Armed Forces. What did they say to you there if you came in late?"

"They said, "Good morning, Admiral, can I get your coffee, sir?'

When beginning an aviation career it is not unusual to be overwhelmed, terrified, suffer from lack of confidence and just plain old be scared. As experience grows, self-confidence replaces fear ... but after a time, when you think you have seen it all, you realize your initial reactions to flying were all too true.

WANTED: PIANO PLAYER

Long before he became a nationally-known songwriter-singer and actor, Kris Kristopherson was an Army Aviator on the way up. He got diverted into the 'Entertainment Industry' where he co-starred with the likes of Barbara Streisand, later forming a country music group "The Highwaymen" with Waylon Jennings, Johnny Cash and Willie Nelson. He is a member of the Country Music Hall of Fame, not the least for his song "Sky King" found at:

http://www.youtube.com/watch?v=i458ZzwpE3w

A ragged, old, derelict shuffled into a down and dirty bar. Stinking of whiskey and cigarettes, his hands shook as he took the "Piano Player Wanted" sign from the window and handed it to the bartender. "I'd like to apply for the job," he said. "I was an F-4 driver and a Lieutenant Colonel in the Air Force, but when they retired the Phantom, all the thrill was gone, and soon they cashiered me as well. I learned to play the piano at O-Club happy hours, so here I am."

The barkeep wasn't too sure about this doubtful looking old guy, but it had been quite a while since he had a piano player and business was falling off. So, why not try him? The seedy ex-Lt. Col. staggered his way over to the piano while several patrons snickered. By the time he was into his third bar of music, every voice was silenced. What followed was a rhapsody of soaring music, unlike anything heard in the bar before. When he finished there wasn't a dry eye in the place.

The bartender took the old fighter pilot a beer and asked him the name of the song he had just played. "It's called "Drop your Skivvies, Baby, I'm Going Balls To the Wall For You!" said the Lt. Col. After a long pull from the beer, leaving it empty, he said, "I wrote it myself." The bartender and the crowd winced at the title, but the piano player went into a knee-slapping, hand-clapping bit of ragtime that had the place jumping. After he finished, the fighter pilot acknowledged the applause, downed a second proffered mug, and told the crowd the song was called, "Big Boobs Make My Afterburner Light Off."

He then excused himself and lurched into the head.

When he came out the bartender went over to him and said, "Look bus driver, the job is yours, but do you know your fly is open and your pecker is hanging out?"

"Know it?" the old fighter pilot replied, "Hell, I wrote that too!"

Twelve Days of Combat

On the first day of combat, the Air Force gave to me…

A pilot in a teak tree.

Two rocket pods.

Three fuel tanks.

Four AIM-9s.

Five thousand pounders.

Six seven-fifties.

From the estate of Robin Olds,
BGEN, USAF (Ret'd)
And who went west, 14 June 2007

On the seventh day of Combat, Ho Chi Minh gave to me…

Seven SAMs a-zinging.

Eight flak sites firing.

Nine MIGs a-diving.

On the tenth day of Combat, the Air Force gave to me…

Ten Sandys searching.

Eleven Jollys whirling.

Twelve days a-waiting.

From The Fighter Pilot's Handbook
TO 1F-FTRPLT-1 Utility, After-Flight Manual

The three best things in life are a good landing, a good shit and a good orgasm. A night carrier landing is one of the few opportunities to experience all three at the same time.

WHEN I MISS FLYING

One more look at airline life. All you young 'uns – see what you can look forward to?

We have a cockpit mock-up in our house.

When I mention to my wife that I miss flying (being retired) she puts me in the mock-up around bed time for 8 hours.

She has a chair in a closet, puts on the vacuum cleaner to simulate cockpit air noise; has a dim night light to simulate cockpit lighting and serves lukewarm chicken with cold vegetables on a tray.

When I get sleepy and attempt to doze off, she knocks twice loudly on the door to simulate the FA's entering the cockpit.

Then, after 6 hours she turns on a flood light directly in front of me to simulate the sun coming up when approaching 20° west.

After two hours of sleep she calls the phone next to the bed from her cell and says its crew scheduling.

I then get a cup of coffee that has been in the coffee-maker all night.

Finally, she lets me out and I have to get in the back seat of her car while she runs morning errands to simulate the crew bus ride to the hotel.

When we get home I tell her I am ready for bed and the bedroom door is locked for an hour to simulate the hotel rooms not being ready.

When I promise to never "complain" about being retired, I am allowed to enjoy my "layover" and go to bed.

Oh, and one more thing, she talks to her friends loudly outside the bedroom door to simulate the hotel maids chattering in the hall in their native language.

Croatia Army Pilot
1941 – 1944
A short-lived independent Croatian air force arose from a dismembered Yugoslavia and allied itself with Nazi Germany. They did not last long, being decimated on the Russian Front.

One peek is worth a thousand instrument cross-checks.

WHERE ARE THE AIRPORT KIDS?

As you read that which follows, consider what we, in aviation, have lost to the past. What a shame.

"Where are the airport kids? They have gone the way of ramshackle hangars, 40 hp Cubs, tattered windsocks and hand-operated gas pumps. Gone with the grey-beard flight instructors who were also the mechanic, book-keeper and janitor for flight schools that operated out of tiny line shacks at the edge of mown grass strips. Gone are the days when a youngster could spend a day at an airport watching the planes drift around the pattern, talk to the pilots and mechanics. Gone are the days when sweeping out a hangar or carefully washing an airplane could be traded for a few precious moments in the sky.

In the name of 'safety', 'security' and 'efficiency' these opportunities to learn the skills and lore of aviation are now denied most of today's young people. Glass and concrete, tall fences and 'security' gates...airports with "No Trespassing" signs and locked doors keep out those who would be the airport kids of today and the aviators of tomorrow."

- Chuck Larsen

I'm in my sixth decade as I'm putting this book together and I guess I'm one of the lucky 'oldsters' who enjoyed that which is lamented above. I recall sweeping hangars and being 'allowed' to clean the belly of round-engine fire-breathers: What excitement! What joy! And then I got to fly with the pilot: "We gotta dry her off from that good wash job you gave her!"

I flew with one of the last of the US Navy enlisted pilots prior to WWII: He had two aircraft carriers sunk out from under him in that war; one was the Yorktown at the Battle of Midway. He cut me no slack whatsoever but sure learned to fly tailwheel airplanes like a Navy pilot [I can to this day plunk her down on the #3 wire, make 3, 2 and 1-point landings and, believe it or don't, make smooth-flaring landings as well]. I got to fly with a gruff old SOB who lived through 30 missions over Germany in B-17's and another 100 or so in F-86's in Korea. He treated me like 'Da Kid' that I was then but as I earned his trust and respect, we became a crew. Ain't nothing higher between two persons in aviation than that. I flew with Frances Gary Powers [Google that name, youngsters, and read about a chapter in aviation and this nation's history] after he returned from his trial and imprisonment in the Soviet Union – now Russia.

All along the way, I have had older pilots – mentors as they're called now – guide my steps, warn me of the pitfalls and traps then send me out into the sky to earn the privilege of wearing wings. As a matter of fact, when the Navy pilot [Chief 'Red' Decker, R.I.P] was preparing to move away, I queried "Red, how can I ever thank you for what you've done for me?"

He replied, cigar at the corner of his mouth, "Kid, ya can't. But someday years from now you're going to be me and there will be some other 'Kid' coming along. Work his ass off like I did to you, but give him the chances to do and understand things like I gave you. That's how you can thank me." This book is part of my obligation to 'Red' to pass along to others what he, through his blood, sweat and tears, learned the hard way and then taught to me.

And I challenge everyone reading this book, everyone who has a history in aviation, to help, assist and encourage the young ones coming along so they learn the lessons that everyone who has gone before has paid so dearly for. For only by doing that can we guide aviation into the future. For only by bringing along those who are, or will be, the future of aviation can we insure its continued existence as one of mankind's finest aspirations, and achievements.

An airplane may disappoint a good pilot but it should never surprise him.

WHO PACKED YOUR PARACHUTE?

There is a lot of ego in aviation, especially in the cockpit. A good pilot has to believe they're the best out there or else why suit up and go commit aviation? But we should, we MUST, respect and be appreciative of all those whose job is to support us in the furtherance of our mission, for without them we're just little kids making airplane noises and cleaning our side of the windscreen [think about it!]. The following story I'm told is true, but it serves to make the point:

Sometimes, in the daily challenges that life deals us, we miss that which is really important. We may fail to say hello, please and thank you. We might miss congratulating someone who achieved a goal or who had something wonderful happen to them. We may forget to give a complement or commit a random act of kindness.

Charles Plumb, a USN Academy graduate, was a fighter pilot during Vietnam. On his 75th combat mission he was shot down; he ejected and parachuted into enemy territory where he was subsequently captured, spending years in a communist Vietnamese prison. He survived that Hell and, at last word, still lectures on the lessons learned during that ordeal. One day, Plumb and his wife were dining at a restaurant when a man approached them: "You're Plumb! You flew off the Kitty Hawk and were shot down!" "How in the world did you know that?" asked Plumb.

"I packed your parachute." the man replied.

Plumb gasped in surprise and gratitude as they shook hands. "I guess it worked." said the man. "It sure did. If your chute hadn't worked, I wouldn't be here today." Plumb couldn't sleep that night, thinking about that man, what he might have looked like those many years ago in a Navy uniform: A Dixie Cup hat, bib at the back of his shirt and bell-bottom trousers. "I wonder how many times I might have seen him and not even said 'Good morning' or 'How are you?' or anything because, you see, I was a fighter pilot and he was just a sailor.

Plumb thought of the many hours that man spent down in the bowels of the ship, carefully weaving the shroud lines and folding the silk of each chute, holding in his hands the fate of people he didn't know. Now when Plumb addresses an audience, he asks "Who's packing *your* parachute?" Everyone has someone who provides what they need to make it through the day. Plumb also points out that he required many different kinds of parachutes after his shoot-down. Over enemy territory he needed the physical parachute, but he also needed a mental parachute, an emotional parachute, a spiritual parachute. He called on all of these before returning home.

His experience challenges all and each of us to prepare to weather whatever storms lie ahead. But as you go through this day, week, month and year...recognize - **and thank** - those who pack your parachute!

Your mind is like a parachute – it only works when open.

YOU KNOW YOU'RE A FREIGHT DOGGER IF:

If we haven't been there at some point in rising to the top in aviation, then we've all known someone who has been there or still is. It takes a special breed to be a Dogger – we used to call them "Dalmatians", like the fire station dog - friendly enough but not a brain in their head. Truth to say, they flew through conditions that semi-sane pilots wouldn't go near, yet most live to tell the tale and go on to a higher calling (I could tell you the story of the squall-line that went from deep in the Gulf of Mexico to north of Chicago but I don't have enough time or paper). Let's just admit that clichés become clichés for the mere fact they are true so often.

1. Your airplane was getting old when you were born.

2. You have not done a daylight landing in the past six months.

3. ATC advises you of smoother air at a different altitude, and you don't give a shit.

4. When you taxi up to an FBO they roll out the red carpet, but quickly take it back when they recognize you.

5. You call the hotel van to pick you up and they don't understand where you are on the airport.

6. Center asks you to "keep the chickens down" so they can hear you talk.

7. Your airplane has more than 75,000 cycles.

8. Your company call sign is "Oil Can."

9. The lady at the FBO locks up the popcorn machine because you plan on "making a meal of it."

10. Your airplane has more than eight faded logos on it.

11. You wear the same shirt for a week, and no one complains.

12. Center mispronounces your call sign more than three times in one flight.

13. Your Director of Operations mysteriously changes your maximum takeoff weight during the holiday season.

14. Every FBO makes you park out of sight of their building.

15. You have ever walked barefoot through the FBO because you just woke up.

16. You mark every ramp with engine oil.

17. Everything you own is in your flight bag and suitcase.

18. All the other pilots wait for you to "test the squall line" first.

19. All the other airlines hold to see if you get in.

20. You request the visual approach with 300' overcast and ½ sm vis.

21. You make no attempt to deviate around weather.

22. You don't bother checking the weather 'cause you're going anyway.

23. You have an emotional reunion with your newly assigned Beech 99 because you used to fuel it 25 years earlier when it only had 18,000 cycles on it and the windows weren't painted over.

24. You've slept more nights at Willow Run than in the house you grew up in.

25. Upper management thinks a derelict fuel truck for you to sleep in is a "crew domicile".

26. You hope to someday make it to the big time...Atlas Cargo.

27. You carry your own personal step ladder in the back of the aircraft.

28. You've changed tires, starter generators, and ADI's but you're neither an A&P nor an avionics tech.

29. You have a secret Mexican family in Del Rio, Texas.

30. The tip tanks also serve as an alarm clock when they run dry.

31. You become VERY proficient at night-time aileron rolls to stay awake.

32. You lose your radios and the approach controller says, "Hey, Mailbag 216, wake up! I know you're sleepin' up there!"

33. On a clear night you consider it normal to make a low pass or two to clear the ground fog and deer off the runway at Presque Isle.

34. You fly with a Captain who has both dead-sticked a DC-3 at night to a safe landing and had to declare an emergency because his copilot tried to pee out an old antennae hole on a Convair 580 and was nearly castrated.

———————————————

(The "Old Frontier" Airlines, 1950 – 1986, R.I.P.)

For D.K., D.L., G.M., F.H., W.R., and all you 'old Frontier' pilots and friends, now long since retired.

———————————————

What separates Flight Attendants from the lowest
form of life on earth?
The cockpit door.

YOU MIGHT BE AN AIRPLANE MECHANIC IF:

Pilots and mechanics seem to have relationships of mutual disrespect: Pilots are always breaking 'their' aircraft and the mechanics never can get things done right and on time. And woe betide the poor Nugget who breaks his crew chief's aircraft...

I used to take a couple of six-packs by the maintenance hangar once a month on a Friday afternoon around 4:45 pm and share with the 'wrenches'. They appreciated that courtesy – and when I needed a favor they were predisposed to help rather than blow it off 'til the next day.

You've ever said, "Oh yes sir, it's supposed to look like that."

You've ever sucked LOX to cure a hangover.

You know what JP4/JP5 (jet fuel) tastes like.

You've ever used a piece of safety wire as a toothpick.

You've ever had to say, "My boots are still black!" (Or ever spray-painted them black)

You have ever used soot from the tailpipe to blacken your boots.

You believe the aircraft has a soul.

You talk to the aircraft.

The only thing you know about any city is where the good bars are.

You know more about your coworkers than you do about your own family.

AIRPLANE MECHANIC

ON DUTY

You can't figure out why maintenance officers exist.

You ever wished the pilot would just say, "Great aircraft!"

You think everyone who isn't a Maintainer is a wimp.

You wondered where they keep finding the idiots that keep making up stupid rules.

You consider 'Moly-B' fingerprints on food an 'acquired taste'.

You've ever been told to "go get us some prop wash, a yard of flight line or the keys to the jet.

You have ever jumped inside an intake to get out of the rain.

Little yellow ear plugs are all over your house.

You have ever preflighted in really bad weather only to learn that the flight was canceled hours ago.

Your spouse refuses to watch any aviation shows or attend airshows with you.

You have ever looked for pictures of "your" airplane in aviation books and magazines.

You can't figure out why two weeks of advance per-diem is gone after three days.

You can sleep anywhere, anytime. But as soon as the engines shut down you are wide awake.

You have ever used, wheel chock, or tow bar for a pillow.

You have ever stood on wheel chocks to keep your feet dry.

You have ever used a pair of Dykes to trim a fingernail.

You have ever pulled the gun switch while riding brakes.

You have ever started an airplane inside the hanger!

You have ever wiped leaks right before a crew show.

All you care about is the flying schedule and your days off.

You have ever had to defuel your airplane an hour after fueling it.

Everyone you know has some kind of nickname.

You have used the "Pull Chocks" hand signal to tell your buddies it is time to leave.

You have ever bled hydraulic fluid into a Gatorade bottle or soda can because you are too lazy to go get a hydraulic bucket and the Hazmat keys.

You know in your heart that your jet is female.

You refer to ANY machine as "she."

You refer to QA as "the enemy."

You hate Ops, Maintenance Control, QA, and cops.

You've ever made a new pilot buy you a beer just to put his name on the canopy.

You know the international marshaling sign for "pull your head out of your ass."

You've ever worked weekend duty on a jet that isn't flying on Monday.

You've wanted the jet to start just so you can warm up.

You can't remember half of your coworker's real names... only their nicknames.

You fix 30 million dollar jets, but can't figure out what's wrong with your $150 lawnmower.

Your toolbox at home has wheels and foam cutouts, just like the ones at work.

Some of the tools in your toolbox at home are etched.

The way you measure cost of living in other countries is by the price of a beer at a bar.

YOU MIGHT BE A REDNECK PILOT IF:

You know, there's all kinds of redneck (or if you think you're uptown, it's 'Redneq') jokes disparaging those who earn their living with their hands, or working the land, or any other such 'humble' endeavors. My wife is from "L.A." (That's "Lower Alabama" to you Yankees) and all her family down there could rightfully be called 'rednecks'. And if being a redneck means honoring your word no matter what, saying "Yes, sir" and "Yes, Ma'am" to those older than you, going to church on Sunday (and other days too), loving – and serving - your country, singing the national anthem, saying the Pledge of Allegiance – ALL of it - and standing up when Old Glory passes in the 4th* of July parade… then I'm a redneck too. So help me God.*

You have used ~~duct tape~~ "100 mile-an-hour tape" to repair cowlings, wingtips, etc. or a flattened out Budweiser can and pop rivets for more important parts. *(We did that more than once in Alaska. – ed.)*

Part of your preflight is removing corn stalks from the landing gear.

You estimate the weight of the mud on your airplane into the CG.

Fuel used for the farm vehicles is interchangeable with your plane.

You've never landed at a paved airport although you've been flying for years.

You've ground looped by hitting a cow or deer on your 'runway.'

You consider any flight above 500' agl to be "high altitude."

Some of the more important engine parts have a "John Deere" data plate.

You have never used a sectional but you have all your state's Rand McNally road maps [20+ years old].

Your local blacksmith has made [or remanufactured] some landing gear parts.

You use a Purina feed sack for a windsock.

You refer to formation flying as "We got us a convoy!"

Your stall warning horn plays "Dixie."

You've ever used 'shine' as an avgas substitute.

You choke if you have to say the word "Yankee."

You can't understand why "10-4" is not condoned by ATC.

You don't understand why female controllers object to being called "Darlin'."

You wonder why J C Whitney doesn't come out with an airplane customizing catalog like you've been telling them to.

You wonder why ATC will not accept a readback such as "We-all's cleared from rat cheer to yonder by this heah airway and that-there intersection…"

You think Bubba is right up-town because his hangar has a flush privy.

You wonder why them fools at Telex can't come up with a headset that will fit over your cowboy hat and not crush it down.

Your weight-and-balance includes a gun rack.

United States Army Air Corps – Navigator
1941 – 1947

No-one ever collided with the sky.

YULETIDE FOLLIES

Three aviators all happened to pass away on Christmas Eve. Meeting Peter at the Pearly gates, the old saint said "In honor of this holy season, you must each possess something symbolizing Christmas so you may enter through to Heaven."

The flight engineer fumbles through his pockets and, pulling out a cigarette lighter flicks it into flame. "It's a candle." He says.

"You may pass through yon Pearly Gates." said Saint Peter.

The first officer reaches into his pocket and reveals a set of keys. Jingling them ever so softly, he says "These are Christmas Bells."

Saint Peter, beaming, says "Enter thou the Kingdom of Heaven."

The old Captain began searching desperately through his things. Finally, from deep in a rear pocket, he pulls out a pair of women's panties.

Saint Peter looked at him with raised eyebrows and asked querulously, "And just what do those symbolize?"

The old captain smiled and said, "These are Carol's."

ZERO - ZERO

I conclude this collection with the following story. Yet it's more than merely a 'story'; it is an exemplary tale in honor of professionalism, attention to detail, setting high standards and goals for oneself – and the benefit that comes from perfecting and maintaining those qualities: Not only in one's flying skills, but for life in general. Come sit at the feet of this once-green and callow co-pilot and learn the lessons he learned that day.

ZERO - ZERO
By Charles Svoboda

It happened sometime in 1965, in Germany. I was a copilot, so I knew, everything there was to know about flying, and I was frustrated by pilots like my aircraft commander. He was one of those by-the-numbers types, no class, no imagination and no feel for flying. You have to be able to feel an airplane. So what if your altitude is a little off or if the glideslope indicator is off a hair? If it feels okay then it is okay. That's what I believed.

Every time he let me make an approach, even in VFR conditions, he demanded perfection. Not the slightest deviation was permitted. If you can't do it when there is no pressure, you surely can't do it when the pucker factor increases, he would say. When he shot an approach, it was as if all the instruments were frozen perfection, but no class. Then came that routine flight from the Azores to Germany: The weather was okay; we had 45,000 pounds of fuel and enough cargo to bring the weight of our C-124 Globemaster up to 180,000 pounds, 5,000 pounds below the max allowable.

It would be an easy, routine flight all the way. Halfway to the European mainland, the weather started getting bad. I kept getting updates by high frequency radio. Our destination, a fighter base, went zero/zero. Our two alternates followed shortly thereafter. All of France was down. We held for two hours, and the weather got worse. Somewhere I heard a fighter pilot declare an emergency because of minimum fuel. He shot two approaches and saw nothing. On the third try, he flamed out and had to eject.

We made a precision radar approach; there was nothing but fuzzy fog at minimums. The sun was setting. Now I started to sweat a little. I turned on the instrument lights. When I looked out to where the wings should be, I couldn't even see the navigation lights 85 feet from my eyes. I could barely make out a dull glow from the exhaust stacks of the closest engine, and then only on climb power.

When we reduced power to maximum endurance, that friendly glow faded. The pilot asked the engineer where we stood on fuel. The reply was, I don't know - we're so low that the book says the gauges are unreliable below this point. The navigator became a little frantic. We didn't carry parachutes on regular MAC flights, so we couldn't follow the fighter pilot's example. We would land or crash with the airplane. The pilot then asked me which of the two nearby fighter bases had the widest runway.

I looked it up and we declared an emergency as we headed for that field. The pilot then began his briefing.

This will be for real. No missed approach. We'll make an ILS and get precision radar to keep us honest. Copilot, we'll use half flaps. That'll put the approach speed a little higher, but the pitch angle will be almost level, requiring less attitude change in the flare.

Why hadn't I thought of that? Where was my feel and class now? The briefing continued, I'll lock on the gauges. You get ready to take over and complete the landing if you see the runway that way there will be less room for trouble with me trying to transition from instruments to visual with only a second or two before touchdown? Hey, he's even going to take advantage of his copilot, I thought. He's not so stupid, after all.

Until we get the runway, you call off every 100 feet above touchdown; until we get down to 100 feet, use the pressure altimeter. Then switch to the radar altimeter for the last 100 feet, and call off every 25 feet. Keep me honest on the airspeed, also. Engineer, when we touch down, I'll cut the mixtures with the master control lever, and you cut all of the mags. Are there any questions? Let's go! All of a sudden, this unfeeling, by the numbers robot was making a lot of sense. Maybe he really was a pilot and maybe I had something more to learn about flying. We made a short procedure turn to save gas.

Radar helped us to get to the outer marker. Half a mile away, we performed the Before Landing Checklist; gear down, flaps 20 degrees. The course deviation indicator was locked in the middle, with the glideslope indicator beginning its trip down from the top of the case. When the GSI centered, the pilot called for a small power reduction, lowered the nose slightly, and all of the instruments, except the altimeter, froze. My Lord, that man had a feel for that airplane! He thought something, and the airplane, all 135,000 pounds of it, did what he thought. Five hundred feet. I called out, "400 feet...300 feet...200 feet, MATS minimums...100 feet, Air Force minimums." I'm switching to the radar altimeter....75 feet nothing in sight....50 feet, still nothing...25 feet, airspeed 100 knots.

The nose of the aircraft rotated just a couple of degrees, and the airspeed started down. The pilot then casually said, "Hang on, we're landing." Airspeed 90 knots...10 feet, here we go! The pilot reached up and cut the mixtures with the master control lever, without taking his eyes off the instruments. He told the engineer to cut all the mags to reduce the chance of fire. CONTACT!

I could barely feel it. As smooth a landing as I have ever known and I couldn't even tell if we were on the runway, because we could only see the occasional blur of a light streaking by. Copilot, verify hydraulic boost is on, I'll need it for brakes and steering. I complied. Hydraulic boost pump is on, pressure is up? The brakes came on slowly - we didn't want to skid this big beast now. I looked over at the pilot. He was still on the instruments, steering to keep the course deviation indicator in the center, and that is exactly where it stayed.

Airspeed, 50 knots? We might make it yet. Airspeed, 25 knots? We'll make it if we don't run off a cliff. Then I heard a strange sound. I could hear the whir of the gyros, the buzz of the inverters, and a low frequency thumping. Nothing else. The thumping was my pulse, and I couldn't hear anyone breathing. We had made it! We were standing still! The aircraft commander was still all pilot.

After-landing checklist, get all those motors, radar and un- necessary radios off while we still have batteries. Copilot, tell them that we have arrived, to send a follow me truck out to the runway because we can't even see the edges? I left the VHF on and thanked GCA for the approach. The guys in the tower didn't believe we were there. They had walked outside and couldn't hear or see anything. We assured them that we were there, somewhere on the localizer centerline, with about half a mile showing on the DME.

We waited about 20 minutes for the truck. Not being in our customary hurry, just getting our breath back and letting our pulses diminish to a reasonable rate. Then I felt it. The cockpit shuddered as if the nose gear had run over a bump. I told the loadmaster to go out the crew entrance to see what happened. He dropped the door (which is immediately in front of the nose gear) and it hit something with a loud, metallic bang. He came on the interphone and said "Sir, you'll never believe this. The follow-me truck couldn't see us and ran smack into our nose tire with his bumper, but he bounced off, and nothing is hurt?"

The pilot then told the tower that we were parking the bird right where it was and that we would come in via the truck. It took a few minutes to get our clothing and to button up the airplane. I climbed out and saw the nose tires straddling the runway centerline. A few feet away was the truck with its embarrassed driver. Total damage - one dent in the hood of the follow me truck where the hatch had opened onto it.

Then I remembered the story from Fate Is the Hunter. When Gann was an airline copilot making a simple night range approach, his captain kept lighting matches in front of his eyes. It scarred and infuriated Gann. When they landed, the captain said that Gann was ready to upgrade to captain. If he could handle a night-range approach with all of that harassment, then he could handle anything.

At last I understood what true professionalism is. Being a pilot isn't all seat-of-the-pants flying and glory. It is self- discipline, practice, study, analysis and preparation. It's precision. If you can't keep the gauges where you want them with everything going right, how can you keep them there when everything goes wrong?

United States Army Air Corps – Pilot
1941 – 1947

If you don't gear up your brain before takeoff, you'll probably gear up your airplane upon landing.

END PIECE & AFTERWORD

As a final comment, I commend all you aviators to accomplish some form of training and/or proficiency exercise each and every time you fly.

Give yourselves a task out of the PTS appropriate to your certificate and ratings…and **practice precision.**

Choose a runway stripe and practice until you can land, full stall, centered over the centerline, drift corrected, on that exact stripe.

Choose a heading, then practice stalls and recoveries so the Heading Indicator hardly wavers.

Choose an altitude and transition from cruise airspeeds to Vso and back all within 100'. Then add heading control as above to the mix.

Practice instrument approaches until you think the localizer and glideslope needles are broken and frozen in the crosshairs.

Practice partial-panel approaches until they can be done with 'no sweat'.

Dust off those old textbooks, manuals and yes, the FAR/AIM and read, inquire, study and relearn all you learned those many years ago to get where you are now.

And if you need assistance or advice in polishing your knowledge and skills a little, employ your local CFI for a few hours of scrapping off the rust.

Remember:
You are an Aviator, not just a fly-boy.
Always plan to do your best.

Blue Skies & Tailwinds!

DREW CHITIEA, DPE, MCFI
BLACK HAWK, COLORADO
2014

APPENDIX

ABR Pithy One-Liners

Throughout this book at the bottom of each chapter I have placed a sentence – perhaps two – of aviation observations, truisms and comments. Here below are collected all in one spot these sayings full of Pith…and a little vinegar as well.

Enjoy!

1. If God had meant for Man to fly, he would have made his bones hollow – not his head.

2. Flying is not dangerous – crashing is dangerous.

3. Aviation is not so much a profession as it is a disease.

4. Always keep an 'out' in your back pocket.

5. The worst day of flying beats the best day at work.

6. You cannot be lost if you don't care where you are.

7. Let's do a 360 and get the hell outa here!

8. The medical profession is the natural enemy of the aviation profession.

9. What you know is not so important as what you do with it.

10. Do not spin this aircraft! If a spin occurs, it will return to earth without further attention on the part of the aeronaut.

11. Never trade skill for luck.

12. You will never do well if you stop doing better.

13. The most dangerous part about flying is the drive home from the airport.

14. Luck may stand in for skill occasionally, but not consistently.

15. Any comment regarding how well things are going – or in regards to tailwinds of any velocity – will immediately get things going in the opposite direction.

16. Airspeed, altitude, Brains: Any 2 are required for a successful flight.

17. Keep the aeroplane in such an attitude that the air pressure is directly in the pilot's face.

18. Aviate, navigate, and communicate – in that order.

19. Truly superior pilots are those who use their truly superior judgment to avoid those situations requiring their truly superior skills.

20. Keep flying the airplane until all the moving parts have stopped moving.

21. Death is a small price to pay for looking 'Shit Hot'.

22. There are three simple rules for making good landings – unfortunately, no-one knows what they are.

23. Airspeed is Life – Altitude is Life Insurance.

24. It is far better to break ground and fly into the wind than the other way around.

25. When a flight is going incredibly well, something was forgotten.

26. "IFR" flying – I Follow Roads, Rivers & Railways.

27. Aviation rule #1: First and Foremost – Always fly the plane.

28. 'Tis best to keep the pointy end going forward and the greasy side down.

29. Given a choice, always go for the more conservative option.

30. And so, at the beginning of each day, consider that ATC, the weather-guessers, mechanics, supervisors…and birds…are all trying to kill you. Your job is to not let them.

31. The future is aviation is the next 30 seconds. Long-term planning is the next hour and a half.

32. Much of what you think you know is incorrect.

33. "Happy Hour Landing" – two for the price of one.

34. It has been said that two wrongs don't make a right – but two Wrights can make an airplane.

35. Without fuel, pilots are just pedestrians.

36. To err is human, to forgive divine – neither of which is corporate policy.

37. It is better to die than to look bad; but it is possible to do both.

38. I knew I was in trouble when the tower asked me to climb to field elevation.

39. Flying is not a Nintendo game: You cannot push a button and start over.

40. Murphy's Law of Flight Instruction: If a student can do the wrong thing at the wrong time, he will.

41. FAA regulations prohibit drinking within 8 feet of the airplane and smoking within 50 hours of the flight; or is it the other way around?

42. If you crash because of bad weather, when they bury you it will be beautiful, clear and calm.

43. There is no financial reason in the world why you cannot pass your next flightcheck.

44. Learn from the mistakes of others; you will never live long enough to make them all yourself.

45. Better higher than lower; better faster than slower.

46. The survivability of the landing is inversely proportional to the angle of arrival.

47. You have never been lost until you have been lost above Mach 3.

48. Hovering is for pilots who love to fly but have nowhere to go.

49. Asking a pilot what he thinks of the FAA is like asking a fire hydrant what it thinks of a dog.

50. Never trust a fuel gauge.

51. If you must make a mistake, try to make it a new one.

52. FARs are worded either by the most brilliant lawyers in Washington – or the most stupid.

53. An airplane flies because of a principle discovered by Bernoulli, not Marconi.

54. Good judgment comes from experience: Experience comes from bad judgment.

55. Dyslexic atheist – doesn't believe in dog.

56. Forget all that stuff about Lift, Weight, Thrust & Drag - an airplane flies because of money.

57. The Law of Gravity is not a generalized rule.

58. In thrust I trust [put another way: I feel the need for speed]

59. It is better to be on the ground wishing you were flying than flying wishing you were on the ground.

60. A light twin defined is that airplane when one engine fails the other gets you to the scene of the crash.

61. It is always better to have C-sub-t greater than C-sub-d. Simply put, thrust should always exceed drag.

62. Passengers prefer old captains and young flight attendants.

63. A fool and his money are soon flying more airplane than he can handle.

64. A helicopter is a collection of rotating, oscillating & reciprocating parts going 'round and 'round & up and down – all of them attempting to become simultaneously random in motion.

65. Fighter pilots make movies; attack pilots make history.

66. If it ain't broke, don't fix it. If it ain't fixed, don't fly it.

67. A mechanic's favorite: "It's not a leak…it's a seep."

68. Be nice to your First Officer – he just might be your captain at the next airline.

69. For those who don't care, fly Military Air.

70. The next time war is decided on how well you can land on a carrier, the Navy will clean up. Until then, I'll worry about who spends their training time flying and fighting.

71. Experience is the knowledge that enables you to recognize a mistake when you make it again.

72. Never let an airplane take you anywhere your brain hasn't been to at least 5 minutes prior.

73. Always remember: You fly with your head, not just your hands.

74. If it doesn't work, rename it. If it still doesn't work, the new name isn't long enough.

75. One of the most important skills a pilot must master is ignoring those things in an aircraft which were put there by non-fliers to get the pilot's attention.

76. Out on the line, all the girls are looking for husbands…and all the husbands are looking for girls.

77. A good simulator checkride is like successful surgery on a cadaver.

78. Please don't tell Mother I'm a pilot – she thinks I'm a piano player in a whorehouse.

79. You know you've landed gear up when it takes full power to taxi.

80. Trust in your captain…but keep your seatbelt securely fastened.

81. The owners' guide that comes with a $1,000 refrigerator makes more sense than the one that comes with a $100 million dollar airliner.

82. A 'greaser' landing is 50% luck, two in a row is 100% luck, and three in a row means someone is lying.

83. "Come see me" notes from the Chief Pilot are always distributed on Friday afternoons…after office hours.

84. A kill is a kill.

85. Experience is a tough teacher: First comes the test, then the lesson.

86. Pilots believe in clean living – they never drink whiskey from a dirty glass.

87. Flying is the perfect vocation for the man who wants to feel like a boy – but not for one who still is.

88. Nothing flies without fuel – so let's have some coffee!

89. Fuel in the tanks is limited – Gravity is forever.

90. Assumption is the mother of all screw-ups.

91. There are no atheists in the foxholes.

92. The three most common things heard on the CVR are "Was that for us?", "What did he say?" and "Oh, shit!" since computers are now onboard airplanes, a fourth and a fifth have been added: "What's it doing now?" and "Why is it doing that?"

93. If God had meant for Man to fly, He would have given him green, baggy Nomex skin and full wallets.

94. When you are sitting in the rubber raft looking up at where your airplane used to be, it's too late to check the weather, flight plan or wonder where the emergency checklist is.

95. Flying a twin doesn't make you twice as safe – it merely doubles the chances of suffering an engine failure.

96. The main thing is to take care of the main thing.

97. Every pilot knows the definition of a good landing is one you can walk away from. A great landing is when you can use the airplane again without major maintenance.

98. "It was my ex-wife who drove me to drink. It's the only thing I'm grateful to her for." - W.C. Fields.

99. There will be a day when you walk out of an airplane and two things will be true: You will either know it's your last flight in an airplane, or you won't.

100. "I ran out of altitude, airspeed and ideas all at the same time." Attributed to just about every test pilot who ever survived a crash.

101. Helicopters don't fly – they beat the air into submission. Sometimes the air wins.

102. Tell someone you work for a different airline than the one you really work for, and they'll tell you how much better yours is.

103. One problem is a problem; two problems are a hazard, three problems create accidents.

104. Any attempt to stretch fuel is guaranteed to increase headwinds.

105. The nicer an airplane looks, the better it flies.

106. The sharpest captains are the easiest to work with.

107. Never ask a man if he's a fighter pilot. If he is, he'll let you know. If he isn't, don't embarrass him.

108. How come every ground school class I've ever been in has one ass who, 5 minutes before the end of the day, asks a question requiring a 20-minute answer?

109. Sure, the money is better in the private sector…But then, you can't call in airstrikes.

110. Everything in aviation is accomplished through teamwork until something goes wrong - then one pilot gets the blame.

111. When in doubt, hold on to your altitude; no-one has ever collided with the sky. BUT – did you check about mountains along your route at 'your' altitude?

112. One who flies with fear encourages fate.

113. Any pilot who does not privately consider himself the best in the game is in the wrong game.

114. I hate to wake up and find my co-pilot asleep.

115. A thunderstorm is Nature's way of saying "Up Yours!"

116. Definition of 'Pilot': The first one to the scene of an aircraft accident.

117. When a weather forecaster talks about yesterday's weather, he's a historian. When he talks of tomorrow's weather, he's reading tea leaves.

118. Regarding engine power: Lots is good, more is better & too much is just about right.

119. When beginning an aviation career it is not unusual to be overwhelmed, terrified, suffer from lack of confidence and just plain old be scared. As experience grows, self-confidence replaces fear … but after a time, when you think you have seen it all, you realize your initial reactions to flying were all too true.

120. The three best things in life are a good landing, a good shit and a good orgasm. A night carrier landing is one of the few opportunities to experience all three at the same time.

121. One peek is worth a thousand instrument crosschecks.

122. An airplane may disappoint a good pilot but it should never surprise him.

123. Your mind is like a parachute – it only works when open.

124. What separates Flight Attendants from the lowest form of life on earth? The cockpit door.

125. No-one ever collided with the sky.

126. If you don't gear up your brain before takeoff, you'll probably gear up your airplane upon landing.

Aviation Acronyms

God knows there are plenty of these in Aviation – and those people who over-use acronyms just make me PO'd!

AC   Aircraft Commander
The "HMFWHIC" of a military aircraft.

ADF   Automatic Direction Finder
The flight instructor/instructor pilot.

AFM   Aircraft Flight Manual
The book provided by the manufacturer where all the details of the aircraft are hidden. Required by S/N to be aboard the aircraft, usually missing the first page where the N-number and aircraft S/N are noted with revisions haphazardly inserted therein.

AGL   Above Ground Level
The larger this number, the fewer chances there are of running into the edges of the sky: The upper edge of the sky may be defined as interstellar space; the lower edges are where all the houses, trees, barns, poles, silos, towers, etc. are found.

AIM   Aeronautical Information Manual
The repository of arcane knowledge, procedures and policy written by lawyers for bureaucrats: Of passing interest to pilots.

AME   Aviation Medical Examiner
The person you go to for your aviation medical color test: Red
blood + green money = you pass.

AO   Area of Operations
In essence: "No matter where you find yourself, there you are."

AOG   Aircraft On Ground
The acronym used when ordering a part desperately needed for
an aircraft grounded until the part arrives, usually insuring
delivery by stagecoach and/or snail mail.

APF   Attempts Per Flight
Can be number of landing tries per approach, number of runway
impacts per landing try, number of times the localizer/glide-slope
CDI is pegged per instrument approach. Of interest primarily to
statisticians and those who charge by the hour.

ASI   Air Speed Indicator
Gauge in the cockpit of dubious veracity and trustworthiness as
there are many types of 'airspeed', all subject to interpretation
depending on the state of sobriety of the interpreter.

ATC

> (1) Air Traffic Control (civilian) – A ground-based aerial
> surveillance system in which the operators guide the
> unsuspecting – and trusting - pilot towards opposing traffic
> and/or the red zone(s) depicted on weather radar.
> (2) Air Training Command (military) - The cadre in charge
> of turning snot-nosed civilians into rip-roaring angels of
> death.

BS   Bullshit
An extremely useful word with multiple purposes & meanings:
Can be used as a noun, verb, adverb, adjective, declaratory
statement, statement of opinion and of fact. Usable in polite
society when disguised as a sneeze.
[See also: Au Contraire]

BSR   "Bang – Stare – Red"
The principle – usually in rotorcraft – that dictates the louder the
'Bang' in your aircraft the quicker your eyes will go to the
gauges. The longer you stare at the gauges the quicker the
indicators will go from green to red.

BX   Base Exchange –
A location on a military base where such necessities and
possibles one might need for basic existence may be purchased
out of the paltry pay those in service receive from an overly-
generous government.

C – 4   C – 4
A form of plastic explosive with multiple and myriad number of
uses including livening up a dull day.

CAVU   Ceiling And Visibility Unlimited
The rare and glorious type of flying day where, if you squinted
hard, you can see the back of your own head.

CAFB   Clear As a F***ing Bell
[See: CAVU]

CDI   Course Deviation Indicator
A gizmo attached to the old-fashioned navigational radio which
indicates to the pilot when the boundaries of the airway and/or

approach path have been exceeded. These are unnecessary when the aircraft is equipped with a GPS as no-one looks at it anyway.

CFI   Certificated Flight Instructor
A person who rides in an aircraft with someone who is trying to kill him. All the CFI must do is figure out how this attempt will be made (may be several attempts per flight) and head it off.

CIGARTIPS   Controls, Instruments, Gas, Aircraft status, Run-up, Trim, Ignition, Propeller, Seatbelts & Systems.
A quick-n-dirty before takeoff check.

CRM   Crew (or Cockpit) Resource Management
The concept that Co-pilots and First Officers have something valid to contribute to the flight.

CVR   Cockpit Voice Recorder
A device used by accident investigators to use whatever was said in the last 30 minutes of a flight to prove an accident was pilot error.

DG   Directional Gyro (aka 'Heading Indicator')
One of the 6 primary flight instruments (in the old '6-pack' steam gauges days) guaranteed to precess a degree per minute in VFR and at least twice that in IMC.

DOD   Department Of Defense
Formerly (Civil War – WWII) known as the 'War Department', now a part of the "Military-Industrial complex" President Eisenhower warned about.

DP   Departure Procedure
The routing ATC issues to you when you want to go this-a-way and they want you to go that-a-way.

DZ   Drop Zone
The location where the airborne troopers or equipment were
supposed to land: If dealing with both troops and equipment,
these are mutually exclusive locations.

ER   Efficiency Report
A regularly-scheduled review of one's capabilities in the
performance of their duties. Can range from "Sets low standards
for himself and then fails to achieve them" on up.

EVAL   Evaluation
An estimation of pilot skills, knowledge and abilities by someone
who used to be able to do all that stuff.

FA   Flight Attendant
Formerly 'stewardesses' (female) but now could be anyone
and/or anything.

FAA   Federal Aviation Administration
1. Really nice men and women from the government whose
primary concern is your welfare and well-being as a pilot.
2. "Fear and Alarm."

FAR   Federal Air Regulations
1. Formerly written in blood, now written by blood-sucking
lawyers for the edification of bureaucrats; the sole purpose
of which is to confuse pilots. [See: NPRM – FARCA]
2. Opposite of NEAR.
3. What a pilot from southern states has when raw fuel is
pumped into a hot engine nacelle.

FIGMO   F*** It, Got My orders
Quaint old Anglo-Saxon expression used by 'short-timers' to tell
the neophytes what to do, where to go and how to do it.

FITREP   Fitness Report
Someone else's opinion on how you perform your duties.
[See: Lies, Falsehoods and Fabrications]

FMB   Fermented Malt Beverage(s)
E.g. Beers, ales, porters, stouts, lagers, and so forth.

FNG   F**king New Guy [See: Nugget]
Persons allegedly holding pilot/crew credentials, new to the
squadron, unit, outfit or company, who are not to be placed in
any position of authority or responsibility until they can prove
they're not going to get themselves killed, or get you killed,
within the first few weeks of assignment, deployment or of being
hired.

FO   First Officer [See: Co-pilot]
One who laterally balances the cockpit and is never allowed to
touch the flight controls unless the captain wants a nap or must
exit the cockpit to perform a personal weight-and-balance check.
Oh, c'mon! You can figure that one out, right?

FO   F**k Off
An 'olde' Anglo-Saxon invitation to take yourself and your silly-
assed ideas, thoughts and words to some inhospitable place far,
far from where the exclaimer currently exists, resides or
occupies.

FOM   Flight Operations Manual
The repository of Management's policies and procedures which
insure corporate profits and golden parachutes for those residing
at company headquarters. It has no apparent direct correlation to
flight safety, crew comfort, crew accommodations and the like.
It can also be used as a doorstop.

FSS   Flight Service Station
The place where the specialists who give weather briefings work;
a building with no windows.

FUBAR   F**ked Up Beyond All Recovery
The third level of 'F**ked-up-edness' behind SNAFU and
TARFU.

G   The Force of Gravity
    1. One 'G' is experienced just standing on the planet
(Earth that is). Multiple G's are induced by acceleration.
forces created by maneuvering the aircraft. "I love the feel
of G-forces in the morning!"
    2. String worn by persons attempting to attract members of
the opposite sex (c'mon, it is the 21st century now, ain't it?
–ed.).

GIB   Guy In Back
Anyone in an aircraft aft of the HMFWHIC.

GPS   Global Positioning System
The latest whizzy-gizzy cockpit doo-dad that always indicates
'TO' where you're going. The old 'FROM' days of VOR
navigation are gone…until those GPS satellites go Tango-
Uniform and pilots must revert to ground-based navigational
systems.

GUMPS   Gas, Undercarriage, Mixture, Propeller, Systems &
Seatbelts
A gouge to use for a pre-landing check until it is safe to use the
official checklist.

HMFWHIC   Head Mo-Fo What Him (or Her) In Charge
Usually that poor soul who, when all the fecal matter has been
evenly distributed by the rotating oscillating air movement
device, finds himself (or herself) up to their eyeballs in it.

IAP   Instrument Approach Procedure
The procedure used when the weather conditions are less than
"Clear and a million."
[See: North Pole Approach]

IFR   Instrument Flight Rules
     1. The rules and procedures to follow when you cannot see
     the ground or when wearing a 'view-limiting device'. The
     time to use the advice: "One peek is worth a thousand
     cross-checks".
     2. Methodology for complying with definition 1. above:
     "I Follow Rivers, Roads & Railways."

IMC   Instrument Meteorological Conditions
Where the advice given under 'IFR' doesn't work and your shit
cannot be weak.

IOE   Initial Operating Experience
Experience given to 'Nuggets' prior to actually being allowed to
manipulate the flight controls of an aerospace vehicle.

IP   Instructor Pilot
The military version of the civilian CFI; same duties and
responsibilities except the IP gets to fly cooler aircraft and
receives a steady paycheck.

LOX   Liquid Oxygen
Something you don't want any form of spark or fire around.

LZ Landing Zone
The location where skids touch the ground: If reported 'cold',
they will inevitably be 'hot' by the time you get there.

KMAG YOYO Kiss My Ass Goodbye, You're On Your Own
Pretty self-explanatory if'n you ask me.

MALF Malfunction
An event whereby the aircraft takes revenge on the pilot/aircrew
by failing a critical instrument or equipment, usually at the worst
possible time, thereby generating weighty & lengthy amounts of
paperwork, usually after an 'event'.

MOA Military Operating Area
Airspace wherein there are only two kinds of aircraft: Fighters
and Targets.

MTR Military Training Route
Published routes used by the U.S. Armed Forces where speed
limits below certain altitudes do not apply. *I had 2 F-4's pass
underneath me when I was but 500' AGL – quite a sight!*

NAVAID Navigational Aid
Usually a ground-based electronic navigational equipment placed
either permanently or nearly-so by those well-trained in map,
compass and guesswork; relied upon by those overly-trusting
souls piloting aircraft to get them within crawling distance of the
local watering hole.
[Also see: VOR, TACAN and - most relevant – NDB]

NDB   Non-Directional Beacon
   1. Fancy name for AM radio station.
   2. You have **No Damn Business** doing this kind of
   approach what with all the precision and GPS approaches
   around.

NOTAM   Notice to Airmen
Important aeronautical information issued by the government the
day after the planned event.

NTSBN   ational Transportation & Safety Board
The governmental agency charged with determining how a
particular aviation accident/incident was due to pilot error.

OEM   Original Equipment Manufacturer
Maker of life-limited parts only they can replace

ORI   Operational Readiness Inspection(s)
Something that no combat-ready outfit has ever passed: A
situation in which you stop doing what you were doing in order
to simulate doing what you were doing so that you can show
someone else that you can simulate doing what you were doing
as well as you were doing it before you were interrupted.

OTS   Out of Service
The appended identifier of the only airport for miles around
when you need a close-by fuel or pit-stop.

P – 7   "Proper Prior Preparation Prevents Piss-Poor
Performance"
*Never has a truer statement ever been made so succinctly for so
many.*

PA   Public Announcements

Crew comments to the SLC's pointing out interesting things about the flight, such as "Out of the left side of the aircraft you can see Kansas, Oklahoma and the northern third of Texas."

PC   Proficiency Check

A regularly scheduled event to prove to someone who doesn't fly regularly that you still can.

PC   Politically Correct

A theory spread around the country that it's possible to pick up a turd by the clean end.

PIC   Pilot in Command

The prime suspect when any event occurs.

PEBPAS   Problem Exists Between Panel and Seat

[See also: Short Circuit Between the Headphones]

PLO   Permanent Latrine Orderly

Speaks for itself

PMA   Parts Manufacturing Authority

The authorization given to those who want to make OEM parts, only cheaper

PO   Pissed Off

Meaning: Somewhat disappointed with the current state of affairs, conditions or situations.

POH   Pilot Operating Handbook

Mistakenly used by the uninformed as the last word in operating an aircraft [See: AFM]. While of good general knowledge, it is usually out-of-date with few-to-no revisions past the original publication date.

PTS   Practical Test Standards
The standards used to evaluate pilots in training: Written by office personnel who only see the sky when allowed outside by their supervisors or parole officer(s).

QA   Quality Assurance
Those people who look over the shoulders of those doing the work and tell them how they are not doing it correctly.

QNH   "Cue-En-Aich"
The altimeter setting over Great Britain and the Commonwealth nations given in milibars (Mb)

REMF   Rear-Echelon Mother F**ker
A somewhat disparaging term used by those on the cutting edge for those in cushy jobs far from danger: Those who deal with the gear in the rear.

RON   Remain Over Night
Can mean exactly that to an extended stay.
[Also see: TDY]

RPM   Rotations per Minute
A number referring to the rotational disc either in front, above or behind the aircraft, in the old days (20th century) called a 'Fan'. A high number keeps the pilot cool; if the number is low or worse – zero – he begins to sweat profusely.

SLC   Self-Loading Cargo
Passengers

SHP   Sierra-Hotel-Papa
Shit-hot Pilot (Aren't we all? –ed).

S/N   Serial Number
The numbers placed on aircraft, aircraft parts and aircraft
equipment to identify OEM and PMA approved parts. These
numbers are usually placed in obscure and hard-to-get-to places.

SNAFU   Situation Normal – All F**ked Up
The first status level followed by TARFU and FUBAR.

SOB   Son Of a Bitch
Either an endearing term of respect, or fightin' words.

SOG   Special Operations Group
A collection, gaggle or unit composed of individuals with
'special skills' who, when asked/commanded to perform feats of
questionable legality and unquestionable daring, will have their
existence denied if discovered, killed or captured by the
opposition.

SOF   Supervisor of Flying
Someone charged with negating all the factors mentioned in
"Fighter Pilot's Heaven."

SOP   Standard Operating Procedure
The techniques, methods, practices and procedures to fall back
on when "just winging it" is found inadequate, unsuitable or
downright dangerous. "When all else fails, read the directions."

STC   Supplemental Type Certificate
Authorization given to those who invent better and cheaper ways
to circumvent the OEM/PMA cartels with 'new and improved'
methods, addenda and miscellany about aircraft.

STFU   Shut The F**k Up
Self-explanatory request for silence.

SWAG   Scientific Wild-Ass Guess
A method of empirical observation with causal-dependent results
when trustworthy data is lacking.

TACAN   Tactical Air Navigation
Name for a military VOR.
[See also: VOR & NAVAIDs]

TARFU   Things Are Really F**ked Up
The status level between SNAFU and FUBAR.

TDY   Temporary Duty
Originally meant as short-term duty stationing, it now can mean
anything this side of the second deployment.

TLAR   That Looks About Right
A means to determine if something – like an approach to landing
– is within limits; can also be used as "TSAR" (That Sounds
about Right) and "TFAR" (That Feels About Right). More
precise than the 'SWAG' method.

TU   Tango-Uniform
Otherwise known as "Tit's Up" (How bugs die…on their back
with their T U). Otherwise known as 'Dead.'

UEI   Uniform & Equipment Inspection(s)
Speaks for itself: Ironing just the outer sleeve showing in your
locker doesn't pass anymore…they know this trick.

USAAC United States Army Air Corps
The flying arm of the US Army prior to WWI until 18 September 1947, when it became the (next entry).

USAF United States Air Force
Without munitions would just be an expensive flying club.

VFR Visual Flight Rules
Succinctly summarized in an old Confederate Air Force pre-airshow briefing: "Y'all stay above 5 feet and don't do nuthin' dumb."

VMC Visual Meteorological Conditions
Technically, when the cloud ceiling(s) are higher than 1,000' AGL and 3 miles visibility: Also, the conditions under which most mid-air collisions occur.

VOR Very high frequency Omni-Range
A ground-based navigational system from not only the last century but also the last millennium that has been confusing pilots and vexing the FAA Knowledge Test takers for years.

WTF Whiskey Tango Foxtrot
An expression of incredulity or bemused wonderment.

YGBSM You Gotta Be Shitting Me!
Another expression of incredulity or bemused wonderment.

201 File Personnel File
The repository of every complaint letter, FITREP (good & bad) and scrap of paper with your name on it produced by others and for which there is no appeal, excuse or redress.

Aviation Dictionary

How did the letters of the alphabet get in the order they are? Is it because of that song? And why is that song the same as "Twinkle, Twinkle, Little Star?"

I know you just sang them to yourself – be I right?

Aerial
[Also see: Antennae] That part of the airplane most frequently broken off by the pilot during the preflight inspection when ascertaining if anything is broken off.

Aero
That portion of the atmosphere which overlies Great Britain and any of the Commonwealth nations.

Aerodrome
Where aeroplanes alight on the ground under that portion of the atmosphere overlying Great Britain and any of the Commonwealth nations.

Airframe
What an FAA inspector is doing when he sends his kid out to ask a student pilot for a ride.

Airscrew
1. What the pilots in Great Britain and the Commonwealth nations call the propeller.

2. A flightcheck when the FAA Inspector rides along as an 'observer'.

Airspace Reservation
A geographical location set aside by the U.S. Government for the exclusive occupancy of airspace.

Airspeed
1. The speed of an aircraft through the air.
2. True airspeed plus 20% when talking to other pilots. Deduct 25% when speaking with retired fighter jocks.
3. Measured in furlongs-per-fortnight (FPF) when speaking with a Student Pilot.

Alternate Airport
An airport lying 20 minutes beyond the point of fuel exhaustion.

Altimeter Setting
The place where the altimeter is placed on the instrument panel – usually hidden by the control column when performing an instrument approach to minimums.

Approach
Asking that cute flight attendant out for dinner.
[Also see: Departure]

Arresting Gear
Equipment used by the authorities to keep order at aviation-based parties.

ATC Control Center
Dark, drafty, ill-kept barn-like structures in which nefarious individuals gather for dubious reasons.

Au Contraire
("oh con trair") From the French; an exclamation of disbelief. [Also see acronym: BS]

Autopilot
Someone who busted their flightcheck.

Bail Out
1. Any form of egressing an airplane while in flight.
2. Getting your friend out of the hoosegow after an all-night bender.

Bank
The folks who hold the lien on most pilots' cars.

Barrel Roll
Getting the keg from the car to the hangar for the "safety meeting."

Blind Flying
Having a date with someone you've never seen before.

Bloody Good Show
Aka: "Well done!" as spoken in the British Commonwealth.

Brain Bag
The container carried by pilots (all types) holding a rusted-out E6B, plotter, outdated charts, Dash-one (POH) 6 months out-of-date, pack of 12 year-old chewing gum (still good), cigarettes (or cigars), Hershey bars and three days dirty laundry.

Buzz Job
(aka: "Buzzing") To fly extremely low, "Cut the grass". The final maneuver by many pilots no longer with us.

Caged Gyro
Not much less docile than a wild gyro.

Caging the Gyro
Much easier with the domesticated species.

Captain
Any airline pilot with four stripes on his sleeve; usually found holding his own hand.

Carburetor Icing
A phenomenon mentioned in the report to the FAA/NTSB immediately after a pilot runs out of gas.

Center of Pressure
The location of the FAA knowledge (written) or practical tests.

Chart
> 1. A large piece of paper most useful for protecting cockpit surfaces from food and beverage stains.
> 2. A large piece of paper which, if folded and placed properly in the cockpit window, provides a passable sunscreen.

Chinese Landing
One wing low.

Chock
Pieces of wood or hard rubber which magically appear in the way of the nose wheel just before receiving taxi clearance. [Also see: Gremlin]

Clank Up
State of extreme agitation usually brought on by the recipient hearing such phrases as "Overseas", "Special Mission", "Flightcheck", "The C.O./Chief Pilot would like to see you in their office…NOW."

Clear
A warning to others shouted by the pilot two seconds after hitting the 'Start' button.

Clear the Prop
Moving all the admiring young ladies away from the front of the plane so the dashingly handsome pilot may gain access to same

Cockpit
Where the pilot sits while trying to figure out where he/she is and/or where they are going.

Cone of Confusion
An area about the size of New Jersey, located above the final approach fix at any airport.

Contact
    1. An archaic form of the word 'Clear!' also spoken two seconds after the starter is engaged.
    2. Friend who can find 'cheap' aircraft parts.

Contact Approach
Not to be performed by anyone at any time unless approach clearance has been received and acknowledged. *If you know what I mean.*

Control Tower
A small shack on stilts inhabited by government pensioners who cannot hear; when they become blind they are sent to Centers.

Course
Popular alternate landing field marked by fairways and greens: Curiously, those who land here are said to be 'off course'.

Crab
    1. The squadron Ops Officer or flight school chief pilot.
    2. A technique used by pilots to compensate for crosswinds, usually without success.

Crash
To bed down for the night.
[Also see: Suitable Landing Site]

Critical Engine
That part of the airplane which used to live under the cowling but now is in intensive care at the maintenance shop.

Cross Control
Angry tower operator

Cross Country
Any student flight beyond eyeball acquisition of the home airfield.

Dead Reckoning
Navigational method: You reckon correctly, or you are.

Deicer
Aviation terms for hills, wooded slopes, apartment buildings and trailer parks.

Deicing Boots
Rubber inflatables designed to work under all weather conditions except icing.

Departure
What to do after a "Missed approach".

Destination
Geographical point 30 minutes beyond the pilot's bladder max pressure point.

Dive
Pilot's lounge and/or airport café.

Downwind
Direction of Student Pilot take-offs.

Downwind Leg
The one on the lee side when "seeing a man about a horse."

Drag
Enticing the IP back to the airplane to fly with you. [Also see: Induced Drag]

Dykes
Wire cutters. *Where did your filthy mind take you?*

Elevator
Device by which the tower raises or lowers the approach end of any runway. *Especially useful for playing with student pilots and Navy jocks.*

Engine Failure
A condition which occurs when all fuel tanks mysteriously become filled with low-octane air.

Event
1. An occasion used for the generation of paperwork.
2. An experience the PIC &/or aircrew did not wish to have.

Exceptional Flying Ability
A pilot who has logged an equal number of takeoffs and landings.

Fast
Describes the speed of any high-performance aircraft, especially military; lower-performance and training aircraft are described as "half-fast."

Final Approach
Asking out that cute flight attendant one last time.

Firewall
1. (Noun) Section of the aircraft specially designed to funnel heat and smoke into the cockpit.
2. (Verb) Act of pulling 65 inches of manifold pressure from an engine designed to give only 50.

Fixed Base Operator
Any male instructor after a vasectomy.

Flaps
Spirited discussion(s) between ATC and pilots usually brought on by the phrase "Advise when able to copy a phone number"

Flashlight
A device wherein pilots store dead batteries.

Flight Following
In-trail formation flight.

Flight Instructor
An individual of dubious reputation and sobriety, paid vast sums of money to impart knowledge of questionable value and who has an amazing vocabulary concerning the coordination, intelligence and ancestry of student pilots.

Flight Line
Small diameter twine-like substance used to occupy 'Nuggets', e.g. "Go find me a ball of Flight Line."
[Also see also: Bucket of prop wash]

Flight Service Station
1. The place wherefrom pilots obtain weather briefings prior to flight .
2. A building with no windows from which weather forecasts are issued.

Foxtrot-Oscar
See acronym "FO", 2nd definition.

Frost
Attitude shown by an uncooperative stewardess. [See: Horizontally Opposed]

Gaggle
(noun) A large number of anything headed in the same general direction in the same part of the sky.

Glide Distance
Half the distance from an airplane to the nearest suitable landing field at the point of engine failure.

Glider
Formerly 'airplane', prior to running out of fuel.

Gouge
An easy mnemonic, patois or saying that aids in memory & recall when one cannot remember the real thing.

Green Bag
Flight suit – so named for its fashionable color and fit.

Gremlins
Small invisible beings who enjoy tormenting pilots by putting chocks in front of nose wheels after everyone is aboard, kinking the vacuum lines during instrument flight, shifting weight/cargo to the furthermost aft position while inflight, and other such 'humorous' pranks as they can think of.

Gross Weight
Overweight pilot.

Ground Speed
Average speed from the airport to home and vice-versa.

Hangar
Sheltered area housing several cast-off couches, a comfy chair with no seat cushion support, a coffee pot (which hasn't been cleaned since the Nixon Administration) , coffee cups (ditto), numerous shelves with half-full cans, bottles and containers of gawd-knows-what, a work bench or two with no available flat surface upon which to work, old magazines and Trade-a-Planes

("Hey, here's a Cessna 185 for $35,000!"), a semi-classic old car awaiting restoration…and perhaps an airplane.

Headset
Not scanning for other traffic
[Also see: 'midair' or 'near miss']

Heated Air Mass
Usually found in and about hangars, flight lounges, crew rooms, airport cafes and non-flying members of the opposite sex.

Helicopter
Thousands of parts flying in close formation surrounding oil leaks, waiting for metal fatigue to set in.

Hobbs Meter
The instrument which, when failed during dual instruction, brings the lesson to a screeching halt.

Holding Pattern
Term applied to the dogfight in progress over any navigational facility serving a terminal airport.

Hold Short
The order given by ATC when they want the aircraft to not go where they already are.

Hood Time
Logable flight time when aviating while not looking outside the airplane.

Horizontally Opposed
May be expressed in any of the following ways: "No!" "Hell, No!" or "Are you freakin' kidding me?!" [Also see: Frost]

Hydroplane
An airplane designed to land long and fast on a short & wet runway.

Hyperventilation
Opening one or both windows at cruise airspeeds.

Induced Drag
Getting the instructor to fly with you again, usually by using a bottle of Scotch Whiskey as a lure.

Instrument Rating
A certificate indicating the holder has received enough training – and has all the knowledge, ability & awareness – to know when to stay on the ground.

Instrument Flight
The method of flying by needle, ball and ripcord.

Iron Compass
Railroad lines.

Junkers
1. Type of WWII German airplane.
2. A plane no-one can make airworthy.

Kilometer
Unit of measurement on aeronautical charts to further confuse those pilots who already have trouble with knots.

Landing Flap
A 6,000 foot roll-out on a 5,000 foot runway.

Landing Gear
Those things that stick out from the bottom of the airplane which keep the propeller out of the dirt/concrete/asphalt after landing.

Lazy 8
The airport operator, his four mechanics and three lineboys.

Lean Mixture
Non-alcoholic beer.

Logbook
A small rectangular notebook used by a pilot to record lies ("Fly when you can, log what you need" - BC).

Loop
What a passengers' stomach does when subjected to unexpected aerial 'frivolity'. [Also see: Barf bag]

Max Gross Weight
Maximum permissible takeoff weight plus two suitcases, 10 oil cans, 4 sleeping bags, 4 rifles (with ammo), 8 cases of beer, a bottle of medicinal scotch, whisky and the groceries.

Mini Mag Lite
A device which supports the AA battery industry.

Missed Approach
Being told 'No' by that cute flight attendant.

Mixture Control
The Head Barkeep.

Motor
A word used by the English and Student Pilots when referring to
an aircraft engine.

Nanosecond
The time delay between the low fuel light illuminating and the
onset of carburetor icing. [Also see: carburetor icing]

Navigation
The art of flying from point 'A' to point 'B' while really trying
to get to point 'C'.

Nose Wheel
The wheel at the front of an airplane used by pilots unable and/or
unwilling to fly airplanes with the third wheel at the tail of the
airplane where it should be. [Also see: Training Wheel]

Nuremberg Defense
The defense put forth by the Nazi henchmen during their post-
WWII trials in Nuremberg, Germany:
"I vas only following orders." (It won't work at your hearing or
Review Board either – Ed.)

O-Club
Officer's Club: The base watering hole where commissioned
individuals may imbibe in FMB's and other assorted mind-
altering beverages, tell lies, war stories and otherwise
decompress from the stresses of the day.

Overhaul
Cleaning the top spark plugs, adding a can of 'Upper Lube' and
repainting the crankcase.

P-Factor
What occurs when the IP shuts down one engine and the student feathers the prop on the other one. *What other definition came to your mind?*

Parker Pen
The ONLY proper writing instrument for making 'important' entries in one's logbook.

Parasitic Drag
A pilot who bums a ride and complains about the service or doesn't offer to help with the fuel bill.

Pilot
A misguided individual who – if of the male persuasion – speaks of flying when with women and about women when flying.

Pilot in Command
The person who while seemingly protected by FAR 91.3 is actually the focus of attention when determining the extent of "Pilot error."

Pitch
The story a (male) pilot presents to the 'target for tonight'.

Plotter
Fixed Base Operator who connives to keep fuel prices above average.

Prang
1. (Verb) To damage an aircraft by contact with an immovable object (e.g. the ground).
2. A loud noise immediately preceding the termination of a flight, usually accompanied by a rapid descent.

Prop
What your buddies should do for you when leaving the club; like as not they need it themselves.

Propeller
The fan in front of an airplane that keeps the pilot cool…turn it off and watch him sweat.

Prop Wash
1. A cleaning agent the crew chief or plane captain sends 'Nuggets' in search of.
2. Refers to flying tales overheard in a 'Dive'.

Range
Usually about 30 miles beyond the point where all fuel tanks fill with air.

Rich Mixture
What you order at the other guy's promotion party.

Roger
Used when you're not sure what else to say.

Roll
1. The first design priority for a fully loaded KC-135A.
2. 'Ammo' at the end-of-deployment and/or squadron stand-down dinner (for Walt W. & the 69th SOG)
3. The money needed to take out that cute flight attendant

Rotorhead
A pilot who flies aircraft with the propeller on top of the aircraft rather than in front.

Runway
Cleared surface for departing from and alighting upon the face of the planet. Always too short and not wide enough for student pilots and those not adept at crosswind landings.

Safety Belt
Alcoholic drink for the instructor prior to dealing with a troublesome student.

Scarf Up
(Verb) To grab, rescue or capture (I was scarfed up by the Jolly Greens); unfortunately, can also mean "I was scarfed up by the V.C."

Sectional
Any chart that terminates 25 miles short of your destination. [Also see: Chart]

Service Ceiling
Altitude at which cabin crews can serve drinks.

Slow Flight
That portion of the flight extending beyond bladder limits.

Spoilers
[See acronym: FAA]

Stable Air
Atmosphere found over the stockyards of Chicago, IL; Omaha, NE; Fort Worth, TX; or Greeley, CO.

Stall
Technique used to explain to the bank why your car payment is late.

Steep Bank
Banks that charge pilots more than 10% interest.

Stick Actuator
Pilot

S-Turn
Course flown by a Student Pilot going from point 'A' to point 'B'.

Supercharger
Pilot with eight credit cards (all maxed out).

Sweat
What a pilot does when the 'fan' up front (or above, for you rotorheads) isn't rotating anymore and keeping him 'cool'.

Taildragger
1. An older pilot after a long flight.
2. A young pilot who over-rotates a tricycle-gear airplane during takeoff.

Tail Wind
Results from eating beans and/or cabbage, often causing oxygen depletion in the immediate vicinity.

Takeoff Distance
Length of the runway plus 150'.

Tango-Uniform
[See acronym: TU]

Test Pilot
Any unemployed aviator more than 50 nm from home.

Thermal
Atmospheric phenomenon blamed when a pilot cannot hold altitude.

Trim Tab
A device student pilots use to control the airplane instead of using the flight controls.

Turn & Bank Indicator
An instrument largely ignored by pilots.

Useful Load
  1. Volumetric capacity of the aircraft, disregarding weight
  2. About four scotch whiskeys (doubles, natch!).

WAC Chart
Directions to the Army Post's female barracks. *You must be of a 'certain' age to appreciate this one.*

Walkaround
What to do when waiting for the weather to clear.

Wilco
Roger's brother, the nerd.

Wingman
#2 in the flight who protects the tail of flight lead. The member of the flight or crew who says "You have the steak, Skipper; I'll take the chicken" or "I'll take the fat one, boss."

Wing Span
Pilot with arms long enough to reach the charts on the floor behind the pilot's seat.

Wing Strut
Peculiar, ritualistic walk performed by Student Pilots after their first solo.

Yankee
Any pilot who asks Atlanta tower to "Say again."

Yaw
Answer given by a pilot (mouth full) during happy hour when asked if he's a pilot.

Zero
Style and artistry points earned for a gear-up landing.

Regulation Index

61	57	(a)(b)	Recent Flight Experience: Pilot in Command	Full Stop or Touch & Goes
67	57	(a)	Recent Flight Experience: Pilot in Command	Once a Knight is Enough
67	103		Medical Information*	
67	107		Medical Information*	
67	109		Medical Information*	
91	3	A & B	Responsibility & Authority of the Pilot in Command	Another Aviation Fable
91	3		Responsibility & Authority of the Pilot in Command	Inflight Malfunction Flow Chart
91	15		Dropping Objects	USS Midway's Toilet Bomb
91	17	(1)(2)(3)(4)	Alcohol or Drugs	Future Pilot

91	25		Aviation Safety Reporting Program	Pilot Commandments
91	103		Preflight Action	Checked NOTAMs
91	103		Preflight Action	Fixed Wing Checklist
91	103		Preflight Action	Once a Knight is Enough
91	105	A	Flight Crewmembers at Stations	B-25 Moon
91	105	A, B	Flight Crewmembers at Stations	Airline Captain Dies Enroute
91	107	A. (1)(2)	Use of Safety Belts & Shoulder Harnesses	B-25 Moon
91	111	A. B. C.	Operating Near Other Aircraft	Formation Etiquette
91	117	A. B. C.	Aircraft Speed	Balls to the Walls
91	119	A	Minimum Safe Altitudes: Anywhere	Aviation 101

91	119	A	Minimum Safe Altitudes: Anywhere	Hung Up on Flying
91	119	C	Minimum Safe Altitudes: General	Aircraft Crashes Into Occupied Structure
91	307	C	Parachutes & Parachuting	Activity for Retired Pilots
91	403	(d)	Maintenance: General	Ultimate Darwin Award Winner
105	All		Parachute Operations	Activity for Retired Pilots
AIM 4	Sec. 3	3	Traffic Patterns	Avoiding a Mid-Air Collision
AIM 4	Sec. 3	5	Unexpected Maneuvers in Airport Traffic Patterns	Avoiding a Mid-Air Collision
AIM 5	Sec. 1	3	Notice to Airmen (NOTAM) System	Checked NOTAMs

AIM 7	Sec. 1	23	PIREPs Relating to Turbulence	Turbulence PIREPs
AIM 7	Sec. 4	1, 2, 3, 4, 5, 6	Bird Hazards	Quote From 'Airplane'
AIM 8	Sec. 1	2	Effects of Altitude - Ear & Sinus Block	Earache Remedy
AIM 8	Sec. 1	1 (d)	Alcohol	Future Pilot
NTSB 830	2		Accident & Incident Reporting: Definitions	Anybody Can do Anything With an Airplane
NTSB 830	5		Immediate Notification	Anybody Can do Anything With an Airplane
NTSB 830	5		Immediate Notification	Anybody Can do Anything With an Airplane
CRM		4.1	Defined	Airline Job Description

DUI Reporting Form

The FAA DUI/DWI reporting form is located at:

https://www.faa.gov/about/office_org/headquarters_offices/ash/ash_programs/investigations/airmen_duidwi/

Date: _____

Federal Aviation Administration
Civil Aviation Security Division, AMC-700
P. O. Box 25810
Oklahoma City, OK 73125

Dear Sir or Madam:

I submit the following information in compliance with Federal Aviation Regulation 61.15(e):
1. NAME: _____
      (Last Name, First Name, Middle Name or Initial)

2. DATE OF BIRTH: _____

3. CERTIFICATE #: _____

4. ADDRESS: _____
      (Street Number/Name, Post Office Box, RFD...etc.)

      (City, State, Zip Code)

5. TYPE OF VIOLATION: _____
      (DUI, DWI, DWAI, Refusal to Test...etc.)

6. DATE OF ACTION: _____
      (Date of the Conviction or Administrative Action*)

7. STATE HOLDING RECORD: _____

8. STATEMENT AS TO WHETHER THE MOTOR VEHICLE ACTION AROSE FROM THE SAME INCIDENT OR AROSE OUT OF PREVIOUSLY REPORTED MOTOR VEHICLE ACTION. (Is this action from the same incident or was there more than one arrest, particularly within a three-year period?)

_____

      (Your Signature)

OPTIONAL INFORMATION:

1. DRIVER'S LICENSE NUMBER: _____

2. SOCIAL SECURITY NUMBER: _____

3. TELEPHONE NUMBER(S): _____

*A Motor Vehicle Action is defined as ANY alcohol/drug related administrative action taken against a person's state driver's license-including suspensions, cancellations, revocations, or denials of a license to operate a motor vehicle, or conviction for an alcohol related motor vehicle offense.
    You may print and mail this form or submit it via fax to (405) 954-4989

Websites

Over the years I have discovered some great places to visit on the internet, so I include them here for your edification and enjoyment. Have fun exploring – and if you know of some others, send them along for the hoped-to-be second edition. See the 'Invitation' section up front for the address and how to avoid me deleting your submission out-of-hand as spam.

www.Crashandsurvive.com

Everyone is taught how to fly, but what to do if you are about to meet terra firma away from an airport? My late friend Mick Wilson was an accident investigator for the FAA for years and wondered why some people survived horrific crashes and others did not live through lesser ones. He correlated his findings into a great book and DVD. It has my total and complete recommendation as an asset to pilots.

http://FAL-1.tripod.com

I know many pilots – now retired, sad to say – who began their airline careers at the "Old Frontier" airline. They to this day have a loyalty to that entity which speaks volumes. Here's the site for you 'O.F.' folks.

http://en.wikipedia.org/wiki/Wright_R-3350_Duplex-Cyclone

Explanation of the history and use of the Wright R-3350 engine.

The name was "The Wild Blue Yonder". Oscar Brand with the Roger Wilco Four. There were 8 songs on each side including the one below. They are in order:

Save A Fighter Pilot's Ass
The Goddamned Reserves
Come And Join The Air Force
Barnacle Bill, The Pilot
Give Me Operations
Fighter Pilot's Lament
Itazuke Tower
I Wanted Wings
Sidi Slimane
The Poor Co-Pilot
Army Air Force Heaven
Cigareets And Sake
Bless Em All
Wreck Of The Old Ninety-Seven
Glory Flying Regulations
Lets Have A Party

Also enclosed was a booklet with all the words to each song.

———

Note from Moderator Pete Sofman: Videos of some of these songs can be found at:

http://tinyurl.com/6sla263

http://tinyurl.com/7m9zc26

Santa's Checkride can be found at:

http://youtu.be/50vE47DGEy4

Request for Assistance

If you have in your files, collections or ephemera other materials which you think could be added to another book like this, please feel free in sending them along to me. IF a sequel to this book is produced, IF your item is used, and IF you are the first one submitting it, I will include your name, city & state as contributor credit. Even better would be if you also include any relevant FAR or section from the AIM or any FAA publication so I may relate that which you send to a learning moment. You know – something which 'builds character'.

PLEASE be aware and VERY careful of submitting anything with an obvious copyright such as cartoons, pictures and/or illustrations as my begging for forgiveness in reproducing them can absolve me of just so much – then the copyright owners get pissy and <u>nobody</u> likes it when that happens. If you are sending along an original photo (Meaning: <u>You</u> are the photographer who took it), then I'd be pleased to include not only the picture but will also credit you for your photographic skills. If you photoshop something…ahhh… use your best judgment – and skills - if you submit it.

So, good and faithful reader, should you have something to contribute, <u>please</u> have some class and sense of appropriateness about it. After all, this book is being read by not only hard, cold, steely-eyed aviators who have been there and done that, but also by those innocents whose dreams we do not want dashed just yet. Let them figure it out on their own, okay?

Send what you have to:

Drew@Coloradoskymaster.com

Or if by snail-mail:

Drew Chitiea
PO Box 65
Black Hawk, Colorado
USA
80422-0065

Thanks a lot...Stay cool...Right on...Roger-doger...Over & out.

About Colorado Skymasters:

Colorado Skymasters is a loose – emphasis on 'loose' – confederation of pilots, mechanics, ATC personnel and yes, even retired FAA suits, who wish to remain active in aviation and give back to the community within which they have spent most of their lives.

The retired airline types have flown for airlines now long gone, absorbed by others or fallen by the wayside. The hottest aircraft our military types have flown are now either in museums, on a stick outside the entrance gate to the base or can be found in the 'Old Warbirds' section of fly-ins and airshows. The civil aviation sorts – who at times could hardly be called 'civil' – have logged time in airplanes only seen in the 'Classics' and 'Antiques' sections of Trade-a-Plane. In essence, we know how to start, keep running and maintain round and cantankerous engines in all their permutations.

We specialize in the esoteric and fringe areas of aviation, e.g. tailwheel training, aerobatics/upset-and-recovery, mountain flying in Colorado's Rocky Mountains (your airplane or ours), insurance-required instruction and experience-building for specialized and/or high-value airplanes, and most importantly the mentoring of youg aviators on their way up the aviation ladder. We also have a flight school on Denver's south side whereby those persons with time constraints or who are stalled in their efforts to gain a certificate and/or rating can come for a high-intensity training regime to quickly reach their goal(s) in aviation (Examiner on staff - natch!).

To view our programs or to contact us, please visit our website at:

www.Coloradoskymaster.com

ABOUT THE AUTHOR

Andrew D. "Drew" Chitiea has been a pilot not only since well back in the last century but the last millennium as well. He has enjoyed, endured & experienced enough excitement, endeavors, assignments and so forth to righteously be entitled to say "Been there, done that" to much of aviation (He's got a number of corroborating T-shirts and has a supporting role in the video as further proof). Too modest for his own good, he will admit to nothing unless properly encouraged to spill his guts, usually by the profligate administration of some of Scotland's finest 'medicinal' beverage (Single Malt, Highland, minimum twelve-year old, vast quantities thereof) and or other ~~bribes~~ "creative inducements".

Adept at fooling all the people all the time, he has somehow logged flight time in over 175 different make/model of airplanes, been designated a "Master Instructor" eight times consecutively (soon to be nine) and has sweet-talked the FAA into awarding him the "Designated Pilot Examiner" (DPE) status by which he, in the guise of administering flight checks for the last 14 years from Sport Pilot to Initial CFI to ATP, enjoys the privilege of legally being able to steal from pilots. He provides this 'service' from his secret ~~hideout~~, ~~lair~~, AO in Colorado. He and his wife Peggy own and fly a Cessna P-210 and a Skybolt biplane.

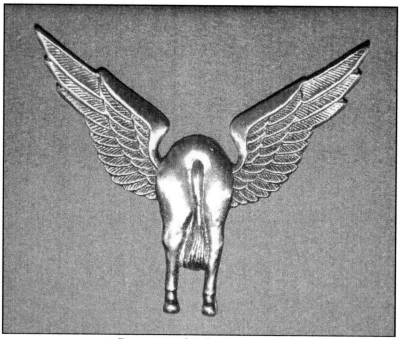

Designated Pilot Examiner
Time Indeterminate
(unauthorized)

HOW & WHERE TO ORDER MORE COPIES

Since everyone you show this book to will ask: "Where did you get this?" You can either show them this page and allow them to copy the information

OR

You may allow them to <u>carefully</u> remove this page from the book and use it to order their own copy. In either case, I appreciate your acting as a sales agent and representative on my behalf.

(That 12 year-old Scotch whisky referred to several times in this book ain't cheap, y'know!)

www.Amazon.com

After entering this website, enter (Aviator's Bathroom Reader) or my last name (Chitiea) and you will be taken directly to the ordering page. Follow their prompts and in a few short days your own copy of this book will be delivered to the address stipulated in your order.

www.Coloradoskymaster.com

This is my company website; click on 'Products & Publications' along the left side, then scroll down until you see the Bathroom reader order page. You may then securely order this using Paypal AND you may ask for an inscription with signature from the author (surely in time to be a collectors' item!)

Send a personal check:

You may send a personal or company check for $22.95 + $4.00 postage ($26.95 total) to:

Colorado Skymaster Publications - ABR
PO Box 65
Black Hawk, Colorado 80422-0065
USA

I must wait until your check clears (+/- 10 days) and then your book will be delivered by a registered agent & operative of the Federal Government. In essence, allow +/- 3 weeks for snail-mail.

If you are an aviation bookstore, flight school or other retailer interested in volume discounts, please contact me at the address above or email:

Drew@Coloradoskymaster.com

Please use "ABR" in the message subject line.